MOJAVE DESERT

Wildflowers

A FALCON GUIDE®

MOJAVE DESERT

Wildflowers

A FIELD GUIDE TO WILDFLOWERS, TREES, AND SHRUBS OF THE MOJAVE DESERT, INCLUDING THE MOJAVE NATIONAL PRESERVE, DEATH VALLEY NATIONAL PARK, AND JOSHUA TREE NATIONAL PARK

by Pam MacKay

FALCON®

GUILFORD, CONNECTICUT
HELENA, MONTANA

AN IMPRINT OF THE GLOBE PEQUOT PRESS

*A***FALCON**GUIDE®

Text design: Sue Cary
Photo credits: All photos by the author unless otherwise indicated.
Map on cover and page 2 provided by the Mojave Desert Ecosystem Program.

Library of Congress Cataloging-in-Publication Data is available.

ISBN 10 : 0-7627-1162-0
ISBN 13 : 978-0-7627-1162-8

Printed in China
First Edition/Second Printing

DEDICATION

In loving memory of Dolores

Contents

Acknowledgments viii
Preface 1
Map 2
Introduction.. 3
   Mojave Desert Geography and Climate 3
   Mojave Desert Topography and Geology 4
   Mojave Desert Soils and Rock Surfaces 7
   Past Vegetation of the Mojave 9
   Past Human Uses of Mojave Desert Plants 11
   Early Botanical Exploration of the Mojave Desert .. 13
   Present Vegetation of the Mojave 17
   Plant Adaptations to Desert Climate 27
   Threats to the Mojave Desert Flora 29
   Present Conservation and Management 34
   How to Use This Book 35
   How Plants Get Their Names 35
Blue, Purple, and Lavender Flowers 41
Pink, Rose, and Magenta Flowers............................... 77
Red and Orange Flowers.. 113
White to Cream Flowers.. 123
Yellow Flowers.. 187
Green and Brown Flowers 265
Non-Flowering Plants... 301
Glossary.. 308
For Further Reading 315
Index 320
About the Author 339
About Some of the Photographers 340

ACKNOWLEDGMENTS

I could not have written this book without the assistance and support of Tim Thomas. He spent countless hours coaching me on how to take quality photographs, accompanying me on photographic excursions, providing me with information, and editing. He helped at every stage, from the original organization and outline to the preparation and packaging of slides for mailing. His expertise on rare plants and conservation was invaluable.

I owe a large debt of gratitude to Andrew Sanders of the University of California at Riverside Herbarium, the technical advisor for this book. For many years he has been my mentor, teaching me the flora of the Mojave Desert and San Bernardino Mountains. He edited species accounts, provided distribution and taxonomic information, and offered many helpful suggestions.

I am especially grateful to my talented photographers, including John Reid, Steve Ingram, RT Hawke, Tim Thomas, Michael Honer, and Wendell Minnich. John Reid also developed film, loaned photographic supplies, and offered valuable feedback on my photographs. Thomas Elder III provided the digital images of the *Cryptantha* nutlets.

Many thanks to Elizabeth Lawlor, anthropology professor at Mt. San Antonio College, and Fran Elgin, librarian at Victor Valley College, who provided information sources and editing for the section on Native Americans and ethnobotany. Technical advice and editing for the topography and geology section was provided by Don Buchanon, professor of geology at Victor Valley College, and Larry Reese, geology enthusiast, world traveler, and retired aerospace engineer. I am grateful to others who provided technical information or told me where to find it, including Rick Everett, Dieter Wilken, Gordon Pratt, and others.

A special thank you to those who gave many words of encouragement. I might never have undertaken this project if it were not for Karen Wiese. My friends, coworkers, and students were extremely accommodating, and my sons, Steve and Greg, always cheered me on. I am especially grateful to my father, John, who instilled in me a love for science and the outdoors.

The map for this book was provided by the Mojave Desert Ecosystem Program (MDEP). The MDEP is an effort to create a comprehensive, shared scientific database that allows land managers and natural resource specialists to ask and answer questions about variables that affect ecosystem dynamics, sustainable land management, and land-use decision making. It enables accurate modeling of environmental factors and facilitates data-driven analysis of the Mojave ecoregion. The MDEP provides all users (federal, state, local, and private) easy Internet access (www.mojavedata.gov) to geospatial natural resource data for the entire ecoregion and is a model for the sharing and integration of resource data and expertise.

Death Valley

PREFACE

This is not just another picture book of the most attractive plants of the Mojave Desert; in fact, many of the plants included here are tiny, drab, and easily overlooked. Nor is this a book of merely the most common species; it also includes many species that are rare and unique to the Mojave Desert. It is intended for the occasional desert wanderer and amateur botanist but should also prove useful to those with some knowledge of botany. No matter what your level of expertise, my hope is that this book will lead you to a deeper and more thoughtful study of plants, not just the ability to call them by name, but also to find out how they interact with their environment and with the other species around them.

Very little is known about many of the plants presented in these pages, especially those that are rare or less attractive. Why do they grow where they do? What pollinates them? What eats them? What species use them for shelter? How many are there in a population? Do their populations remain stable, or are they increasing or declining? What factors influence population sizes? There are many questions that can be asked and answered, not only by professional botanists, but also by amateurs who are willing to spend time observing. Share your observations with others. You can make a significant and valuable contribution to our knowledge and understanding of the Mojave Desert ecosystem.

This book offers a historical perspective on peoples who dwelled in the Mojave Desert and those who explored it. Ways in which native peoples used desert plants are described in the text, and the introduction presents a brief overview of who those peoples were. In addition, many of the species descriptions give information about those individuals for whom the plants were named, often the explorers who first collected the species on their arduous expeditions during past centuries.

I also hope that this book will help you develop an awareness and appreciation of the unique resources of the Mojave Desert, so that you will realize that it is in the best interest of all to preserve it. There are many threats to the desert ecosystem and to rare species within it that are discussed in the introduction and species accounts. The introduction will also discuss present conservation efforts in the Mojave, and how you can become involved. Well, what are we waiting for? Grab your hand lens, and let's go botanizing. . . .

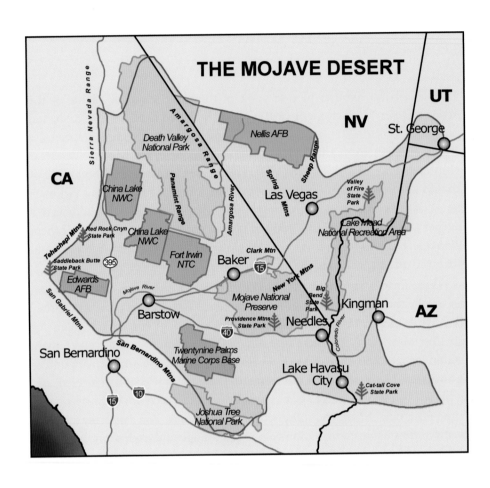

$\mathcal{I}$NTRODUCTION

Mojave Desert Geography and Climate

The Mojave Desert is the smallest North American desert, occupying less than 50,000 square miles. It has a nearly rectangular shape, wedged between the Sonoran Desert to the south and Great Basin Desert to the north. The southern border goes through the middle of Joshua Tree National Park and the Little San Bernardino Mountains, along the San Bernardino and Riverside County line. The Garlock and San Andreas Faults and Tehachapi Mountains define the western border. On the north, the Mojave has small extensions into Eureka, Saline Owens, and Death Valleys in California. In Nevada the Mojave Desert includes most of Clark County, with fingers extending north into Nye and Lincoln Counties north of Beatty, into Tikaboo and Pahranagat Valleys, and at Elgin. A small corner of Washington County in southwestern Utah, extending to near St. George, is also considered part of the Mojave. The Mojave also occupies the northwestern portion of Arizona to Kingman, with an extension into the lower Grand Canyon area. In the southeast the Colorado River divides the Mojave from the Sonoran Desert. The map provides a generalized regional view of the area covered in this book.

This area is considered a desert because there is little precipitation and significant water loss due to evaporation; in fact, the Mojave is the driest of the North American deserts. The mountains along the southern and western desert borders effectively block many of the moisture-bearing westerly winds from the coast. This "rain shadow" limits the amount of precipitation that reaches the desert. Lowland areas of the western Mojave average about 5 inches of precipitation per year, while the drier areas in the eastern Mojave average only 2 inches per year. Death Valley's average is only 1⁹⁄₁₀ inches per year. In some years, less than ½ inch of rain occurs. When it does rain, prevailing dry air masses and winds quickly facilitate evaporation from the soil surface. Most of the rain in the western Mojave occurs during the winter months, whereas the eastern Mojave has a greater chance of receiving summer monsoon rains. Many areas east of Twentynine Palms receive more than half of the annual precipitation in the summer months. Rains in summer and fall often bring cloudbursts, which cause flash floods that may temporarily provide water for plant roots but also cause erosion and landscape alteration.

The presence or absence of atmospheric water and cloud cover has a tremendous influence on temperature. Water efficiently absorbs and releases heat, so moisture in the atmosphere tends to buffer temperatures. Since the Mojave Desert has little precipitation, it is a land of temperature extremes; it is very hot in summer and cold in winter. Winter storms may bring snow to the higher elevations of the Mojave. On these rare occasions, the snow normally melts within a very short time.

Mojave Desert Topography and Geology

Complex geologic processes have formed the varied topography and soil types in the Mojave Desert, creating many different microclimates that contribute to the plant diversity present today. The movements of tectonic plates have resulted in the formation of the numerous north-south mountain ranges and valleys in the eastern and northern Mojave Desert and Great Basin. This landscape is called horst-and-graben, where "horst" refers to the mountainous uplifted or tilted blocks, and "graben" means "grave," referring to the sunken valleys between the mountain ranges. The lowest graben is Death Valley, with over 550 square miles below sea level, including Badwater, the lowest spot in the nation with an elevation of 282 feet below sea level. Some of the uplifted mountains are quite high, such as Telescope Peak in the Panamint Range (elevation 11,049 feet), which overlooks Badwater to the east. The action of the Garlock and San Andreas Faults has caused a rotation of the mountain ranges in the western and southwestern Mojave, resulting in more of an east-west than a north-south orientation.

There is evidence of extensive volcanic activity in various parts of the Mojave Desert and in the adjacent Owens Valley and Sierra Nevada Range. This is primarily a result of molten materials emerging through faults in the thinning crust. You will find recent lava flows at Lavic and Amboy and in the far northern Mojave and Owens Valley. The Sierra Nevada volcano, Mammoth Mountain, is an example on a larger scale. Cinder cones or craters are prevalent at Cima, Pisgah, Amboy, and other sites. The numerous faults have also allowed submerged molten materials (magma) to heat water below; hot springs form when the hot water surfaces. These hot

Wet playa

springs are home to thermophilic (heat-loving) bacteria that can tolerate temperatures well above 122 degrees F, a water temperature that will scald your hand if you immerse it. The soils around hot springs are often salt encrusted, where only the salt-tolerant plants called halophytes can grow.

Runoff waters from mountains in and bordering the Mojave Desert have no route to the ocean, so the interior drainage collects in low valleys. At the end of the last glacial maximum, the melting of glaciers caused so much water to accumulate in these low spots that a large proportion of the northern Mojave was covered by a series of lakes from Owens Valley to Death Valley. The gigantic Lake Manly, which covered what is now Death Valley, was over 600 feet deep and 90 miles long. There were numerous smaller lakes, including Lake Searles, Lake Panamint, China Lake, and just north of the Mojave Desert, Owens Lake. Lake Mannix stretched along the Mojave River from Barstow to the Cave Mountain area. With the retreat of the glaciers and drying of the climate, these lakes have dried up; they are now called **playas**. The ancient shorelines of many of these relic lakes are visible as strand lines on some hillsides above the playas. During

STEPHEN INGRAM

Dry playa

wetter periods, runoff laden with salts and minerals reaches these playas. Because of heavy sedimentation and clay deposits in the underlying soil, the runoff water tends to pool on top. This water evaporates, leaving the salts and minerals on the playa surface. Many of the playas have a high accumulation of compounds that behave like common baking soda, causing "self-rising" soil that puffs up and forms an upper crust. The high salt content prevents plants from growing on the surface in the center of the playa, but salt-tolerant (halophytic) plants often occupy margins. These are called wet playas, and an example is Soda Lake. Other playas (called **dry playas**) retain claylike properties, forming large cracks in the mud as the water evaporates. An example is El Mirage Dry Lake in the western Mojave.

Alluvial deposits, caused by the erosion of sand and debris from mountains in and surrounding the Mojave Desert, reach a depth of at least 4,000 feet in the Antelope Valley, with a decrease in depth toward the eastern Mojave. Alluvial deposition also occurs in the canyons through which the water flows out of the mountains. These sloping accumulations of debris that form skirts at the bases of mountains are called **alluvial fans,** or **bajadas,** when they coalesce. Runoff water can channel down bajadas on its way to basins, forming washes or gullies, often called **arroyos.** In some areas, eroded and windblown decomposed granite and sediments can accumulate to form **sand dune systems,** which are discussed under desert dune vegetation, below.

Mojave Desert Soils and Rock Surfaces

Soil formation in the Mojave Desert occurs primarily by physical weathering of parent rock material by wind and water. A small amount of biological weathering can also take place when acids from lichens dissolve minerals on rock surfaces, or when plant roots fracture bedrock. Since there is very little water in the Mojave, soils tend to be poorly developed and very thin. The most weathered portion on the surface, called topsoil, is usually less than 6 inches deep, compared to fertile farmlands where the topsoil can be several feet deep. Many plant species need a deep topsoil layer and cannot grow in the desert for this reason.

Texture in relation to soil nutrients and water: Soil texture refers to the relative proportions of different-size particles in the soil. The smallest particles are clay, silt particles are midsized, and sand particles are relatively large. Since the Mojave has poor weathering of parent rock material, the soil texture is sandy, with large spaces between particles that allow water and dissolved minerals to quickly percolate. Cold winter temperatures, lack of water, and sparse vegetation result in poor conditions and slow rates of decomposition by soil microorganisms such as bacteria and fungi; this contributes to the paucity of nutrients in sandy desert soils.

Cryptobiotic soil crusts form when strands of cyanobacteria (formerly called blue-green algae) hold soil particles together, forming a stable matrix where algae, lichens, and mosses can infiltrate. This crust prevents the strong desert winds from blowing away the soil, especially the smaller particles, so the soil can hold more mineral nutrients. These crusts may be the only source of nitrogen for plants in many desert areas. The cyanobacteria are able to take atmospheric nitrogen and change it into a form that can be used by plants, through a process called nitrogen fixation (this function is also carried out by bacteria living in root nodules on many Pea Family plants). These crusts are necessary for the establishment of some species, yet they also function as a barrier to other seeds. The seeds of the invasive Red Brome *(Bromus madritensis* ssp. *rubens)* are unable to penetrate crusts, which can explain why this plant is prevalent in disturbed areas where the crusts have been broken. Off-highway vehicles, grazing, and other types of soil disturbance are destructive to cryptobiotic crusts, which are essential to proper arid land ecosystem functioning.

Some Mojave Desert soils have **caliche,** an impenetrable subsurface layer of accumulated calcium carbonates and other salts. As water is drawn to the soil surface by evaporation, these materials are left behind, hardening into a crust. Water does not soak through this layer, it is difficult for plant roots to penetrate, and it is nearly impossible to dig through it if you are trying to plant a garden. **Carbonate outcrops** (limestone, dolomite, and marble) are scattered throughout the mountains of the Mojave Desert and on low, north-facing slopes of the Transverse Ranges. The chemical makeup of these carbonate soils is a stressful environment for plants, yet some are able to adapt. Many of our rare and endemic Mojave Desert species are found on these soils.

Desert varnish is a dark reddish brown or black coating on the outer surfaces of rocks and boulders in many parts of the Mojave. Turning the boulders over often reveals a reddish or orange varnish coating on the rock undersurfaces as well. Desert varnish is extremely thin, sometimes less than $\frac{1}{100}$ millimeter. Several theories for its formation have been proposed, one of which involves the absorption of atmospheric iron and manganese by bacteria that live on the rock surfaces. These minerals are slowly oxidized and deposited with clay particles onto the rock surfaces over tens of thousands of years. The effects of desert varnish on plant growth are unclear, although there are some desert plants that seem to be found mostly in areas where desert varnish exists. The amount of accumulated desert varnish can help geologists and archeologists date landforms and human artifacts. It is thought that the alkaline dust that becomes airborne from the passage of off-highway vehicles may inhibit desert varnish–producing bacteria.

Lichen crusts are apparent on many rock surfaces in the Mojave Desert. These come in many shades from greens and grays to bright reds, oranges, and yellows. They consist of algae and fungi that live in an intertwined symbiotic relationship called obligate mutualism, in which both organisms benefit and one cannot survive without the other. The alga carries out photosynthesis, providing food for both itself and its fungal partner. The fungus provides protection from wind and scorching sun and may also secrete weak acids that can help the lichen absorb mineral nutrients from the rock. When conditions are dry, the lichen remains inactive, but when there is moisture available, it sucks up water like a sponge and begins making food. Lichens fulfill the very important ecosystem function of crumbling rock surfaces so that mosses and grasses can become established, which in turn facilitates the growth of larger plants. This process is called primary succession. Lichen colonies probably live for hundreds of years, but they eventually absorb and concentrate toxic compounds so that the fungal component dies. They are very sensitive to air pollution and have been used as pollution indicators.

Past Vegetation of the Mojave

How can we know what the Mojave Desert vegetation was like in the past? Fossilized remains of giant ground sloths, camels, and three-toed horses and extensive stromatolites from shallow-water lake systems throughout the region indicate that the vegetation was much more dense and lush in ancient times. There is also evidence from the more recent past, from the time since the last full glaciation, which can help explain and account for the vegetation that we see today.

Ancient homes of pack rats give us a glimpse of what species were present since the last glacial maximum, about 18,000 to 20,000 years ago. To understand this evidence, it is important to know about pack rat physiology, ecology, and behavior. The most common species in the Mojave is called the Desert pack rat *(Neotoma lepida)*. This is a New World rodent that is not related to the European rat associated with filth and overcrowded cities. Desert pack rats are light beige, weigh less than one pound, and have large ears and prominent eyes. They are not as well adapted to desert living as their common name suggests, for they urinate copiously, losing valuable water. Since they live in a place where water is scarce, they compensate by eating green, moist vegetation. Unfortunately, this type of diet doesn't provide them with much energy, making it difficult to cope with the temperature extremes of the desert. Natural selection has favored individuals who are active at night and who build nests. A nest can decrease the energy costs of regulating body temperature, protecting the animal from excessive heat and cold. A nest can also provide a place to hide by day, minimizing water loss and offering protection from predators.

The nests are built in crevices, caves, and under dense vegetation. The pack rat makes improvements by dragging in sticks, green plant parts, animal droppings, bones, and just about whatever else is available. Cactus joints are frequently added, which are effective at deterring predators, especially coyotes. If you listen at night, you can hear them hauling items to the nest, making quite a racket! As pack rats die, new generations of pack rats continue to build nests at the same site, adding materials to the older nests. In some places, this has gone on for millennia. The abundant urine that is added to the nest components tends to crystallize, solidifying and preserving the remains of woody plant species used in nest construction, so that they are still identifiable millennia later. These remains from numerous middens have been identified, quantified, and radiocarbon-dated to give a picture of what the vegetation was like during the last 18,000 years in the Mojave Desert and in other areas where middens are found.

Consider that the last full glacial period was around 20,000 years ago. Current models show that the average temperature was cooler by at least 6 degrees C. and that there was at least 40 percent more precipitation. About 16,000 to 12,000 years ago, the glaciers began to retreat, and from 12,000 to 10,000 years ago there was a warming trend, marking the beginning of the modern interglacial age called the Holocene. In the middle Holocene there was a drying trend, called the xerothermic, that favored more xeric (dry adapted) species. Midden data from various sites in the Mojave Desert paint different pictures of vegetation change in response to these climate changes. This is not surprising, since topography, latitude, and climate varied site to site. However, there are general trends that will be described here.

During the last glacial period, vast lakes covered much of the Mojave Desert. Pinyon-Juniper woodland and Juniper woodland were much more widespread, occurring at much lower elevations than at present, sometimes even on the desert floor in moist areas. But now there are small, isolated pockets of woodland, which are restricted to the middle and upper elevations of scattered mountain ranges. In the northern Mojave, Limber Pine *(Pinus flexilis)* and Western Bristlecone Pine *(Pinus longaeva)* were also found at much lower elevations on upper slopes. Now they occur only on the highest slopes, north of the Mojave. On the lowest and very driest sites, desert scrub was present. However, it did not consist of heat-tolerant species that we see in desert scrub today, but of species that are better adapted to cold (here called steppe species), such as Big Sagebrush *(Artemisia tridentata)* and Winter Fat *(Krascheninnikovia lanata)*. As conditions became hotter and drier in the xerothermic period of the middle Holocene, the woodlands retreated to higher altitudes and latitudes. Steppe species also migrated to moister, cooler areas. The number of succulent species decreased. With this decline in woodland and steppe species at low elevations came a corresponding increase in heat-loving species, such as Creosote Bush *(Larrea tridentata)*, White Bur-Sage *(Ambrosia dumosa)*, Pygmy-Cedar *(Peucephyllum schottii)*, and Honey-Sweet *(Tidestromia oblongifolia)*. Some species were present before the retreat of the glaciers, but many were new, and they arrived at different times in different locations in the Mojave Desert. The Creosote Bush *(Larrea tridentata)* arrived very early after the glacial retreat in some locations, evidently migrating north from the Chihuahuan and Sonoran Deserts. The King Clone Creosote near Lucerne Valley is estimated to be over 11,000 years old, and is probably the oldest living plant on Earth. This is evidence of its early arrival in the Mojave Desert, yet in its most northern present range, the earliest Creosote Bush midden record is only 5,500 years old. At the end of the middle Holocene there was a temporary increase in precipitation, allowing the immigration of more mesic (water-requiring) species such as Mormon Tea *(Ephedra* species), Rhatany *(Krameria* species), and Desert Almond *(Prunus fasciculata)*, which contribute to the species richness present today.

Past Human Uses of Mojave Desert Plants

Ethnobotanical information is given in the comments section for numerous plants in this book. In many cases, details are included about how the plant was used by specific groups that occupied different areas of the Mojave Desert. The groups mentioned are those that existed in historical times, not the most ancient desert dwellers. These groups were primarily hunter-gatherers, relying mostly on plant foods and supplementing their diets with meat when it was available. Because there is little rainfall in the desert, food items were not plentiful, and so populations of most of these bands were also small. Because of the seasonal availability of resources, desert dwellers of the past often had annual migration patterns, occupying lowlands in winter months and higher elevations in summer. The populations were also scattered, with nuclear family groups as the main social structure. Occasionally larger groups would come together for rabbit drives or hunts, and some groups developed trade routes. In areas of richer and more reliable resources, larger extended family groups were common.

The **Western Shoshone** primarily lived in the Great Basin, but they also inhabited the northern Mojave Desert, including northern portions of the Panamint Range, Death Valley, and Funeral Mountains, east to the Pintwater Range and present-day Beatty, Nevada. The **Southern Paiute** occupied present-day Las Vegas and its surrounds, including the Spring Mountains, Clark Mountain, and the eastern flanks of the Black and Avawats Mountains, to the upper stretches of the Colorado River and northwestern Arizona. Both the Paiute and Shoshone were hunter-gatherers and made annual migrations to harvest pine nuts and mesquite pods. Many plant resources were managed by pruning, scattering seeds, and burning to increase yields. The tribes closest to the Colorado River had limited agriculture, while the closely related Owens Valley Paiute used Owens River water to irrigate native plants.

The **Chemehuevi** lived in the areas west of the Colorado River and in the eastern and southern Mojave Desert, south of Clark Mountain to the north-facing slopes of the Little San Bernardino Mountains. They were hunter-gatherers who were skillful at making and using willow hunting bows. This enabled them to hunt big game, including deer and bighorn sheep, which supplemented their diet of seeds, berries, yucca fruits, cacti, reptiles, and rabbits. They later added a few cultivated crops to their diet. They are known to have made long journeys to visit neighboring groups, using extensive trail systems, including the Mohave Trail. They are also renowned for making very fine baskets.

The **Mohave** settled in the Colorado River Valley, north and south of Needles, but south of the territory occupied by Southern Paiute. Their language ties them to Arizona groups to the east. They are noted for farming pumpkins, corn, beans, and tobacco. They also fished and gathered large quantities of mesquite pods. With time for leisure activities, they developed trade routes, such as the Mohave Trail, which went from Needles to the Mojave River with stops at springs, including Rock Spring, Cedar Spring, Soda Lake, Dagget, and Barstow. This same trail was later called the Mohave Road, and was used by trappers, settlers, and gold seekers. They also had time for fighting with neighbors! They fought extensively with the

Chemehuevi to the west, and the territory occupied by these groups constantly shifted.

The **Kawaiisu** lived from Bakersfield, through the Tehachapi Valley, and into the northwestern Mojave Desert, to Red Rock Canyon, and north almost to Little Lake. Most artifacts in this part of the Mojave are from 500 to 1,500 years old, leading to speculation that ancestors of this group left the southern Sierra Nevada during the mini-ice-age of 3,000 years ago, and may have began migrating back to the Sierra during a global warming period 700 to 800 years ago. The Kawaiisu territory encompassed a wide range of habitat types, through which they migrated to take advantage of seasonal food resources such as elderberries, manzanita, chia, and acorns. They hunted deer, antelope, and bear. They also had an extensive trail system to contact the neighboring Paiute and Chemehuevi, making seasonal trips east as far as the Mojave and Amargosa Rivers.

The **Serrano** occupied the San Bernardino Mountains, including the northern desert slopes. The **Vanyume** were likely an extension of the Serrano, since they spoke nearly the same language, but very little is known about their culture. They lived along the Mojave River to at least Barstow, and in pockets on the desert slopes of the San Gabriel Mountains, as at Pearblossom. They did not cultivate crops, but survived on mesquite pods, various seeds, insects, reptiles, and rabbits, and also likely gathered pine nuts from the foothills. Evidently their impoverished lifestyle did not favor population growth, for there were very few Vanyume when Father Francisco Garcés traveled through the Oro Grande area in 1776, providing the Vanyume their first contact with whites. By 1900 they were extinct, evidently the victims of several smallpox epidemics, raids by other tribes, and assimilation into white culture.

Early Botanical Exploration of the Mojave Desert

This section gives information about some of the bold, adventurous individuals who explored and collected plants in the Mojave Desert during the past two to three centuries. Many of them sent plant specimens to university botanists, especially Asa Gray of Harvard, who often named plants in honor of the collector. These are arranged in alphabetical order by last names. Unfortunately it is impossible to include all the collectors on this list, especially those who have made important contributions in the last fifty years. You will find more information under the comments section for many of the species accounts.

Annie Montague Alexander (1867–1950) and her friend, **Louise Kellogg** (1879–1967), collected museum specimens of over 20,000 plants, animals, and fossils throughout the northern and eastern Mojave in the 1940s. Annie funded research for Joseph Grinnell, John C. Merriam, and other well-known scientists, and she was a benefactress of the University of California at Berkeley Museum of Paleontology.

William Whitman Bailey (1845–1915) studied botany under Asa Gray of Harvard, and later became a botany professor at Brown. He was a botanist on the United States Geological Survey of the 40th parallel, and he made vast collections in southern Nevada.

Ira Waddell Clokey (1878–1950) collected throughout southern Nevada, culminating in the production of a noteworthy flora of the Spring Mountains (Mount Charleston) in the 1930s.

Frederick Vernon Coville (1867–1937) was the Chief of Botany for the United States Department of Agriculture, an instructor at Cornell University, and curator of the National Herbarium before and after it was transferred to the Smithsonian. He made extensive plant collections on the Death Valley expedition of 1891.

Mary DeDecker (1909–2000) made botanical explorations throughout the northern Mojave Desert and Owens Valley. She collected nearly 6,500 specimens, many of which she sent to Philip A. Munz when he was working on *A California Flora*. She started the Owens Valley Committee to protect Owens Valley water from the Los Angeles Department of Water and Power, she founded the Bristlecone Chapter of the California Native Plant Society, and she wrote the *Flora of the Northern Mojave Desert*.

John Charles Frémont (1813–1890) worked with the United States Topographical Corps on surveys in the eastern United States. In the 1840s he was appointed to lead three expeditions to map routes to the West, including one in 1844 that took him from the Tehachapis, across the Mojave Desert in southern California, and northeast through southern Nevada. Although he was not a botanist, he made many important collections, one of which was the Pinyon Pine he found near Cajon Pass. Numerous plant species are named for Frémont.

Father Francisco Garcés was a Franciscan priest who was the first white man to journey through the Mojave Desert. He followed what is now known as the Mojave Road, passing through Piute Creek, the Providence Mountains, the New York Mountains, and Soda Springs. He encountered the Vanyume at the Mojave River in 1776, near the present-day Oro Grande, and reported on their use of native plants.

M. French Gilman (1871–1944) was a longtime caretaker and naturalist at Death Valley. He made numerous plant collections and ornithological observations.

Edmund Carroll Jaeger (1887–1983) was head of the zoology department at Riverside City College from the 1920s to the 1950s. He made botanical collections throughout the Mojave and Colorado Deserts, finding new species and documenting species ranges. He authored *The California Desert, Desert Wild Flowers, Desert Wildlife, A Naturalist's Death Valley*, and *Deserts of North America*. He made the first botanical collections in the Clark Mountains and an important report of plants from the Spring Mountains. Numerous Mojave Desert plants are named in his honor.

Willis Linn Jepson (1867–1946) collected throughout the Mojave Desert in the early 1900s, including Victorville, Barstow, Stoddard Wells, the Ord Mountains, the Panamint and Funeral Mountains, and along the Colorado River. He founded the California Botanical Society and wrote *Trees of California, Manual of the Flowering Plants of California*, and the unfinished, multivolume *Flora of California*.

Marcus Eugene Jones (1852–1934) was a self-educated mining engineer and botanist who worked for a Salt Lake City railroad company. He collected plants throughout the West, including the Mojave Desert and San Bernardino Mountains. He questioned the authority of Asa Gray and other prominent botanists by publishing *Contributions to Western Botany*, making it possible for western botanists to publish on their own.

George H. Goddard (1817–1906) was a cartographer from Great Britain. He served as a naturalist to assist Lieutenant Tredwell Moore on an expedition to eastern California in the 1850s to find a route for a railway that would pass over the Sierra Nevada range. He made the first map of Death Valley, and he collected hundreds of botanical specimens from that region.

Joseph Christmas Ives (1828–1868) participated in the Whipple Expedition and was then assigned to explore the Colorado River. He made botanical collections around the present-day Lake Mead and into the Grand Canyon. He erroneously predicted that white settlers would leave that area alone, as it resembled the "gates of hell."

Clinton Hart Merriam (1855–1942) was the head of the Division of Ornithology and Mammalogy for the United States Department of Agriculture. One of the first of his many biological surveys of the West was the department's Death Valley expedition in the 1890s. He developed the life zone concept to explain distributions of plants with the purpose of determining the suitability of land for farming.

Philip A. Munz (1892–1974) collected throughout the Mojave Desert, often with other important botanists including Marcus E. Jones and John C. Roos. He wrote *A California Flora* and *A Flora of Southern California.*

Aven Nelsen (1859–1952) was a professor of botany and college president at the University of Wyoming. He was primarily interested in the flora of the Rocky Mountains but collected extensively throughout the Western states, including parts of the Mojave Desert.

Edward Palmer (1831–1911) was born in England but spent most of his life collecting over 10,000 species of plants in the Americas. In 1891 he led an expedition across California through Death Valley, and he collected extensively in southwestern Utah. Many plant species are named in honor of him.

Samuel Bonsall Parish (1838–1928) and **William Fletcher Parish** (1840–1918) were brothers from San Bernardino, California. They made extensive botanical collection trips throughout the local mountains and deserts, including the Mojave. Samuel was in contact with many of the leading botanists, and many species were named for him.

Charles Christopher Parry (1823–1890) worked for the Pacific Railroad and Mexican Boundary Surveys and made many plant collection trips to the deserts and mountains of the American Southwest. He discovered numerous new species, and quite a few are named in his honor.

Carl Albert Purpus (1853–1941) was a German-born horticulturalist who made extensive collection trips to many parts of the United States and Central America. From 1895 to 1899 he explored southern and western Nevada, northern and western Arizona, western Utah, and the northeastern portion of the Mojave Desert in California. He was an approved collector for the University of California at Berkeley Herbarium, although he was not paid. He supported himself by selling seeds and unusual plants that he collected to German horticulturalists.

Sereno Watson (1826–1892) was a camp cook who was appointed as plant collector when William Bailey left the Clarence King expedition of the 40th parallel. He later was one of the botanists on the Josiah D. Whitney expedition, where he collected and described many species across Utah, Nevada, and the eastern Sierra Nevada Range.

George M. Wheeler (1842–1905) conducted surveys in the 1870s for the United States Corps of Engineers. The first large survey documented geological, botanical, zoological, and archeological information on vast areas of southern Nevada, southwestern Utah, and eastern California, including the Mojave Desert. He received such acclaim for the first survey that Congress decided to fund a second survey through Death Valley to the Colorado River.

Lt. Amiel Weeks Whipple (1817–1863) commanded the Pacific Railroad Survey of the 35th parallel. He made numerous important botanical collections through the Mojave Desert with the survey surgeon and botanist, **Dr. John Milton Bigelow** (1804–1878). The survey route was that of the historic Mohave Road and later Highway 66, but it was not the ultimate location of the transcontinental railway.

Carl B. Wolf (1905–1974) collected in Kern County and the northwestern Mojave Desert. He was a botanist at the Rancho Santa Ana Botanic Garden and author of several works on oaks and cypress.

Present Vegetation of the Mojave

Although the Mojave Desert does not sustain lush vegetation, the rich topographic variation supports high species diversity with over 2,600 species of plants (this excludes elevations above 7,500 feet in the Panamint, Spring, and Sheep Ranges). Some of the most common plant families in the Mojave include the Sunflower Family (Asteraceae), the Grass Family (Poaceae), the Pea Family (Fabaceae), the Mustard Family (Brassicaceae), the Figwort Family (Scrophulariaceae), the Buckwheat Family (Polygonaceae), and the Goosefoot Family (Chenopodiaceae).

About one-fourth of Mojave Desert plants are endemic, meaning they are found nowhere else. Some endemic species with restricted ranges and/or low abundance are considered to be rare. Less than 10 percent of Mojave Desert plants are considered special-status plants; that is, rare enough to be protected by state or federal listing as threatened or endangered or considered rare by other programs or organizations, such as the California Native Plant Society. This is a far lower proportion of special-status plants than the 35 percent reported in the entire state of California. This may be due to lower human population size and less habitat fragmentation in the Mojave Desert, but it may also be explained by the fact that botanical exploration of the Mojave is not yet complete. Because it can be so hot and dry, and there is so much ground to cover, even the most dedicated botanists tend to stick to the roads while collecting specimens. There are so many Mojave Desert canyons and mountain areas where the flora has not yet been documented. There may be rare species left to discover!

Where plants occur depends on elevation, amount of precipitation, soil type, temperature, slope aspect, and many other variables, including the past history of dispersal. Because different species have individual ranges of tolerance to environmental conditions, each species grows only where it is able. Plants are often found in assemblages of those that have similar tolerances, called vegetation types. The species accounts commonly mention the vegetation type in which a species is found; these are described below.

Vegetation types are determined by the dominant species present. Dominant species are often the largest plants, the most abundant plants, or those that occupy the most area, or a combination of these traits. In addition to the dominant species, nearly all of the vegetation types have ephemerals, which are annuals that respond to seasonal rain. In the Mojave Desert, most of these annuals germinate in late winter and appear in the spring and early summer, but occasionally there is a late summer to fall crop, especially in Creosote Bush scrub. The sizes of the annuals often vary with the amount of rain. The species accounts may often give the upper size limit that has been recorded, but in a dry year the plant can be much smaller. Many of the spring annuals that germinate in response to winter rain have seed coat compounds that inhibit germination. There must be enough rain to completely wash away these compounds before germination can occur. The summer to fall annuals also germinate in response to rain, but they also require high temperatures. Many of them are capable of a special type of photosynthesis (called C_4) in which the enzyme to fix carbon dioxide works more efficiently in the heat. The species diversity of spring annuals is much greater than that of summer to fall annuals.

The vegetation types described below are not discrete, but blend into one another across environmental gradients, such as an elevation or moisture gradient. Areas where the vegetation types overlap and blend are called ecotones. In general, the vegetation types are presented in order of increasing elevation, beginning with those vegetation types found in the lowest areas of the Mojave Desert, except for riparian and dry wash vegetation types, which can cover wide elevation ranges.

Alkali sink vegetation generally occurs in the lowest areas of the Mojave, at or below 2,000 feet. These are areas where rainwater drains and collects, but it doesn't penetrate the soil rapidly due to the presence of a clay layer or caliche layer under the surface. Alkaline dry lake beds (playas) are an example of such an area. The water pools on the surface and eventually evaporates, but the salts that were washed in with the water accumulate, giving the soil a very high pH. Salt presents a problem for plants in that it tends to

Alkali sink

STEPHEN INGRAM

draw water out of their roots. Plants that live in alkali sinks have methods to deal with salt (see plant adaptations section); such plants are called halophytes. A species that tolerates extremely high salt concentrations and that you will often find in alkali sinks is Saltgrass *(Distichlis spicata)*. Other common alkali sink species include Iodine Bush *(Allenrolfea occidentalis)*, Bush Seepweed *(Suaeda moquinii)*, Yerba Mansa *(Anemopsis californica)*, Honey Mesquite *(Prosopis glandulosa)*, and the introduced Salt Cedar *(Tamarix ramosissima)* and Russian Thistle *(Salsola tragus)*.

Saltbush scrub vegetation is often found beyond the extreme halophyte zone around alkali sinks, and alkali sink vegetation often grades into Saltbush scrub. The species here must also deal with salt, but not in as high concentrations as found in the alkali sink. Dominant species often include members of the Goosefoot Family (Chenopodiaceae), such as Four-Wing Saltbush *(Atriplex canescens)*, Shadscale *(Atriplex confertifolia)*, and Allscale *(Atriplex polycarpa)*. These species can also be found in **Shadscale scrub** vegetation that occurs in higher elevations in the northern Mojave and near Death Valley. Shadscale scrub also commonly includes Hop-Sage *(Grayia spinosa)* and Winter Fat *(Krascheninnikovia lanata)*.

Saltbush scrub

Creosote Bush scrub

Creosote Bush scrub vegetation covers the bulk of the desert floor and lower alluvial fans. It is characterized by shrubs that seem evenly spaced, with enough distance between so that bare ground is seen between them. Possible reasons for the spacing pattern are discussed under the Creosote Bush *(Larrea tridentata)* and White Bur-Sage *(Ambrosia dumosa)* entries of this book. Areas with this type of vegetation typically receive between 2 to 8 inches of rainfall a year. Since Creosote Bush can withstand a broad range of environmental conditions, it is the dominant species and has a very wide range not only in the Mojave but in the Sonoran and Chihuahuan Deserts as well. In different parts of its range in the Mojave, there are codominant shrubs with smaller ranges of tolerance, so that in different areas you will see different shrub species mixed with the Creosote Bush. Some of its most common associates include White Bur-Sage *(Ambrosia dumosa)*, Brittlebush *(Encelia farinosa, Encelia actoni, Encelia virginensis)*, Cheesebush *(Hymenoclea salsola)*, Mojave Yucca *(Yucca shidigera)*, Silver Cholla *(Opuntia echinocarpa)*, and Beavertail *(Opuntia basilaris)*.

Desert dune vegetation often occurs within Creosote Bush scrub in areas of high sand concentrations. The sand is either from ancient beaches or due to decomposed rock that has been eroded and transported by wind and water to accumulate over millennia. Desert dunes are unique in that the sand readily absorbs water like a sponge. The water can be retained beneath the surface, protected from evaporation by layers of sand above. The plants on desert dunes must have deep roots to take advantage of the water. Dominant dune species include Honey Mesquite *(Prosopis glandulosa),* Desert Willow *(Chilopsis linearis),* Big Galleta *(Pleuraphis rigida),* Desert Sand-Verbena *(Abronia villosa),* Bugseed *(Dicoria canescens),* and Sandpaper Plant *(Petalonyx thurberi).*

Joshua Tree woodland vegetation occurs between 2,500 and 4,500 feet, in areas that receive between 6 to 15 inches of rainfall per year. The Joshua Tree *(Yucca brevifolia)* is not only the dominant plant of this vegetation type, it is also unique to the Mojave Desert. Edmund C. Jaeger asserted that if you drew a line around the entire range of the Joshua Tree, you would be drawing a line around the Mojave Desert. Common associates of the Joshua Tree include Mojave Yucca *(Yucca shidigera),* Paper-Bag Bush *(Salazaria mexicana),* box thorn *(Lycium andersonii, Lycium cooperi),* sage *(Salvia dorrii, Salvia mohavensis),* and buckwheat *(Eriogonum* species).

Blackbush scrub vegetation can occur on its own or as an understory of Joshua Tree woodland or Pinyon-Juniper woodland. It has a wide elevational range. The dominant species is Blackbush *(Coleogyne ramosissima),* which often occurs in vast, somewhat dense stands, making the landscape appear almost a uniform dark gray

STEPHEN INGRAM

Joshua Tree woodland

Blackbush scrub

color. The species that are commonly associated with Blackbush are mostly found in several vegetation types. These include ephedra *(Ephedra nevadensis, Ephedra viridis)*, Hop-Sage *(Grayia spinosa)*, Turpentine Broom *(Thamnosma montana)*, horsebrush *(Tetradymia species)*, Cheesebush *(Hymenoclea salsola)*, and Winter Fat *(Krascheninnikovia lanata)*.

Sagebrush scrub is the dominant vegetation type of the Great Basin Desert, but some can be found along the margins of the Mojave, such as in the southern Sierra Nevada foothills and northern slopes of the Transverse Ranges. There is also a small amount in the eastern Mojave Desert. Sagebrush scrub vegetation can occur on its own or as an understory of Pinyon-Juniper woodland. The dominant species is Big Sagebrush *(Artemisia tridentata)*, and in some places it can form nearly pure stands. Other species that may be present include saltbush *(Atriplex* species), Rubber Rabbitbrush *(Chrysothamnus nauseosus)*, Green Ephedra *(Ephedra viridis)*, Hop-Sage *(Grayia spinosa)*, and Bitterbrush *(Purshia glandulosa)*. There are also numerous species of grasses, including perennial bunch grasses, making this desirable grazing land. However, grazing of Sagebrush scrub negatively impacts the perennial grasses and increases the shrub cover. Cheat-Grass

(Bromus tectorum) is a frequent invader, which competes with the native grasses and is thought to increase the fire frequency.

Pinyon-Juniper woodland vegetation is found between 4,500 to 8,000 feet in areas that receive 12 to 20 inches of precipitation each year, some of which may be in the form of snow. The summer and winter temperatures in this vegetation area are generally lower than those of the desert floor, and it is here that we find a dominant tree, the Pinyon Pine *(Pinus monophylla,* or in a few areas in the eastern Mojave, *Pinus edulis).* The vegetation cover here is denser than at lower elevations, and it can support fire, although the fire frequency is very low, naturally occurring every 150 to 300 years. Once burned, this vegetation type may take up to 100 years to recover. Pinyon Pines need nurse plants to become established, since cold temperatures and frost heaving destabilize the soil and harm fragile roots of seedlings. Once they germinate and become established, they grow very slowly. A codominant in this vegetation type is the California Juniper *(Juniperus californicus)* or in some areas, usually in the eastern Mojave, Utah Juniper *(Juniperus osteosperma).* Some locations have both juniper species, while infrequently they are both absent, and occasionally the junipers occur without Pinyon

Pinyon-Juniper woodland

Pine. Other associates include Bitterbrush *(Purshia glandulosa)*, Apache Plume *(Fallugia paradoxa)*, Big Sagebrush *(Artemisia tridentata)*, Green Ephedra *(Ephedra viridis)*, mountain mahogany (*Cercocarpus* species), and buckwheat (*Eriogonum* species). Pinyon-Juniper woodland is also a common vegetation type in mountains of the Great Basin.

Desert riparian vegetation occurs where there is year-round water. These areas are not very common in the Mojave but include some stretches along the Mojave and Colorado Rivers and some of the larger springs, such as Pachalka Spring at Clark Mountain. More than 80 percent of desert wildlife species use these ecologically important areas. Large trees are dominant, especially Fremont Cottonwood *(Populus fremontii)*. Several willow species may be present, including Red Willow *(Salix laevigata)*, Goodding's Willow *(Salix gooddingii)*, Arroyo Willow *(Salix lasiolepis)*, and Sand-Bar Willow *(Salix exigua)*. Arizona Ash *(Fraxinus velutina)* is often encountered in riparian areas, especially along the Mojave River, and in the eastern Mojave, Single-Leaf Ash *(Fraxinus anomala)* may be found. In many areas the introduced Salt Cedar *(Tamarix ramosissima)* is a problem, as it is able to more efficiently extract water than cottonwoods or willows. Efforts are

Desert riparian

STEPHEN INGRAM

underway to eradicate Salt Cedar from many of the springs and drainages. Along the Mojave River, the introduced Giant Reed *(Arundo donax)* and Russian Olive *(Eleagnus angustifolia)* are also frequent, although they do not seem to spread nearly as rapidly as Tamarisk. Since many isolated springs throughout the Mojave were old home sites, you may find various introduced species that were planted purposely, including elm, fruit trees, and Black Locust.

Desert dry wash vegetation occurs in canyons and drainages with infrequent but severe flooding. These areas are usually in the foothills, where severe thundershower runoff can quickly accumulate from mountains above. The plants inhabiting these unstable sites must be able to recolonize the area quickly after a flood and become established before the next major flooding event. Some of the species adapted to this lifestyle include the Smoke Tree *(Psorothamnus spinosus)* and Catclaw *(Acacia gregii)*. The tough coats on the seeds of these members of the Pea Family need to be abraded, or scarified, before they can absorb water and germinate. The tumbling of the seeds with gravel and sand during a flash flood accomplishes this. Then the seedling must grow roots quickly to tap water deep in the soil before the next flood

STEPHEN INGRAM

Dry wash

STEPHEN INGRAM

Dry wash post flood

occurs. The seeds have large reserves of stored food in the form of "seed leaves" or cotyledons, which enable them to rapidly send down a taproot. Other species frequently found in dry washes include Desert Waterweed *(Baccharis sergiloides),* Cheesebush *(Hymenoclea salsola),* Desert Willow *(Chilopsis linearis),* and Arrowweed *(Pluchea sericea).*

Plant Adaptations to Desert Climate

The Mojave Desert environment presents many difficulties for plants. Plants must adapt to temperature extremes, salty soils, and most of all, lack of water. Plants make their own food by a process called photosynthesis, which requires sunlight, carbon dioxide from the atmosphere, and water that is absorbed from the soil by plant roots. The carbon dioxide must enter the plant tissues through tiny holes called stomates. Unfortunately, when the stomates are open, water readily evaporates from the inside of the plant, through the stomates, to the outside air. Also, photosynthesis can take place only within a certain temperature range. When the temperatures get too high, the plant must cool down if it is going to take advantage of the sunlight available for photosynthesis. The only method the plant has to cool itself is to open its stomates and allow water to evaporate from the leaf surface. The evaporating water carries heat with it, just as it does when humans sweat. Thus, water loss is the inevitable result of making food and staying cool. Plants in the desert cannot afford this water loss, so they have evolved various structural and physiological features (adaptations) to help minimize it. Plants adapted to dry desert climates are called xerophytes. There are three basic xerophyte strategies. A plant can escape drought, avoid drought, or endure drought.

The **drought escapers** are the annual plants that will germinate only when enough water is available to wash away germination-inhibiting chemicals from their seed coats. They then quickly mature and produce flowers, fruit, and seeds. Their individual lives are over when the drought ensues, but their offspring wait beneath the soil for the next rainy season.

Drought avoiders have vegetative parts that stay alive during the dry season, but they are inactive. By keeping metabolic processes and aboveground leaf surfaces to a minimum, they can avoid water loss. Such plants can be drought-deciduous, losing leaves in summer to minimize evaporative surfaces during hot, dry seasons. Other successful drought avoiders are perennials with some vegetative parts, such as a bulb, surviving underground during the hot, dry seasons.

Drought endurers remain alive and metabolically active during drought. Some adaptive features include hairy leaf surfaces that can trap humidity and form a moist boundary layer to minimize evaporation. A waxy or gummy coating on leaf surfaces also traps moisture in the leaf. Many desert species have either very small leaves, or larger leaves, which are divided into smaller leaflets. This effectively minimizes leaf surfaces from which water can evaporate. Plants with green stems don't need water-evaporating leaves at all, since the stem carries on the photosynthesis. Many desert plants have tough, fibrous tissues in their leaves, which prevent wilting when water is lacking. There are also anatomical adaptations such as the stacking of multiple layers of photosynthetic cells into small leaves; in areas with greater moisture availability, usually only one such layer is present. The stomates are located only on undersurfaces of leaves to avoid wind that increases evaporation rate, or the stomates may be sunken into hollows to keep them from direct contact with wind. Often these sunken stomates have hairs surrounding the hole to trap moisture. Some grasses have special cells on the upper surface called bulliform cells that will lose water during drought, allowing the leaves to fold or curl to trap humidity. The roots of some species may go very deep to tap groundwater or spread very far to collect as much surface water as possible in a short amount of time when it is available. Some species access a nearly constant water supply in this manner; these are called pheatophytes. There are also physiological adaptations to drought. Some plants open their stomates only at night when temperature is lower to reduce evaporation. In this case the carbon dioxide that is needed for photosynthesis enters at night and is stored until morning when light is available; this is called crassulacean acid metabolism.

Some heat-tolerant plants, called **C$_4$ plants,** use an enzyme for photosynthesis that is very efficient at high temperatures, while most other plants (C$_3$ plants) use a less efficient enzyme. Examples of C$_4$ plants include many native grasses as well as the competitive, introduced, and invasive grass species. The annuals that come up only following summer rainfall are also mostly C$_4$ species.

Plants that have adaptations to salty conditions are called **halophytes.** Some halophytic species, such as Saltgrass *(Distichlis spicata),* can tolerate high salt concentrations by secreting salt from leaves and stems. Other species, such as the Iodine Bush *(Allenrolfea occidentalis),* can store excess salt in organs and tissues until those parts die and fall off.

Threats to the Mojave Desert Flora

Development and urban expansion with the associated pollution and wastes are obvious threats to any ecosystem. The Mojave Desert ecosystem also faces a suite of other challenges, some of which are exacerbated by slow recovery rates due to extremely arid conditions.

Utility corridors: The width of individual utility corridors is often relatively narrow, but the desert is crisscrossed by thousands of miles of these, adding up to a considerable total acreage. Vegetation is completely removed where underground pipelines are installed, and studies have documented slow recovery, although there may be a temporary increase in annual species in the cleared zone. These corridors may restrict species migrations and impede gene flow, leading to smaller population sizes and decreased genetic diversity. Corridor construction crews can inadvertently introduce invasive plants, and power-line roads increase the potential for unpatrolled entry, illegal collection, and vandalism. New utility corridors could be placed next to existing roads or corridors to minimize impacts.

Mining: Vegetation is removed at mine sites for roads, piles of tailings, and quarry pits. These direct and localized effects have caused substantial habitat loss for certain endemic plants, especially where there are large mining operations, as at carbonate mines on the desert slopes of the San Bernardino Mountains. Although many effects of mining are quite localized, there are often off-site effects as well. Eroded soil, runoff water carrying toxic materials, problems with windblown dust, and animal deaths at cyanide-pit gold-extraction mines have all been documented in the Mojave Desert.

Off-highway vehicles: Motorcycles, dune-buggies, and four-wheel-drive vehicles have been shown to cause soil compaction, increased erosion, disruption of cryptobiotic soil crusts, damage to plant roots, altered hydrology, and reduced soil-percolation rates, as well as significant reductions in vegetation cover. Scars from off-highway vehicle tracks are expected to persist for many years, as vegetation recovery rates are very slow in arid environments.

Military activities: Military bases, including Fort Irwin, China Lake, Twentynine Palms, Edwards Air Force Base, and Nellis Air Force Base and the Nevada Test Site occupy extensive areas of the Mojave Desert. Intense damage has occurred from military training exercises, tanks and vehicles, bomb tests, and tent areas. On the other hand, many military-controlled areas are protected because the public does not have access. The expansion of Fort Irwin is expected to negatively impact the majority of known Lane Mountain Milkvetch *(Astragalus jaegerianus)* populations. One hundred percent of the known Clokey's Cryptantha *(Cryptantha clokeyi)* populations are on China Lake and Fort Irwin, and there is no protection for this species.

Grazing: Public lands in the Mojave Desert have been grazed by sheep and cattle since the 1800s. The numbers of grazing animals are declining; Arizona, Nevada, and Utah do not sponsor grazing on public lands in the Mojave Desert, and there is currently pressure in California to stop this activity. Positive effects of grazing in the desert have been suggested but not substantiated, such as fertilization of desert plants, facilitation of seed dispersal, and soil aeration. Grazing has been shown to cause a decrease in plant cover and biomass due to destruction of above-ground plant parts, with effects varying according to season, soil condition, and land-use history. Compaction of soil by trampling results in altered surface and subsurface water flow and decreased water availability to plant roots, as well as a redistribution of soluble mineral nutrients. Trampling and compaction also decrease the cover of cryptobiotic soil crusts, which are important in retention of mineral nutrients and water, preventing wind erosion, and thwarting establishment of non-native grasses. Grazing can lead to altered species composition of some plant communities. Recovery from grazing is slow, since the effects of grazing do not stop immediately when animals are removed; the disturbed soil continues to be eroded by wind and invaded by weedy species, and the effects of compaction may permanently alter water flow.

Wild burros and horses: These non-native animals have severely damaged sensitive desert habitats, especially riparian areas and springs. They eat large amounts of vegetation, compact the soil and alter hydrology, and foul water sources, sometimes to the exclusion of native wildlife. Under the poorly thought-out Wild Horse and Burro Act, the Bureau of Land Management has a mandate to provide for these animals that are not native to the Mojave Desert ecosystem. Advocates for burros and horses claim that these are part of our Western cultural heritage, but the historic population sizes were much smaller than they are now, and the damage was nowhere near as severe. Although some springs are being fenced to exclude burros, the vegetation recovery rate is slow, and in some places fences are vandalized, making them ineffective barriers.

Altered water flow: Hydroelectric power and flood control along rivers is a threat to riparian vegetation. If rivers are dammed and water flow controlled, cottonwoods may decline. They require the periodic scouring of a flood, since it brings essential nutrients into the system.

Non-native species invasions: The most common woody invasive in the Mojave Desert is Salt Cedar *(Tamarix ramosissima)*. Salt Cedar outcompetes native riparian vegetation, especially cottonwoods and willows, by numerous means. It has a great tolerance to high salt concentrations and low water availability. Its taproots readily draw deep groundwater, lowering the water table and causing water stress for other species. When it takes in excessive water and evaporates it through its leaves, salts become more concentrated in the soil, creating a hostile environment for other species that are less tolerant to salt. Its dense canopy can exclude seedlings of its competitors and can also cause an increase in fire frequency by creating a continuous fuel load; unfortunately it resprouts very well after fire. Since it evolved elsewhere, its natural herbivores are not around, so not much eats it. It is not surprising, then, that in a 1995 study of riparian vegetation along the Mojave River, Salt Cedar was the dominant species in over 50 percent of the 10,000 acres surveyed.

How can Salt Cedar be eradicated? It is a difficult, labor-intensive process to mechanically remove it, and it is useless to try to burn it out. However, a study on the Colorado River showed that Salt Cedar could not tolerate being flooded for more than 70 days, but the native species Goodding's Willow (Salix gooddingii) survived the flooding. This suggests that if natural water flow were restored, perhaps the resultant flooding may help suppress Salt Cedar invasion. However, this would not be feasible along the Colorado River, as flooding would threaten agricultural lands and developments. Dam removal on the Mojave River would likely be ineffective, as there is probably not enough water available to cause extensive enough flooding.

Annual invasive species also can alter the functioning of Mojave Desert ecosystems. The worst pests are the European grasses, including Red Brome (Bromus madritensis ssp. rubens), Mediterranean Grass (Schismus barbatus), and Cheat Grass (Bromus tectorum). Red-Stemmed Filaree (Erodium cicutarium) is also problematic, as is Sahara Mustard (Brassica tournefortii). These likely compete with native annuals, but more studies are needed. Some of these have been implicated in increasing fire frequency in desert vegetation, which did not evolve with fire. In addition, air pollution can cause an increase of nitrogen deposition in desert soils. This has been linked to an increase in invasions of non-native species that require high nitrogen levels, especially Red Brome. Soil bacteria, fungi, and mycorrhizae (fungi associated with plant roots) could be affected, altering litter decomposition rates and further changing species composition.

What affects the population sizes of these annual invasive species? Recent research shows that Red Brome cannot survive without high nitrogen levels, and it declines following drought. Mediterranean Grass and Red-Stemmed Filaree are not dependent on increased nitrogen, and they are more adapted to dry conditions and therefore likely to survive drought. Spring fires can suppress invasive grasses in chaparral, but prescribed burning is not practical in the Mojave Desert, as some of the native species are not adapted to fire and are adversely affected by it.

Climate change and global warming: What does the future hold? Many climate change models predict a future global warming trend. This is likely associated with the natural cycles of warming and glaciation that have been occurring for millennia, although it may be somewhat intensified by human activities that add to atmospheric greenhouse gases, such as carbon dioxide. The increase in carbon dioxide that is associated with global warming has the potential to increase rates of photosynthesis. Models predict that desert vegetation should have a 50 percent increase in primary productivity (amount of photosynthesis per area per year) with increased carbon dioxide levels. This was tested in a Department of Energy study in Nevada, in which carbon dioxide–rich air was piped into a tented natural desert area. The result was indeed an increase in biomass compared to the control area, but there was an accompanying increase in Red Brome (*Bromus madritensis* ssp. *rubens*), an introduced European grass that uses C_4 photosynthesis, making it very efficient at high temperatures. An increase in this species is implicated as a cause of increased fire frequency in the Mojave Desert and altered function of soil microbes. Global warming, then, is likely to change species compositions in the Mojave Desert, with unpredictable consequences for ecosystem function.

Global warming may cause increased evaporations and storms, providing more water for plants. However, models show that there will not be increased precipitation everywhere; some areas are expected to become more arid. It is not certain what will happen in the Mojave, so it is difficult to predict how the Mojave Desert flora will fare. We know from the past that species ranges shift in response to climate change, but when the climate changes occurred in the Holocene, there were very few barriers to species migration. With human development and landscape manipulation, we may have created impediments to species migration that will not allow them to shift ranges and adapt to future change, perhaps resulting in species extinctions. Development and land use have also caused habitat fragmentation, which is associated with decreased gene flow between populations, genetic drift associated with smaller population sizes, and loss of genetic diversity, which could alter the capability of a population to adapt to change.

Present Conservation and Management

The unique plant resources of the Mojave Desert need protection, but the success of conservation efforts depends on the land-use policies of agencies in charge of public lands. Enormous tracts of ecologically critical land are managed by the military, and the National Park Service has developed general management plans for Death Valley and Joshua Tree National Parks and the East Mojave National Preserve. The United States Bureau of Land Management oversees the largest proportion of the Mojave Desert. This agency is required to manage for multiple uses and is responsive to public input. Many user groups have paid lobbies supported by industry, such as mining, grazing, and off-highway vehicle recreation. However, those who are interested in participating in conservation and education-oriented activities do not have industries to back them; most who get involved in lobbying the management agencies are largely unpaid volunteers. It is important to pay attention and voice your opinion on plans and policies for the management of public lands.

It is also difficult for the agencies to adequately patrol the lands they manage, mostly because they do not receive adequate funding to provide rangers and other personnel. Those who spend a lot of time in the Mojave Desert can take an active role by watching the activities taking place on public lands. When you see destructive actions and events, be sure to report these to the management agency and to the California Native Plant Society, a statewide watchdog organization with many chapters, including the new Mojave Desert Chapter. You can reach them at their website, www.cnps.org, to find out about conservation issues, field trips, meetings, and horticultural uses of native plants. There are also native plant societies in Arizona and Nevada. Get involved! You can play a vital role in the protection of the unique resources of the Mojave Desert.

How to Use This Book

This book groups plants by flower color, and within each color the species accounts appear in alphabetical order by family. Keep in mind that a book of this size cannot cover all of the plants in the Mojave Desert, so you may not find an exact match. Species descriptions have been simplified by minimizing the number of botanical descriptive terms used. A glossary of these terms is found in the back of this book. Following the introduction you will find illustrations of the parts of a leaf, variations of leaf shape, arrangement, and venation. Basic diagrams of flower parts for several flower types are also included. You may wish to purchase a 10X hand lens to see some of the delightful details up close! These are often available at stamp collecting shops, jewelers, and forestry suppliers.

The reader is encouraged to compare plants found in the field to herbarium specimens to confirm identification. An herbarium is a museum collection of dried and pressed plant specimens that are used to study ranges, habitats, taxonomy, and genetics of specific plants and to assess and document species diversity of a region. Numerous major herbaria with Mojave Desert specimens are open to the public, including those at University of Nevada at Las Vegas, University of California at Riverside, and Rancho Santa Ana Botanic Garden in Claremont, California. Smaller collections are available locally at Victor Valley College in Victorville, the Maturango Museum in Ridgecrest, the Desert Studies Center at Soda Springs, and the University of California Granite Mountains Reserve. Collectors are required to obtain permission to collect from local land management agencies and private landowners.

How Plants Get Their Names

In the 1700s Carl Linnaeus developed a system to inventory and name species, which, although modified somewhat, is still in use today. This system arranges species into taxa (categories) according to their similarities. The taxa are ranked in seven hierarchical levels. All plants belong to the plant kingdom. Members of this kingdom are arranged into smaller taxa called phyla (singular phylum). All of the members of a phylum are arranged into smaller taxa called classes, classes are sub-grouped into orders, orders are sub-grouped into families, families are divided into genera (singular genus), and genera are made up of individual species. The scientific name (also called Latin name or binomial name) of a plant is a combination of the genus and species names. Corn has the scientific name of *Zea mays*. The genus name is capitalized, and the species name is lowercase. The entire scientific name is italicized or underlined. In this book, the scientific name appears in italics under the common name for each plant described.

Scientists need a universal way to communicate to other scientists around the globe about their research. One problem with using common names of species is that the common name is usually not understood in another language. Another problem is that a particular species may have more than one common name, or that the same common name may apply to several species. For example, in this book there are three unrelated species that can have the common name of Bladderpod. Scientific names solve these problems.

The first botanist who publishes a formal plant description in a scientific journal gives the plant its scientific name. This person, the author, must follow rules outlined in *The International Code of Botanical Nomenclature*. The author's name is customarily written after the scientific name. The specimen used to make the official description of a species is called the type specimen. Sometimes it is interesting to find out where the type specimen was collected, and by whom.

Scientific names are sometimes changed. One reason is that new information, especially molecular data, may reveal similarities between species that were not previously suspected by external appearance or internal anatomy. Sometimes it is discovered after a name is published that the plant was previously named, in which case the earliest published name must be applied. In any case, when a name is changed, the original author's name may be in parentheses, followed by the author of the new name or combination. An example, Bigelow's Linanthus, is written: *Linanthus bigelovii* (Gray) Greene. Gray named this plant *Gilia bigelovii*, but Greene later placed it into the genus *Linanthus*, renaming it.

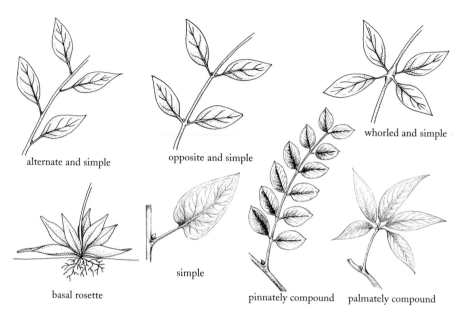

alternate and simple

opposite and simple

whorled and simple

basal rosette

simple

pinnately compound

palmately compound

Figure 1. Leaf type and arrangement

toothed

double-toothed

entire

lobed

cleft

wavy

Figure 2. Leaf margins

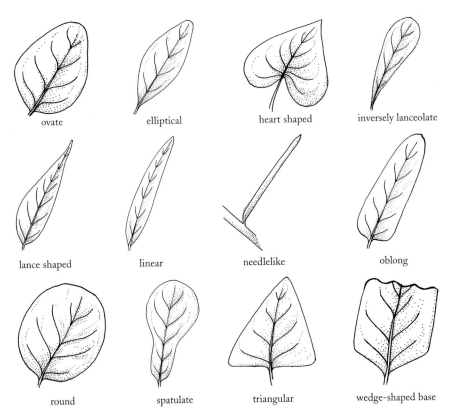

ovate   elliptical   heart shaped   inversely lanceolate

lance shaped   linear   needlelike   oblong

round   spatulate   triangular   wedge-shaped base

Figure 3. Leaf shapes

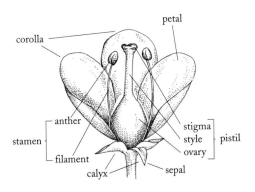

corolla

petal

anther

stamen

filament

calyx

stigma
style
ovary

pistil

sepal

Typical flower in longitudinal view

Figure 4. Flower parts

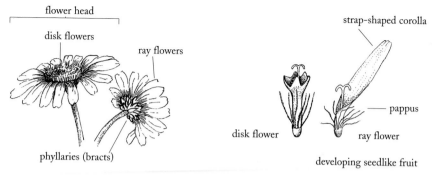

Figure 5. Flowers of the Sunflower Family (Asteraceae)

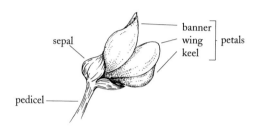

Figure 6. "Pea" Flower of the Bean Family (Fabaceae), side view

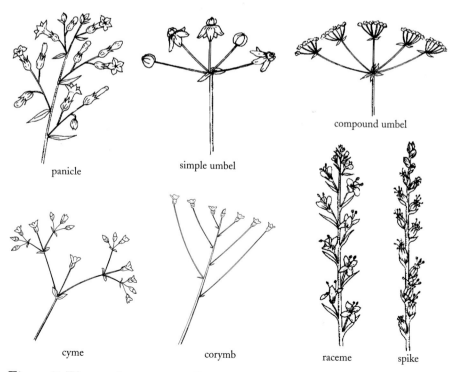

Figure 7. Flower clusters, or inflorescence

BLUE, PURPLE, AND LAVENDER FLOWERS

Flax

STEPHEN INGRAM

This section includes flowers ranging from light blue to dark blue and those that are lavender to deep purple. Since pink, rose, and magenta colors grade into lavenders and purples, check that section if you cannot find what you are looking for here. Blue and purplish flower colors are produced by variations of water-soluble pigments known as anthocyanins.

TIM THOMAS

Desert Cymopteris

DESERT CYMOPTERIS
Cymopteris deserticola Brandegee
Carrot Family (Apiaceae)

Description: This stemless, 4–6" tall perennial has finely dissected, 1–2" long leaves that grow from the root crown on leaf stalks that are the same length as the blades. Purple flowers occur in tight, ball-like clusters, followed by hairy, flattened, ¼" fruits with narrow wings.

Flowering Season: April

Habitat/Range: This rare species occurs in Creosote Bush scrub and Joshua Tree woodland from east of Victorville to Kramer Junction in California. More than 90% of the known populations and individuals occur on Edwards Air Force Base.

Comments: Desert Cymopteris is threatened by habitat alteration from historic sheep grazing, urbanization, and vehicles. With its limited distribution and multiple threats throughout its range, this species meets the requirements for listing as an endangered species, but it is not listed at this time.

Desert Parsley

RT HAWKE

DESERT PARSLEY
Lomatium mohavense (J. Coulter & Rose) J. Coulter & Rose
Carrot Family (Apiaceae)

Description: This thick-rooted, lacey, 4–12" tall perennial has 3–4 times pinnately divided leaves on 1–5" leaf stalks. The tiny, purplish to yellow flowers are produced in a compound umbel on a 3–8" flower stalk. The round, flattened, ¼–½" fruits have wings that are at least as wide as the fruit body.

Flowering Season: April to May

Habitat/Range: Desert Parsley is common on dry slopes and flats from 2,000 to 5,000 feet in Creosote Bush scrub, Joshua Tree woodland, and Pinyon-Juniper woodland. It occurs along the northern base of the San Gabriel Mountains and the western Mojave Desert to Barstow and Inyo County, and south along the western border of the Colorado Desert to Baja California, Mexico. It also occurs in coastal ranges of southern California.

Comments: Although this plant bears the name of Desert Parsley, it is not considered edible. Many plants in this family are poisonous.

Hoary Aster

HOARY ASTER

Machaeranthera canescens (Pursh) A. Gray var.
leucanthemifolia (E. Greene) Welsh
Sunflower Family (Asteraceae)

Description: This annual or short-lived perennial is less than 4' tall. The short-haired, glandular stems have an open branching pattern, producing an almost bushy effect. The 1–4" long leaves vary from linear to obovate, and they may have toothed to nearly entire margins. The flowers are produced in ¼–½" heads. Each head has numerous yellow disk flowers and lavender to purplish ray flowers.

Flowering Season: May to June, and September to October following summer rainfall

Habitat/Range: This variety of Hoary Aster is found from 3,000 to 6,000 feet in Creosote Bush scrub, Joshua Tree woodland, and Pinyon-Juniper woodland in the mountains of the Mojave Desert and the White and Inyo Ranges to Oregon and Utah.

Comments: A variety of insects can often be found on the flowers of Hoary Aster, including colorful Flower Long-Horn beetles in the family Cerambycidae. Some of these beetles have colors and shapes resembling wasps, and many have narrow heads to probe flower parts for pollen and nectar.

STEPHEN INGRAM

Mojave-Aster

MOJAVE-ASTER
Xylorhiza tortifolia (Torrey & A. Gray) E.
Greene var. *tortifolia*
Sunflower Family (Asteraceae)

Description: This 1–2' tall perennial is branched from the woody base. The soft-hairy, elliptical leaves with toothed margins and white midveins are larger near the base of the plant and smaller toward the top of the stem. The stalked, 2½" flower heads have up to 60 light blue ray flowers surrounding numerous yellow disk flowers, and 4–5 rows of 1" phyllaries beneath.

Flowering Season: March to May and sometimes in October following late summer rainfall, especially in the eastern Mojave

Habitat/Range: Mojave-Aster is found on rocky desert slopes, canyons, and washes in Creosote Bush scrub. It is common throughout the Mojave Desert except in the most western areas, and it also occurs in the Sonoran Desert.

Comments: Mojave-Aster is a food plant for larvae of Neumoegen's Checkerspot *(Chlosyne neumoegeni),* one of the more common desert butterflies. The mature larvae are black with gray dots and have 9 rows of black, branching spines.

RT HAWKE

Desert Candle

DESERT CANDLE
Caulanthus inflatus S. Watson
Mustard Family (Brassicaceae)

Description: This distinctive annual has a leafless, inflated, yellowish green stem that can grow to 2' tall. Dark green, oblong, 1–3" leaves clasp the stem at the base of the plant. The conspicuous, dark purple buds open to reveal ½" long flowers with 4 white petals, and the stout, linear fruits are 2–4" long.

Flowering Season: March to May

Habitat/Range: Desert Candle is locally common in flat areas between shrubs in Creosote Bush scrub and Joshua Tree woodland below 5,000 feet. It ranges from Barstow to western Fresno County in California. It is locally common in areas around Boron and Opal Mountain.

Comments: Native Americans and early settlers boiled the young plants with meat to make a palatable stew.

Freckled Milkvetch

FRECKLED MILKVETCH
Astragalus lentiginosus Hook.
Pea Family (Fabaceae)

Description: Freckled Milkvetch is highly variable with pinnately divided leaves and typical "pea" flowers with a banner petal, 2 wing petals, and 2 petals fused to form a boat-shaped keel. The 2-chambered fruits are sessile, strongly inflated, and narrowed abruptly to form a triangular beak.

Flowering Season: April to June or July

Habitat/Range: Freckled Milkvetch is common throughout the Mojave and much of California to Oregon, Wyoming, and northern Mexico. It occurs in dry, open areas in a variety of habitats below 11,700 feet.

Comments: Numerous varieties of Freckled Milkvetch are recognized in the Mojave Desert. Most are herbaceous perennials, and most will hybridize freely at the edges of their ranges. *Astragalus lentiginosus* var. *variabilis* is widespread in sandy sites below 5,200 feet in the southern and western Mojave. It has a keel over ¼" long and an upcurved fruit beak. The common var. *fremontii* occurs in open sand or gravel in the eastern Mojave. It has hairless fruits, an upcurved fruit beak, and keels under ¼" long. Var. *albifolius* has dense white hairs, white petals, and a downcurved beak. It grows in clay flats and alkaline areas in the western Mojave. The rare var. *micans* has silky white hairs, is woody at the base, and is found only on Eureka Dunes.

Arizona Lupine

BAJADA LUPINE, ELEGANT LUPINE
Lupinus concinnus J. Agardh
Pea Family (Fabaceae)

Description: This densely hairy, compact, 4–10" tall annual has palmately divided leaves with 5–9 soft-hairy leaflets. The reddish purple flowers with white to yellow banner petal spots are spirally arranged into 1–3" clusters on 2–3" stalks. The narrow, hairy, ½" long pods have 2–4 seeds.

Flowering Season: March to May

Habitat/Range: Bajada Lupine occupies dry sandy soil in open and often disturbed sites such as roadsides and burned areas. It is found in Creosote Bush scrub and Joshua Tree woodlands from Inyo County to Imperial County and east to New Mexico.

Comments: Plants that were previously called *Lupinus agardhianus,* a more erect form with fewer hairs, are now considered to be indistinct from *Lupinus concinnus.*

ARIZONA LUPINE
Lupinus arizonicus (S. Watson) S. Watson
Pea Family (Fabaceae)

Description: This somewhat fleshy, branched annual is generally 1–2' tall. The palmately divided leaves have 5–10 inversely lanceolate, ½–1½" long leaflets. Magenta "pea" flowers with yellowish banner spots occur in 2–12" long clusters, followed by shiny, ½" long pods.

Flowering Season: March to May

Habitat/Range: Arizona Lupine is common in sandy washes and open areas below 2,000 feet in Creosote Bush scrub in both the Mojave and Sonoran Deserts. This species is especially abundant and conspicuous along highways, even in low rainfall years.

Comments: The genus name, which means "wolf" in Latin, was given because it was mistakenly believed that this plant robbed the soil. However, many members of the Pea Family actually add nitrogen to the soil with the aid of symbiotic bacteria that are housed in root nodules. These bacteria take atmospheric nitrogen and convert it into a form that plants can assimilate and use by a process called nitrogen fixation.

Bajada Lupine, Elegant Lupine

Grape Soda Lupine, Adonis Lupine

GRAPE SODA LUPINE, ADONIS LUPINE

Lupinus excubitus M. E. Jones var. *excubitus*
Pea Family (Fabaceae)

Description: The handsome Grape Soda Lupine is usually around 3' high, although in some areas it grows up to 6'. Its silvery color is due to dense, shiny, flattened hairs covering the foliage. The alternate, palmately divided leaves have 7–9 leaflets on 1½–4" stalks. Blue-violet flowers with yellowish banner spots occur atop the plant in branched clusters, followed by silky, 2" long pods with 5–8 seeds each.

Flowering Season: April to June

Habitat/Range: This species is found in rocky, gravelly, and sometimes sandy soils from 3,000 to 7,500 feet in Creosote Bush scrub, Joshua Tree woodland, and Pinyon-Juniper woodland. It is common along the north-facing slopes of the San Bernardino, San Gabriel, and Little San Bernardino Mountains in California. Its range extends north to the Tehachapis and the mountains of Inyo County.

Comments: The flowers of this plant have a distinctive sticky-sweet odor resembling grape soda, thus the common name.

Desert Lupine, Shockley Lupine

DESERT LUPINE, SHOCKLEY LUPINE
Lupinus shockleyi S. Watson
Pea Family (Fabaceae)

Description: Desert Lupine may have a stem up to 4" long or may appear stemless. The leaves are palmately divided with 7–10 narrow, spoon-shaped leaflets on 1½–5" long stalks. Upper leaflet surfaces are hairless except at the margins, and the undersurfaces have silky, flattened hairs. The dark blue-purple flowers with yellow-spotted banner petals, hairless keels, and white-hairy sepals occur in scattered clusters. The upper seams of the pods are wavy with stiff, long hairs, and there are 2 wrinkled seeds in each pod.

Flowering Season: March to May

Habitat/Range: This plant occurs in dry sandy soils below 1,200 feet in Creosote Bush scrub. It is widespread and fairly common in both the Mojave and Sonoran Deserts.

Comments: This species was named in honor of William H. Shockley (1855-1925), who was one of the first botanical collectors in the White Mountains.

PARRY DALEA
Marina parryi (Torrey & A. Gray) Barneby
Pea Family (Fabaceae)

Description: This slender, 8–20" tall, glanddotted subshrub has purple stems with gray hairs. The alternate pinnately divided leaves have 13–35 round leaflets. Blue and white "pea" flowers with hairy sepals are produced in loose clusters, followed by small 1-seeded fruits.

Flowering Season: March to June

Habitat/Range: Parry Dalea is found in disturbed habitats such as roadsides and washes and also on rocky slopes below 300 feet in Creosote Bush scrub in the southeastern Mojave Desert to Baja California, Mexico.

Comments: This species is named in honor of Dr. Charles C. Parry, who collected on both the Pacific Railway Survey and Mexican Boundary Survey in the 1800s.

STEPHEN INGRAM

Parry Dalea

Indigo Bush

INDIGO BUSH
Psorothamnus arborescens (A. Gray) Barneby
var. *minutifolius* (Parish) Barneby
Pea Family (Fabaceae)

Description: Indigo Bush is a spreading, somewhat spiny shrub around 2–3' tall. The pinnately divided leaves have 5–7 lanceolate leaflets that are ¼–½" long. Showy, deep blue-violet flowers are produced in dense clusters at the branch tips, followed by 2-seeded, gland-dotted fruits that narrow to a long beak.

Flowering Season: April to May

Habitat/Range: Indigo Bush is found on flats and in washes from 500 to 3,000 feet in Creosote Bush scrub in the northern and central Mojave Desert.

Comments: Mojave Indigo Bush *(Psorothamnus arborescens var. arborescens)* is distinguished from var. *minutifolius* by its larger, hairy calyx. It occurs in the western Mojave Desert, where it is threatened by the Fort Irwin military base expansion. It is on the California Native Plant Society watch list.

JOHN REID

Desert Canterbury Bell

DESERT CANTERBURY BELL

Phacelia campanularia A. Gray ssp. *vasiformis* Gillett.

Waterleaf Family (Hydrophyllaceae)

Description: This erect, glandular-hairy, branched annual can grow to 2' tall when there has been plenty of rainfall. The deep green, ovate, 1–2" long leaves with saw-toothed margins are alternately arranged along the full length of the stem, but they tend to be larger near the base of the plant. Gorgeous deep blue, 1–1½" tubular flowers with open throats are produced in large, loose clusters along the upper stems. The protruding stamens each have a hairless, dilated base. The dry, 2-chambered pods contain many tiny, pitted seeds.

Flowering Season: March to May

Habitat/Range: Desert Canterbury Bell can be found in dry, sandy, and gravelly places in Creosote Bush scrub below 500 feet. The range of this subspecies extends from the Victorville region and Morongo Valley to the Providence Mountains and Cottonwood Springs.

Comments: Wild Canterbury Bell *(Phacelia minor)* is similar, but the flower tube is constricted at the throat. It sometimes occurs on desert margins in chaparral. Many people develop contact dermatitis after handling *Phacelia* species. The most glandular species cause the worst problems, and highly sensitive individuals can develop a rash as severe as that caused by Poison Oak.

Notch-Leaved Phacelia

NOTCH-LEAVED PHACELIA
Phacelia crenulata Torrey
Waterleaf Family (Hydrophyllaceae)

Description: This foul-smelling annual grows from 4–24" tall. The dark green, 1–5" leaves are pinnately divided or lobed into segments with scalloped margins. The stems are very glandular above the middle and bear bell-shaped, bluish purple flowers with white throats and protruding stamens on the upper flattened edges of the coiled flower stalks. The fruits are ovate capsules with 2–4 black, pitted seeds, each with a central ridge that separates 2 longitudinal grooves.

Flowering Season: March to May

Habitat/Range: Notch-Leaved Phacelia occurs in open areas and rocky washes below 6,000 feet in Creosote Bush scrub, Joshua Tree woodland, and Pinyon-Juniper woodland in the Mojave and Sonoran Deserts to the eastern Sierra Nevada, Modoc Plateau, and northwestern Mexico.

Comments: Contact dermatitis may develop after exposure to Notch-Leaved Phacelia. If you have sensitive skin, it is best to avoid contact with this and other *Phacelia* species.

RT HAWKE

Washoe Phacelia

WASHOE PHACELIA
Phacelia curvipes S. Watson
Waterleaf Family (Hydrophyllaceae)

Description: This glandular-hairy, 1½–6" tall annual has soft, inversely lanceolate, entire basal leaves that are ½–1¼" long. The upper leaves are much smaller and few in number. The flower cluster is not strongly coiled as in many *Phacelias*, and it has relatively few flowers. Each bell-shaped, ¼" long flower is bluish with a white throat. The hairy, 2-chambered capsules are less than ¼" long, and they contain 6-16 tiny, pitted seeds.

Flowering Season: April to June

Habitat/Range: Washoe Phacelia is found on sandy and rocky hillsides from 3,000 to 6,000 feet in Joshua Tree woodland, Pinyon-Juniper woodland, Sagebrush scrub, and Yellow Pine forest. It occurs in the Tehachapi Mountains and on the desert slopes of the Transverse Ranges and the eastern Sierra Nevada Range to southwestern Utah and northwestern Arizona.

Comments: The type locality for Washoe Phacelia is near Carson City and Washoe in western Nevada.

Lace-Leaf Phacelia, Fat-Leaf Phacelia

FREMONT PHACELIA
Phacelia fremontii Torrey
Waterleaf Family (Hydrophyllaceae)

Description: This 8–20" annual usually has small hairs and glands on the upper half of the plant. The somewhat succulent, 2–5" leaves are deeply pinnately lobed or divided with rounded segments. The 5-parted, violet flowers with yellow throats are produced in coiled clusters at the ends of branches, followed by ovate fruits with 10–18 seeds, each with 6–9 crosswise furrows.

Flowering Season: March to June

Habitat/Range: Fremont Phacelia is common in sandy or gravelly soils below 7,500 feet in the Mojave Desert and elsewhere in California, Arizona, and Utah.

Comments: The corolla color of Fremont Phacelia seems to vary from magenta to violet or blue in different locations. Since soil acidity or alkalinity is known to affect the flower color of some species with anthocyanin pigments, it would be interesting to find out if soil chemistry is responsible for the color variation in this and other *Phacelia* species, such as Round-Leaf Phacelia.

LACE-LEAF PHACELIA, FAT-LEAF PHACELIA
Phacelia distans Benth.
Waterleaf Family (Hydrophyllaceae)

Description: This annual has sparse, stiff hairs and small glands, especially on the upper half of the plant. The alternate, 1–4" long leaves are once or twice pinnately divided with toothed segments, and they occur on short stalks. The blue to white, 5-parted, bell-shaped flowers are in coiled clusters; these fall off as the fruit develops. Each round fruit is on a stalk that is ¹⁄₁₆–³⁄₁₆" long. There are 2–4 pitted seeds per fruit, each with inner surfaces that are not clearly ridged or grooved.

Flowering Season: March to June

Habitat/Range: Lace-Leaf Phacelia often occurs under shrubs in Creosote Bush scrub, Joshua Tree woodland, and Pinyon-Juniper woodland. It is very common throughout the Mojave and Sonoran Deserts to northern Mexico.

Comments: Tansy Phacelia *(Phacelia tanacetifolia)* is similar to Lace-Leaf Phacelia, but it has fruit stalks than are less than ¹⁄₁₆" long, ovate fruits, and corollas that remain attached as the fruits develop.

Fremont Phacelia

RT HAWKE

Parish's Phacelia

PARISH'S PHACELIA
Phacelia parishii A. Gray
Waterleaf Family (Hydrophyllaceae)

Description: This 2–6" tall annual has elliptic to obovate ⅓–1¼" long basal leaves, with leaf blades that are longer than the leaf stalks. The flower stalks are glandular and hairy, and they are not tightly coiled like those of many *Phacelia* species. The lavender, bell-shaped flowers have yellow tubes and are less than ¼" long. The short-hairy fruit contains 20–40 finely pitted seeds.

Habitat/Range: Parish's Phacelia inhabits alkaline or clay soil around playas from 2,500 to 4,000 feet. It is known only from Coyote Dry Lake in California and a few scattered locations in northwestern Arizona and southern Nevada.

Comments: Parish's Phacelia was presumed extinct in California until rediscovered by Mark Bagley in 1989. Although it is threatened by military vehicle activity on the Mannix Tank Trail, it is not listed as endangered or threatened. *Phacelia pachyphylla*, a more common species, may be mistaken for Parish's Phacelia since it looks similar and occupies the same habitat. It is distinguished by having leaf blades shorter than the leaf stalk, round leaf blades, and fruits with over 60 seeds, each with 6–11 cross furrows.

Specter Phacelia

SPECTER PHACELIA
Phacelia pedicillata A. Gray
Waterleaf Family (Hydrophyllaceae)

Description: Specter Phacelia is an erect, thick-stemmed annual that grows to 20" tall. The lower leaves have 3–7 pinnate, rounded or toothed leaflets, while upper leaves are often lobed. The bell-shaped, pink to bluish, ¼" flowers are on the upper surfaces of the split, hairy, coiled flower stalk. Each fruit has 4 seeds that are grooved, pitted on the back, and ridged on the inner surface.

Flowering Season: March to May

Habitat/Range: This species occurs in sandy and gravelly gullies and washes below 4,500 feet in all the deserts of California to Nevada, Arizona, and Baja California, Mexico.

Comments: The species name means "with a pedicel" in Latin, referring to the individual flower stalks.

DESERT-LAVENDER
Hyptis emoryi Torrey
Mint Family (Lamiaceae)

Description: This 3–9' tall shrub has erect to spreading gray branches and twigs with dense, stellate hairs. The opposite, ovate, ½–1" long leaves on ¼" petioles have a minty odor when crushed. The fragrant, lavender, 2-lipped, ¼" long flowers are produced in bracted clusters.

Flowering Season: March to May

Habitat/Range: Desert-Lavender occurs in sandy canyons and washes below 3,000 feet in the eastern and southern Mojave Desert, but it is more common in the Sonoran Desert to Arizona and northwest Mexico.

Comments: Data from fossilized pack rat middens provide evidence that Desert-Lavender moved into the southernmost Mojave Desert during the warming trend of the Middle Holocene, and cold temperatures found in the Mojave now likely prevent it from expanding its range northward and into higher elevations. This plant has smaller leaves with denser hairs during hot summer months when less water is available. Larger leaves with sparser hairs are better able to absorb light for photosynthesis, and these are produced when more water is

Desert-Lavender

available. Various species of native bees are the most effective pollinators, although hummingbirds are also frequent visitors. Stems often swell, turn black, and die due to a rust fungus *(Puccinia distorta)*.

TIM THOMAS

Bladder Sage, Paper-Bag Bush

BLADDER SAGE, PAPER-BAG BUSH
Salazaria mexicana Torrey
Mint Family (Lamiaceae)

Description: This 1½–3' shrub has a distinctive branching pattern, with opposite branches forming right angles to the main stem. The younger stems are light green and covered with fine hairs, while older stems turn grayish brown. The opposite, deciduous, entire leaves are usually up to ½" long, and they are present only when water is available. The flowers have white to light purple upper lips, purple, 3-lobed lower lips, and rose-colored calyces that become inflated and papery in fruit, giving this the common name of Paper-Bag Bush. The fruit inside the calyx is composed of 4 nutlets, a characteristic of the Mint Family, but Bladder Sage lacks the minty odor and square stems that are also common family features.

Flowering Season: March to June

Habitat/Range: Paper-Bag Bush is found on sandy and gravelly slopes, canyons, and washes below 5,000 feet in Creosote Bush scrub and Joshua Tree woodland. It is widespread and common throughout much of the Mojave Desert to Inyo County. It also occurs in the Sonoran Desert to New Mexico and Texas.

Comments: This genus was named in honor of Don Jose Salazar, a Mexican representative and officer on the Mexican Boundary Survey.

STEPHEN INGRAM

Thistle Sage

THISTLE SAGE
Salvia carduacea Benth.
Mint Family (Lamiaceae)

Description: Some consider this white-woolly annual to be among the most beautiful in the Mojave Desert, although it is not unique to the Mojave. Erect, 1–3' stems arise from a basal rosette of 1–4" pinnately lobed and toothed leaves. Spiny bracts subtend 1–4 round clusters of intricate flowers along the stem. The petals are lavender with fringed, 2-cleft upper lips. The lower lateral petal lobes are irregularly toothed, and the lower central lobe is fringed and fan-shaped. The protruding stamens have anther sacs of a striking orange-red color.

Habitat/Range: Thistle Sage is locally common in sandy to gravelly soils below 4,500 feet in Creosote Bush scrub and Joshua Tree woodland in the western Mojave Desert. Its range extends to coastal California and Baja California, Mexico.

Comments: The genus name, *Salvia,* is derived from the Latin word for healing and wellness, since many of the sages have medicinal value. The species name literally means "thistlelike."

Chia

CHIA
Salvia columbariae Benth.
Mint Family (Lamiaceae)

Description: This 4–20" tall annual has a basal rosette of 1–4" long, bristly, bumpy-textured leaves that are once or twice pinnately lobed. The square, erect flowering stalks bear 1–3 dense, round clusters of blue, 2-lipped, ½" long flowers with protruding stamens, and each flower cluster has rounded, bristle-tipped bracts beneath.

Flowering Season: March to June

Habitat/Range: Chia is a common species in dry, open, and disturbed areas below 4,000 feet in Creosote Bush scrub in the Mojave Desert. It is found throughout southern California to Mexico.

Comments: Chia seeds were an important dietary staple of Shoshone, Paiute, and other Native American groups. Seeds were beaten from dried plants into baskets, ground into meal, and mixed with water to form a nutritious mush. Whole or ground seeds were also placed in the eye to ease soreness.

DESERT SAGE, GRAY BALL SAGE

Salvia dorrii (Kellogg) Abrams var. *pilosa* (A. Gray) J. L. Strachan & Rev.
Mint Family (Lamiaceae)

Description: This low, rounded shrub is usually 1–2' high. Its distinctive blue-gray color and opposite, entire, spoon-shaped leaves make it easy to identify. Blue, 2-lipped flowers occur in 1–2" ball-like clusters up the stems. Beneath each cluster is a whorl of hairy, magenta bracts.

Flowering Season: May to July

Habitat/Range: Desert Sage is found on alluvial slopes and in washes from 2,500 to 8,500 feet in Joshua Tree woodland and Pinyon-Juniper woodland. Its range includes the desert slopes of the San Bernardino and San Gabriel Mountains and scattered locations throughout the Mojave Desert to Lassen County.

Comments: *S. dorrii* var. *dorrii* in the northern Mojave Desert has hairless or scaly bracts and calyces, distinguishing it from var. *pilosa*.

Desert Sage, Gray Ball Sage

Death Valley Sage

DEATH VALLEY SAGE

Salvia funerea M. E. Jones
Mint Family (Lamiaceae)

Description: This intricately branched shrub grows to 3' high. Its overall white appearance is due to woolly hairs covering the stems and leaves. The opposite, ovate, sessile leaves are ¼–1" long and often have 2-4 lateral spiny teeth. The deep purple, 2-lipped, ½" long flowers are in 1–3" leafy spikes in leaf axils, and are partially hidden by tufts of wool.

Flowering Season: March to May

Habitat/Range: This uncommon plant is associated with limestone soils. Death Valley Sage is found in dry washes and narrow canyons in Inyo County on the western slopes of the Funeral, Black, and Granite Mountains, in Titus Canyon in the Grapevine Mountains, and in the northern portions of the Panamint Mountains. Its southernmost known location is in the south end of the Bristol Mountains.

Comments: Although there are potential threats from limestone mining, the largest populations of Death Valley Sage are protected within Death Valley National Park.

STEPHEN INGRAM

Mojave Sage

MOJAVE SAGE
Salvia mohavensis E. Greene
Mint Family (Lamiaceae)

Description: This rounded shrub has opposite, ovate, ½–1" long leaves with a puckered texture, dark green color, and small, rounded teeth on the margins. Headlike whorls of pale blue flowers occur singly at stem tips, with white ovate bracts beneath them. Each 2-lipped flower is around ½" long with protruding stamens.

Flowering Season: April to June

Habitat/Range: Mojave Sage is found on dry walls of canyons and washes and in steep, rocky areas from 1,000 to 5,000 feet in Creosote Bush scrub and Joshua Tree woodland. It occurs along desert slopes of mountains within and bordering the Mojave, including the Sheephole, Clark, Turtle, and Little San Bernardino Mountains to northwestern Sonora, Mexico.

Scaly-Stemmed Sand Plant

SCALY-STEMMED SAND PLANT
Pholisma arenarium Hook.
Lennoa Family (Lennoaceae)

Description: This fleshy herb is parasitic on roots of several shrub species. The above-ground portions of the whitish stem are 4–8" tall, and the ½" long leaves are whitish brown and scaly. The narrow, funnel-shaped flowers are in a spikelike cluster on the top swollen stem portions, and the petals are purple with white margins.

Flowering Season: April to July, and in October following summer rain

Habitat/Range: Scaly-Stemmed Sand Plant occurs at elevations below 5,000 feet in Creosote Bush scrub and Joshua Tree woodland in the Mojave Desert, where its host plants include Yerba Santa *(Eriodictyon trichocalyx),* Goldenbush (*Ericameria* species), Rabbit-brush (*Chrysothamnus* species), Cheesebush (*Hymenoclea salsola),* and White Bur-Sage *(Ambrosia dumosa)*. Its range also includes the Colorado Desert and coastal California from San Luis Obispo County to Baja California, Mexico.

Comments: Sand Food *(P. sonorae)* is a related plant of the Algodones Dunes in the Sonoran Desert. The roots of its host plant are more than 5 feet deep, but the tiny seeds don't store enough food to germinate on the surface and penetrate that far underground. Ants and rodents may store the seeds in their burrows, bringing them closer to their host.

Desert Hyacinth

DESERT HYACINTH
Dichelostemma capitatum (Benth) A.W. Wood
ssp. *pauciflorum* (Torrey) Keator
Lily Family (Liliaceae)

Description: This perennial grows from an underground corm that is coated with brown, fibrous tissue. There are 2–3 linear, 4–16" long leaves that grow from the base, each with a groove on the lower surface. The erect stem bears a dense cluster of blue-lavender flowers with 6 spreading segments. The individual flower stalks are longer than the whitish or purple-striped bracts found below the flower cluster.

Flowering Season: March to May

Habitat/Range: Desert Hyacinth inhabits open areas below 7,500 feet in Creosote Bush scrub, Joshua Tree woodland, and Pinyon-Juniper woodland in the Mojave Desert. Its range extends to the Great Basin, the western Colorado Desert, and east to New Mexico.

Comments: *D. capitatum* ssp. *capitatum* has erect flower segments, and the flowers are on stalks that are shorter than the dark purple bracts below, distinguishing it from var. *pauciflorum*.

Flax

STEPHEN INGRAM

FLAX

Linum lewisii Pursh
Flax Family (Linaceae)

Description: Entire, linear, ½–1" long leaves occur along the length of the 6–30", wandlike stems of this perennial. The blue, 5-parted flowers occur in 1-sided, leafy, stalked clusters, and they are very quick to wither and fall. The fruit is a ¼" long capsule with 10 gelatinous seeds.

Flowering Season: May to September

Habitat/Range: Although usually considered a species of higher elevations, Flax is locally common in Pinyon-Juniper woodland in the eastern Mojave Desert. Flax has a widespread distribution in the West from northern Mexico to Alaska.

Comments: Flax had a variety of uses in Western Shoshone culture. They boiled plant parts to make eyewash, boiled stems for a tea to relieve gas, applied crushed leaves to swollen body parts, and made string from the fibers. Other species are widely used today for linen, flaxseed oil, and linseed oil. A species with coppery orange-yellow flowers, *Linum puberulum*, occurs in Pinyon-Juniper woodland of the New York and Clark Mountains of the eastern Mojave Desert.

Cooper's Broom-Rape

COOPER'S BROOM-RAPE
Orobanche cooperi (A. Gray) A. A. Heller
Broom-Rape Family (Orobanchaceae)

Description: Cooper's Broom-Rape is a 4–12" tall, purplish brown root parasite with stout, fleshy, sticky-hairy stems that are unbranched above the ground. Small, overlapping, scalelike leaves cover the lower stem. The upper stem terminates in a dense, spikelike cluster of lavender to yellowish flowers, which are somewhat hidden by bracts. Each flower is ¾–1½" long, with a 3-lobed lower lip and an erect, 2-lobed upper lip.

Flowering Season: March to May

Habitat/Range: This species occurs in flat sandy areas and washes below 4,000 feet in all deserts of southern California to Utah, Arizona, and Baja California, Mexico.

Comments: Hosts of Cooper's Broom-Rape are often members of the Sunflower Family, including Burrobush *(Ambrosia dumosa)*, Cheesebush *(Hymenoclea salsola)*, and Brittlebush *(Encelia* sp.). It has also been reported as a parasite of Creosote Bush *(Larrea tridentata)*, and in the Imperial Valley it has been observed on roots of cultivated tomato plants.

STEPHEN INGRAM

Perennial Eriastrum

PERENNIAL ERIASTRUM
Eriastrum densifolium (Benth.) H. Mason *ssp.*
mohavense (Craig) H. Mason
Phlox Family (Polemoniaceae)

Description: Erect, branched, 6–18" tall stems arise from the woody base of this grayish white woolly perennial. Pinnately lobed and toothed leaves from ¾–2" long occur along the entire stem length. Dense heads of pale blue flowers with protruding anthers are produced on the stem tips, and each ½" long flower has a slender tube which abruptly expands into 5 flattened lobes.

Flowering Season: June to October

Habitat/Range: Perennial Eriastrum inhabits dry slopes and sandy areas from 2,500 to 8,500 feet in Joshua Tree woodland and Pinyon-Juniper woodland in the Mojave Desert. Other subspecies occur in adjacent areas of southern California to Baja California, Mexico.

Comments: There are also several annual species of *Eriastrum* in the Mojave Desert, including Sapphire Eriastrum *(Eriastrum sap-*

pharinum), with intense blue, nearly bilateral flowers with yellow throats and protruding stamens that are attached equally in the upper part of the ¼" flower tube. Desert Eriastrum *(E. eremicum* ssp. *eremicum)* has ½-¾" long bilateral flowers with protruding, unequal stamens that are bent toward the lower corolla lobe. Many-Flowered Eriastrum *(E. pluriflorum)* has a ½-¾" long radial corolla with a yellow to white tube and protruding stamens inserted between the corolla lobes instead of in the tube. Diffuse Eriastrum *(E. diffusum)* has a ¼" long corolla with lobes that are conspicuously shorter thatn the tube. The stamens are inserted unequally at the top of the throat, and they do not protrude farther than the corolla. Few-Flowered Eriastrum *(E. sparsiflorum)* has pale blue to pink or cream, ¼-½" long flowers with equal, non-protruding stamen that are inserted in the lower throat or upper tube.

Broad-Flowered Gilia

BROAD-FLOWERED GILIA
Gilia latiflora (A. Gray) A. Gray
Phlox Family (Polemoniaceae)

Description: The basal rosette leaves of this 4–12" tall annual are toothed or lobed and have cobwebby hairs. A few short, tapered, inconspicuous leaves may clasp the hairless stem. Loose clusters of 1" long lavender flowers with protruding stamens, a tubular throat, and spreading lobes with white bases are produced on the upper stems. The 3-chambered capsule is longer than the calyx.

Flowering Season: April to May

Habitat/Range: Broad-Flowered Gilia is common in deep sandy soils in Creosote Bush scrub and Joshua Tree woodland in the central and western Mojave Desert.

Comments: *Gilia latiflora* ssp. *davyi* in the western Mojave Desert has deep purple corollas with yellow and white throats, which are 2–3 times the calyx length. Ssp. *latiflora* has a widely expanded throat with yellow at the base; it occurs on desert slopes of the San Bernardino and San Gabriel Mountains. From north of Barstow to the El Paso Mountains ssp. *elongata* is found, with stems that have cobwebby hairs near the base and corollas that are up to 1½" long.

Lilac Sunbonnet

TIM THOMAS

LILAC SUNBONNET
Langloisia setosissima (Torrey & A. Gray) E.
Greene ssp. *punctata* (Cov.) S. Timbrook
Phlox Family (Polemoniaceae)

Description: This 1–3" tall, tufted annual has
alternate leaves with 3–5 bristle-tipped teeth
at the widened apex, and clusters of 2–3 bristles at the base. The 5-parted, radial, bell-
shaped flowers have ½–1" long, white to light
blue corollas with numerous purple markings
and 2 yellow spots in the middle of each lobe.
The flowers also have protruding stamens and
bristle-tipped calyx lobes. The fruit is a 3-
sided capsule with angled seeds.

Flowering Season: March to June

Habitat/Range: Lilac Sunbonnet is common
in washes, flats, and slopes with gravelly or
sandy soil below 5,500 feet in the Mojave
Desert to the eastern Sierra foothills and
Nevada.

Comments: Large Bee Flies (Bombyliidae)
are known to visit these flowers. The genus
Langloisia was named after the Louisiana
botanist, Rev. A. B. Langlois. A related
species, Bristly Langloisia *(L. setosissima* ssp.
setosissima), has ½" long, lavender to blue
petals without spots or markings. It is more
widespread than Lilac Sunbonnet, occurring
in both the Mojave and Sonoran Deserts to
the eastern Sierran foothills and northern
Mexico.

Mojave Linanthus

MOJAVE LINANTHUS
Linanthus breviculus (A. Gray) E. Greene
Phlox Family (Polemoniaceae)

Description: This slender, erect, 4–10" tall annual has opposite, palmate leaves with 3–5 linear lobes. Flowers are produced in dense, compact clusters. Each flower has a deeply cleft, ¼" long calyx with membranes connecting the lobes for over half of their length, and a slender, maroon, ½–1" long corolla tube that spreads abruptly into 5 flattened pink, blue, or white lobes. The style is 3-parted, and the stamens are short with the anthers at the opening of the throat.

Flowering Season: May to August

Habitat/Range: Mojave Linanthus is found in dry, open areas below 7,800 feet in Joshua Tree woodland, Pinyon-Juniper woodland, and Yellow Pine forest on north slopes of the San Bernardino and San Gabriel Mountains to the Ord and Liebre Ranges.

Comments: Mojave Linanthus is often seen blanketing recently burned areas.

PARRY'S LINANTHUS
Linanthus parryae (A. Gray) E. Greene
Phlox Family (Polemoniaceae)

Description: Tufted clusters of Parry's Linanthus are only 2–3" tall. The opposite, crowded leaves have 3–7 linear, palmate segments. The funnel-shaped, 5-parted flowers come in blue and white, and both colors can occur within the same population.

Flowering Season: March to May

Habitat/Range: This species occupies sandy flats below 3,500 feet in Creosote Bush scrub and Joshua Tree woodland from the western Mojave Desert to Mono County. It also grows in southern California's inner coastal ranges north to Monterey County. In years with ample spring rains, this species can be seen covering large areas between Phelan and Lancaster.

Comments: This plant has been the subject of several population genetics studies (see comments in white to cream flower section on page 174). The flower color appears to be determined by one gene locus.

Parry's Linanthus

Desert Larkspur

STEPHEN INGRAM

DESERT LARKSPUR
Delphinium parishii A. Gray ssp. *parishii*
Buttercup Family (Ranunculaceae)

Description: This erect, 6–24" tall perennial arises from woody roots. The basal leaves are triangular in outline, have 3–5 linear to oblong lobes, and are usually wilted by the time the flowers appear. The stem leaves have up to 20 lobes that are under ¼" wide at the widest point. The fuzzy, light blue to azure blue flowers with tubular nectar spurs are produced in a long, branched cluster at the tops of the stems. The fruit is made up of 3 segments, and it contains winged seeds. Observation of the seeds with a 10X hand lens will reveal that seed coat cells have wavy margins.

Flowering Season: April to June

Habitat/Range: Desert Larkspur occurs in gravelly areas below 7,500 feet in Creosote Bush scrub, Joshua Tree woodland, and Pinyon-Juniper woodland in the Mojave and Sonoran Deserts to Mono County and Baja California, Mexico.

Comments: The Kawaiisu mixed the dried, ground roots of Desert Larkspur with water to make a paste they applied to swellings. Most larkspurs are very toxic to humans and livestock.

Turpentine Broom, Desert Rue

TURPENTINE BROOM, DESERT RUE

Thamnosma montana Torrey & Fremont
Rue Family (Rutaceae)

Description: Turpentine Broom is a yellowish green, 1–2' tall shrub related to citrus fruits. The tiny leaves fall off early, so its glandular stems appear leafless most of the year. The ½" long flowers are deep purple with a somewhat leathery texture. The rounded, 2-lobed fruits resemble tiny, greenish yellow grapefruits. All parts of the plant yield an oily compound with a pungent odor.

Flowering Season: March to May

Habitat/Range: Turpentine Broom is fairly common on dry slopes below 5,500 feet in Creosote Bush scrub, Joshua Tree woodland, and Pinyon-Juniper woodland. It is found throughout the Mojave and Sonoran Deserts.

Comments: The Kawaiisu and Western Shoshone ascribed special powers to this plant, believing it would keep snakes away and make trouble for their enemies. The Southern Paiute used a tea brewed from it as a laxative, but they said it could also make one crazy for a while. Smoking the bark was supposed to induce sleep.

Chinese Houses

CHINESE HOUSES

Collinsia bartsiifolia Benth. var. *davidsonii*
(Parish) V. Newsom
Figwort Family (Scrophulariaceae)

Description: This 2–8" tall annual has opposite, entire, ½–1½" long leaves, often with slightly scalloped edges that roll under. Dense whorls of nearly sessile flowers have short bracts below. Each 2-lipped, ½–¾" long, pink to lavender flower has a pouch on the upper side and 2 upper lobes that are bent back. The middle lower lobe is folded around the 4 stamens and style, and the 2 lateral lower lobes are spreading. The fruit is a dry capsule.

Flowering Season: April to June

Habitat/Range: Chinese Houses are found in open sandy areas below 4,000 feet from the western Mojave Desert to the Sierra Nevada foothills.

Comments: The genus name honors Zaccheus Collins (1764–1831), who was an authority on lower plants and the vice-president of the Philadelphia Academy of Natural Sciences. The species name refers to the resemblance of the leaves to *Bartsia,* another member of the Figwort Family that is parasitic on the roots of grasses.

Panamint Penstemon

PANAMINT PENSTEMON
Penstemon fruticiformis Cov. var. *fruticiformis*
Figwort Family (Scrophulariaceae)

Description: This hairless, 1–2' tall shrub is highly branched and usually wider than tall. The thick, entire, narrow leaves are 1–2½" long and often folded lengthwise. The 2-lipped, 1" long flowers have a cream-colored tube and lavender limb with purple nectar guides.

Flowering Season: May to June

Habitat/Range: Panamint Penstemon can be found in dry, rocky canyons and gravelly washes from 3,500 to 7,000 feet in Creosote Bush scrub, Joshua Tree woodland, and Pinyon-Juniper woodland in the Panamint, Argus, and Inyo Mountains of the eastern Mojave Desert.

Comments: The related Death Valley Beard-tongue *(Penstemon fruticiformis* var. *amargosae)* occurs from the Kingston Range to western Nevada. The flowers have external glandular hairs, are hairless inside, and are generally less than 1" long. This variety is rare in California and threatened in Nevada.

STEPHEN INGRAM

Palmer's Penstemon

PALMER'S PENSTEMON
Penstemon palmeri A. Gray var. *palmeri*
Figwort Family (Scrophulariaceae)

Description: This erect, grayish perennial is 2–6' tall. The oblong, toothed, basal leaves are on long stalks. The clasping upper leaves have almost entire margins, and the uppermost pairs are united across the stem by their bases. The 2-lipped, 1–1½" long flowers are lilac to pink and white, with darker nectar guides extending into the abruptly inflated throat. The fifth, sterile stamen (staminode) has yellow, shaggy hairs.

Flowering Season: April to June

Habitat/Range: Palmer's Penstemon occurs on roadsides and in canyon floors and washes from 3,500 to 7,500 feet in Creosote Bush scrub, Joshua Tree woodlands, and Pinyon-Juniper woodland. It is found in the mountains of the eastern Mojave Desert.

Comments: The genus name means "fifth stamen," referring to the sterile staminode, a stamen without an anther. This species was named in honor of Edward Palmer (1831–1911), a Department of Agriculture botanist who made numerous collection expeditions to Mexico, South America, and the western United States. More than 200 plants have been named for him.

STEPHEN INGRAM

Goodding's Verbena, Southwestern Verbena

GOODDING'S VERBENA, SOUTHWESTERN VERBENA
Verbena gooddingii Briq.
Vervain Family (Verbenaceae)

Description: Goodding's Verbena is an 8–18" tall perennial with several erect or spreading branches from the base. The opposite, ½–1 ½" long, hairy leaves are divided into 3 segments, which are each pinnately divided again and coarsely toothed. The flowers are produced in rounded, showy, spikelike clusters with ⅓" long bracts. Each flower has a 5-ribbed calyx and light purple, tubular corolla with radial symmetry.

Flowering Season: April to June

Habitat/Range: This species grows in dry, sandy canyons and rocky slopes from 4,000 to 6,500 feet in Joshua Tree woodland and Pinyon-Juniper woodland in the eastern Mojave Desert to Sonora, Mexico.

Comments: This genus was named for Leslie Newton Goodding (1880–1967), one of the first botanists to collect in southern Arizona.

Pink, Rose, and Magenta Flowers

Death Valley Monkeyflower, Rock Midget

RT Hawke

These colors are produced by water-soluble anthocyanin pigments, which can vary according to the acidity or alkalinity inside the cells. Pinks and magentas may grade into lavenders, purples, and blues. Be sure to check the blue, purple, and lavender section if you cannot find your plant here.

Fringed Amaranth

FRINGED AMARANTH
Amaranthus fimbriatus (Torrey) Benth.
Pigweed Family (Amaranthaceae)

Description: This slender, erect, summer annual has pink to reddish stems and alternate, bright green, 1-4" long, linear to narrowly lanceolate leaves on 1" long stalks. Numerous small, male and female flowers are produced in loose, leafy, axillary and terminal spikelike clusters. The pink sepals are around ¹⁄₁₀" long and fringed at the tips. The dried stalks are often quite noticeable in the spring, while most desert annuals are in full bloom.

Flowering Season: August to November, following summer rainfall

Habitat/Range: Fringed Amaranth is found in washes and gravelly or sandy soils below 5,000 feet in Creosote Bush scrub and Joshua Tree woodland in the central, eastern, and southern Mojave Desert. It also occurs in the Colorado Desert to Mexico.

Comments: Most of the summer annuals are absent or uncommon in the western Mojave Desert because the western desert usually does not receive the summer rain that they require. Other members of the genus are cultivated for their edible seeds.

Climbing Milkweed

CLIMBING MILKWEED

Sarcostemma cyanchoides Decne ssp. *hartwegii*
(Vail) R. Holm
Milkweed Family (Asclepiadaceae)

Description: This twining, rank-smelling perennial is filled with milky sap. It has opposite, narrow, arrowhead-shaped leaves that are about 1–1½" long. The pink to purplish flowers are produced in umbels that are on ½-2" stalks in the leaf axils. Each 5-parted flower, with ¼" long corolla lobes, has a ring of white tissue on the inside base of the corolla, and white, oval, filament appendages that are not attached to the ring. The tan, tapering, 3-4" long fruit has flattened, tufted, ¼" long seeds.

Flowering Season: March to May

Habitat/Range: Climbing Milkweed is found clambering over shrubs and draped over trees at the edges of washes below 2,000 feet. It occurs in the eastern Mojave Desert and the Colorado Desert.

Comments: This is one of the food plants for the Striated Queen butterfly *(Danaus gilippus strigosus)*, a relative of the Monarch butterfly. It breeds mostly in the Colorado Desert, although it can be found as far north as Mono County. Twining Milkweed *(Sarcostemma hirtellum)* is similar to Climbing Milkweed, but it has leaves with tapering bases and white to light green flowers, each with white, oval, filament appendages that are attached to the ring. The dry, tan fruit is 1¼-2" long.

Mojave Thistle

MOJAVE THISTLE
Cirsium mohavense (E. Greene) Petrak
Sunflower Family (Asteraceae)

Description: A stout, 2–5' tall flower stalk develops from the basal rosette of this short-lived, white-haired perennial. Long, yellow spines trim the tips of the narrow, pinnately lobed, 4–10" long basal leaves. The leaves decrease in size and become less spiny up the stem. Numerous pink, lavender, or white tubular flowers are produced in 1" wide, stalked heads at the tops of stems and upper leaf axils. The hairless, erect phyllaries have gummy, vertical lines on their keels, ending in spines that spread backward.

Flowering Season: July to October

Habitat/Range: Mojave Thistle is found in canyons, streambeds, springs, and alkali seeps from 1,400 to 7,000 feet in Creosote Bush scrub and Pinyon-Juniper woodland in the Mojave Desert.

Comments: The fresh, young shoots of many species of thistle were peeled and eaten by Native Americans. Desert Thistle *(Cirsium neomexicanum)* is similar to Mojave Thistle, but it has leaves that are fuzzy on both surfaces, and larger flower heads with white flowers that protrude from the spreading, hairy phyllaries. It is found in the eastern Mojave Desert. Western Thistle *(C. occidentale)* has purple to red flowers that are barely longer than the hairy phyllaries. It occurs in the western Mojave Desert.

STEPHEN INGRAM

Hole-in-the-Sand Plant

HOLE-IN-THE-SAND PLANT
Nicolletia occidentalis A. Gray
Sunflower Family (Asteraceae)

Description: This hairless, 4–12" tall perennial emerges in spring from deep, twisted, woody roots. It has succulent, bluish gray foliage with translucent glands and a very pungent odor. The alternate, pinnate, 1–2" long leaves are divided into linear segments, and there is a bristle at the tip of each leaflet. The flower heads have 1 row of 8–12 gland-tipped, ½" long phyllaries. The disk flowers are yellow with purple tips, while the ray flower color varies from pink to purple, salmon, or almost orange.

Flowering Season: April to June

Habitat/Range: Hole-in-the-Sand Plant has a scattered distribution in very sandy soils in Creosote Bush scrub and Joshua Tree woodland. It seems to be most abundant in big, sandy washes emptying out of the north slopes of the San Bernardino and Little San Bernardino Mountains. Its range extends from northeastern Kern County to northern Baja California, Mexico.

Comments: This genus was named for the astronomer and geologist J. N. Nicollet, who was hired by the United States government to explore areas west of the Mississippi River. He was also John C. Frémont's first science teacher.

Desert Needles

DESERT NEEDLES
Palafoxia arida B. Turner & M. Morris var.
arida
Sunflower Family (Asteraceae)

Description: This erect, rough-textured, 1–2'
tall annual has branched stems and alternate,
entire, linear leaves that are 1–4" long. The
cylindrical flower heads are produced in
branched, flat-topped clusters. Each head has
10–20 light pink to white, 1" long disk flowers
with protruding, dark pink styles, subtended
by numerous linear, pointed, ½–¾" long phyllaries.

Flowering Season: March to May

Habitat/Range: Desert Needles are widespread in sandy areas below 3,000 feet in Creosote Bush scrub and alkali sinks in the eastern
and southern Mojave Desert and throughout
the Colorado Desert to Mexico.

Comments: The similar Giant Spanish Needle *(Palafoxia arida* var. *gigantea)* occurs in the
Algodones Dunes of the Colorado Desert
south to Sonora, Mexico. It is threatened by
off-highway vehicles and is designated a California species of concern.

Parry's Stephanomeria, Parry Rock-Pink

PARRY'S STEPHANOMERIA, PARRY ROCK-PINK
Stephanomeria parryi A. Gray
Sunflower Family (Asteraceae)

Description: This 8–16" tall perennial seems almost fleshy, with bluish, hairless stems that are filled with milky sap. The thick leaves are 1–3" long with teeth that point toward the base. The flowers are produced in open clusters of heads on short stalks. Each head has 10–14 pink to whitish, straplike flowers that are ½–¾" long. The phyllaries occur in 2 rows, the inner over ½" long and the outer much shorter. The pappus bristles are united at the bases into groups of 2 or 3, and they are a dirty-looking brownish or yellowish color.

Flowering Season: May to June

Habitat/Range: Parry's Stephanomeria is found in dry, open soil from 2,000 to 7,000 feet in Creosote Bush scrub and Joshua Tree woodland from the western Mojave Desert to Mono Country, California, to Utah and Arizona.

Comments: Charles Christopher Parry (1823–1890) worked for the Pacific Railroad and Mexican Boundary Surveys and made many plant collection trips to the deserts and mountains of the American Southwest. He discovered numerous new species, and quite a few are named in his honor, including Parry's Stephanomeria.

STEPHEN INGRAM

Wire Lettuce, Desert Straw

WIRE LETTUCE, DESERT STRAW

Stephanomeria pauciflora (Torrey) Nelson
Sunflower family (Asteraceae)

Description: This 12–24" tall pale-stemmed perennial has an intricate, angled, branching pattern, forming a short, rounded shrub. The 1–3" long basal leaves have sharply incised lobes that point toward the leaf base, while the upper leaves are entire, small, and often scale-like. The solitary heads have 3–5 pinkish, straplike flowers and 5 phyllaries that are about ⅜" tall. The 5-angled akenes have a pappus of bristles with a brownish, dirty tinge.

Flowering Season: May to August

Habitat/Range: Wire Lettuce is common in open areas, washes, and disturbed areas below 6,000 feet in Creosote Bush scrub, Joshua Tree woodland, and Pinyon-Juniper woodland in both the Mojave and Sonoran Deserts and the adjacent mountains to Kansas, Texas, and Baja California, Mexico.

Comments: Rounded, dried clumps of Wire Lettuce are reported to be favorite food items of the introduced burros in the eastern Mojave Desert.

Desert Willow

DESERT WILLOW
Chilopsis linearis (Cav.) Sweet ssp. *arcuata*
(Fosb.) Henrickson
Bignonia Family (Bignoniaceae)

Description: Desert Willow is a deciduous, 6–18' tall shrub with alternate, slightly curved, lanceolate, 4–6" long leaves. The fragrant lavender to pink flowers have 2-lipped, inflated corollas with purple markings. The fruit is a narrow, 6–12" long capsule, which splits apart to release numerous thin, flattened seeds with tufts of hairs at both ends.

Flowering Season: May to September

Habitat/Range: This common desert shrub occupies washes and other habitats below 5,000 feet where subsurface water is found. It occurs throughout the central and eastern Mojave Desert and the Colorado Desert to Texas and Mexico.

Comments: Desert Willow is not a true willow but is so named because its leaves resemble those of true willows (*Salix* species), and also because of its tendency to grow in washes. Like true willows, the Desert Willow is dependent on subsurface water and can grow roots as deep as 50'. It loses its leaves when temperatures drop to 41 degrees F., or with the onset of drought. This plant cannot self-pollinate, and the style folds shut after being touched. Known pollinators include bumble-bees *(Bombus)* and hummingbirds. Desert Willows are commonly cultivated in gardens, and the dried flowers are brewed to make cough syrup in northern Mexico. It is purported to have anti-fungal properties, useful in treating cuts and scrapes.

Tequilia

TEQUILIA
Tequilia plicata (Torrey) A. Richardson
Borage Family (Boraginaceae)

Description: This low, creeping, evergreen perennial spreads by means of a woody rhizome. The 4-16" stems have opposite branches with small, glandular hairs. The round to ovate leaves are about ¼" long, silvery-hairy, and distinctively fan-folded (plicate). The 5-parted, lavender, ¼" long flowers are produced in leaf axils.

Flowering Season: April to June

Habitat/Range: Tequilia grows in sandy soil and dunes below 3,000 feet in Creosote Bush scrub in the eastern Mojave Desert and the Colorado Desert to Baja California, Mexico.

Comments: Two similar species occur in the Mojave Desert, neither of which have prominent leaf folds. *Tequilia nuttallii,* an annual without a rhizome or glandular hairs, occurs from the Mojave Desert to Washington and Wyoming. *T. canescens* has alternate branches and occurs in the mountains of the eastern Mojave.

Hedge-Hog Cactus, Calico Cactus

HEDGE-HOG CACTUS, CALICO CACTUS
Echinocereus engelmannii
Cactus Family (Cactaceae)

Description: The erect, cylindrical, 8–12" tall stems of the Hedge-Hog Cactus usually occur in groups of 5–15, forming a 2–3' diameter mound. Each stem has 5–13 prominent ribs. This is also called the Calico Cactus because the straight spines are of multiple colors, including yellow, pink, gray, and black on the same plant. The flowers, which occur singly at the tops of stems, come in shades of magenta, lavender, or purple. The inner flower segments are sharp pointed, and the anthers are yellow. The flowers close at night. The round, sweet, edible, 1" diameter fruits with fat-rich seeds turn red when ripe, attracting birds and rodents.

Flowering Season: April to May

Habitat/Range: Hedge-Hog Cactus occurs in gravelly soil below 7,500 feet in Creosote Bush scrub, Joshua Tree woodland, and Pinyon-Juniper woodland in the Mojave Desert. It is also found in the Sonoran Desert.

Comments: Plants need both water from the soil and carbon dioxide from the atmosphere to make food by photosynthesis. However, if plants in the hot, dry desert open their pores (stomates) to let the carbon dioxide in, too much precious water evaporates out through the open stomates. Many cacti and other succulent plants deal with this problem by opening stomates only at night. The carbon dioxide is stored in the form of an acid until the next day, when light can provide the energy to complete photosynthesis. This water-conserving strategy is called crassulacean acid metabolism (CAM).

Nipple Cactus

NIPPLE CACTUS
Mammillaria tetrancistra Engelm.
Cactus Family (Cactaceae)

Description: This 3–10" tall and 1½–3" wide, cylindrical cactus is very inconspicuous and uncommon. It has dense, whitish radial spines and 3–4 curved, ¾–1" long central spines with dark, hooked tips. Short-lived, white to rose-colored flowers with central lavender stripes and fringed outer petals are produced in a circular pattern at the tops of stems. The red, cylindrical fruits are ½–1¼" long.

Flowering Season: April

Habitat/Range: Nipple Cactus is found on dry, sandy soil pockets on rocky desert hillsides and upper alluvial slopes below 4,000 feet in the Mojave Desert, from the Panamint Mountains and eastward.

Comments: This species was once placed in its own genus, *Phellosperma*, because it has a very peculiar, large seed with a thick, corky base. Nipple Cactus and other cacti respond to drought with contractile roots that pull them down into the soil, making them very inconspicuous until they become rehydrated.

Beavertail Cactus

BEAVERTAIL CACTUS
Opuntia basilaris Engelm. & Bigel.
Cactus Family (Cactaceae)

Description: Beavertail Cactus has clumps of flat, bluish gray to purplish, transversely wrinkled pads that are generally 3–8" long and 2–5" wide. The plants appear to be spineless, but clusters of short bristles (glochids) cause a painful surprise if this plant is handled. Rose to magenta, 1–1½" long flowers with dark red-purple filaments and white stigmas are produced along the upper edges of the pads. The dry, tan fruits are 1–1½" long.

Flowering Season: March to June

Habitat/Range: Beavertail Cactus is very common on dry slopes below 6,000 feet in Creosote Bush scrub, Joshua Tree woodland, and Pinyon-Juniper woodland throughout the Mojave and Colorado Deserts to Sonora, Mexico.

Comments: Fossilized pack rat middens record the presence of Beavertail Cactus in Death Valley 19,500 years ago. Native Americans used the pulp of Beavertail Cactus on cuts and wounds to promote healing and alleviate pain. Fruits were de-spined by brushing with twigs, baked in a stone-lined pit until soft, and then eaten. The rare Short-Joint Beavertail *(Opuntia basilaris var. brachyclada)* is distinguished by having short, club-shaped segments rather than flattened ones. It has a limited distribution between 4,000 to 7,500 feet on the desert slopes of the San Gabriel and San Bernardino Mountains. It is threatened by residential development and off-highway vehicles and is considered a species of concern by the state of California.

Desert Live-Forever

DESERT LIVE-FOREVER
Dudleya saxosa (M. E. Jones) Britton & Rose
ssp. *aloides* (Rose) Moran
Stonecrop Family (Crassulaceae)

Description: Desert Live-Forever produces a basal rosette of 10–25 succulent, lanceolate 1–4" long leaves that are nearly round in cross section. The pinkish red, 2–8" flower stalk bears a branched cluster of red-tinged, greenish yellow, 5-parted flowers, and the terminal branches of the flower cluster are often wavy.

Flowering Season: May to June

Habitat/Range: This species inhabits crevices on rocky, dry slopes at elevations from 3,500 to 7,000 feet in Creosote Bush scrub, Joshua Tree woodland, and Pinyon-Juniper woodland. It tends to favor sheltered areas on north-facing slopes. It is found in the mountains of the central, eastern, and southern Mojave Desert and also in the San Jacinto and Laguna Mountains to Baja California, Mexico.

Comments: The Panamint Dudleya *(Dudleya saxosa* ssp. *saxosa)* is generally smaller than Desert Live-Forever, and it does not have wavy flower cluster branches. This rare species is endemic to granite and limestone slopes of the Panamint Mountains, but it is not threatened at this time. This genus was named in honor of William Russell Dudley (1849-1911), the first botany professor at Stanford University.

Newberry Milkvetch

NEWBERRY MILKVETCH
Astragalus newberryi A. Gray var. *newberryi*
Pea Family (Fabaceae)

Description: This stemless, tufted perennial has 1-5" long, divided leaves with 3-13 pinnate, ovate, ¼-½" long leaflets. Flat, silky hairs cover the stems and foliage, giving the plant a silvery appearance. Pink to purple "pea" flowers are produced on stalks that are shorter than the leaves, followed by densely hairy, 1" long pods with 1 compartment.

Flowering Season: April to June

Habitat/Range: Newberry Milkvetch occupies dry, stony places from 4,000 to 7,600 feet in Sagebrush Scrub and Pinyon-Juniper woodland in the eastern Mojave Desert.

Comments: Look for the very tiny exit holes that Seed beetles (Bruchidae) make in the pods of many species of milkweed and other Pea Family plants. The ovate adults with clubbed antennae, striate wings, toothed hind legs, and concealed heads are common on flowers and foliage, but with an average size of less than ⅛", the beetles are seldom noticed. After the eggs are laid on the plant, the larva hatch, tunnel into pods, and eat the seeds. Some species cause serious damage to field crops and stored beans and peas.

Silk Dalea

SILK DALEA
Dalea mollisma (Rydb.) Munz
Pea Family (Fabaceae)

Description: The sprawling, 4–12" long stems of Silk Dalea are covered with fine, soft hairs. The pinnately divided leaves have 8–12 round to oblong, ¼" long leaflets that have gland-dots along the wavy margins. The pink to white "pea" flowers are produced in dense, 1" long spikes. The shaggy-haired, ¼" long calyx is the same length as the corolla or longer, and the calyx lobes are longer than the calyx tube.

Flowering Season: March to June

Habitat/Range: Silk Dalea is common throughout the Mojave and Sonoran Deserts in coarse or gravelly flats and washes in Creosote Bush scrub below 3,000 feet.

Comments: A similar annual species, *Dalea mollis*, does not have wavy leaf margins, the calyx is usually less than ¼" long, and corolla is longer than the calyx. It generally occupies lower, sandier sites than Silk Dalea, and its range extends to Mexico. This genus was named for T. Dale, an 18th-century botanist.

Red-Stemmed Filaree, Cranesbill

RED-STEMMED FILAREE, CRANESBILL

Erodium cicutarium (L.) L'Her.
Geranium Family (Geraniaceae)

Description: This introduced annual develops a basal rosette of twice-divided leaves. Slender, decumbent, 4–20" stems grow from the rosette to bear clusters of 5-parted, ¼" long, rose to lavender flowers. The distinctive fruit has 5 loosely fused, ¼" long lobes at the base, each with a 1–1½" extension that forms the long fruit beak. These 1-seeded lobes split apart, and as they dry, their beak extensions coil. This results in a twisting action that digs the seeds into the soil.

Flowering Season: February to May in the Mojave Desert and nearly year-round in other parts of southern California

Habitat/Range: Red-Stemmed Filaree is common in dry open areas below 6,000 feet. It can be found just about anywhere in California and also occurs throughout the United States. It is especially abundant in disturbed sites and along roadsides.

Comments: This species was introduced into California from the Mediterranean region several hundred years ago. Pieces of Red-Stemmed Filaree have been identified from adobe bricks manufactured in 1771 to build the Spanish mission at Jolon in San Luis Obispo County, providing evidence that this species was established in California by that time. Identification of pollen in layered mud deposits in the Central Valley confirmed the arrival of this species in the 1700s. The genus name is derived from the Greek word for heron, *erodios,* since the fruit shape resembles a heron's bill.

Desert Heron's Bill

DESERT HERON'S BILL
Erodium texanum A. Gray
Geranium Family (Geraniaceae)

Description: The 4–16" long branches of this sprawling annual spread flat and curve up at the tips. Dark green, 3-lobed, ½–1" long leaves with triangular stipules occur on long, hairy petioles. The magenta flowers are unusual in that the ¼–½" long petals are not all the same length on 1 flower, and the sepals are silver with purple veins. The conspicuous, erect, beaked fruits are 1½–3" long.

Flowering Season: March to May

Habitat/Range: Desert Heron's Bill grows on gravelly or sandy soil below 3,500 feet in Creosote Bush scrub in the eastern and southern Mojave Desert and also in the Colorado Desert to Texas and Baja California, Mexico.

Comments: The flowers seem to be responsive to varying levels of light. On a sunny day they often will not open until the afternoon, while on a cloudy day they tend to open earlier.

PURPLE MAT
Nama demissum A. Gray var. *demissum*
Waterleaf Family (Hydrophyllaceae)

Description: The slender, glandular-hairy, 1–8" long stems of this spreading, prostrate annual have a forked branching pattern. Narrow, sessile, spoon-shaped leaves appear in dense clusters at the stem tips. The funnel-shaped, magenta to rose-purple flowers occur singly in the branch axils and are numerous at leafy stem tips.

Flowering Season: April to May

Habitat/Range: Purple Mat is widespread and common in sandy or gravelly soils in Creosote Bush scrub below 4,000 feet from Inyo County south to Imperial County and east to Arizona.

Comments: *Nama demissum* var. *covillei*, which occurs around Death Valley, has winged leaf petioles and gray-hairy leaves.

Purple Mat

Pima Rhatany

STEPHEN INGRAM

PIMA RHATANY
Krameria erecta Shultes
Rhatany Family (Krameriaceae)

Description: This spreading, grayish green, 1–3' tall shrub with blunt stem tips is partially parasitic on the roots of other plants. The simple, linear, sessile leaves grow to ½" long and are alternate on the stems. The bilateral, magenta and green, ¼" long flowers are produced on ½" long, leafy-bracted stalks. Each has cupped sepals and 3 somewhat fused, clawed flag petals. Each spherical, greenish fruit has red spines with downward-pointing barbs along the upper half.

Flowering Season: March to May

Habitat/Range: Pima Rhatany is found on dry, rocky ridges below 5,000 feet in the central, eastern, and southern Mojave Desert, as well as the Sonoran Desert to Texas and northern Mexico.

Comments: A similar species, White Rhatany *(Krameria grayii)*, has spiny branch tips, the flower buds are curved upward, and the purple-red flowers have reflexed sepals. The spherical fruits have spines that are barbed only at the tip. It occupies much of the same range as Pima Rhatany but prefers lower slopes and valleys with sandy soils, often with Creosote Bush. Some groups of Native Americans ate the tiny seeds of Pima Rhatany, and a dye was made from the roots. This genus was named for Johann Georg Kramer (1684–1744), an Austrian botanist and physician.

Mojave Pennyroyal

MOJAVE PENNYROYAL
Monardella exilis E. Greene
Mint Family (Lamiaceae)

Description: This erect, 4–16" tall annual has purplish stems that branch at the base or below the middle. The opposite, lanceolate leaves have a pleasant smell. Several rounded flower clusters up to 1" across are produced along the upper portion of the main stem. These have broad, pointed, purple-veined bracts below. Each small white flower has an erect, 2-lobed upper lip, a 3-lobed lower lip, and 4 stamens.

Flowering Season: April to June

Habitat/Range: Mojave Pennyroyal is found in sandy areas from 2,000 to 6,000 feet in Creosote Bush scrub, Joshua Tree woodland, and Pinyon-Juniper woodland in the central and western Mojave Desert.

Comments: This genus and the genus *Monarda* were named in honor of Nicholas Monardes (1493–1588), a Spanish botanist and physician.

Alkali Mariposa Lily

STEPHEN INGRAM

ALKALI MARIPOSA LILY
Calochortus striatus Parish
Lily Family (Liliaceae)

Description: This elegant perennial has linear, 4–8" long leaves that wither early. The flowers occur singly or in clusters of 1–5 on long, slender stems with ½–1" bracts below. Each 3-parted, bell-shaped, ¾–1¼" long flower has lavender, pink, or white toothed petals with purple veins. The fruit is a narrow, erect, angled, 2" long capsule.

Flowering Season: April to June

Habitat/Range: Alkali Mariposa is found in springs and alkali seeps from 2,500 to 4,500 feet along the desert slopes of the San Bernardino and San Gabriel Mountains. It also occurs in Kern and Tulare Counties and in western Nevada. This species is most concentrated in the southwestern portion of Edwards Air Force Base, where over 10,000 individual plants are present.

Comments: Alkali Mariposa is a fairly rare species that is threatened by downdrafting of water tables from nearby development. It is a California species of concern and is on the watch list in Nevada.

Small-Flowered Eremalche

SMALL-FLOWERED EREMALCHE
Eremalche exilis (A. Gray) E. Greene
Mallow Family (Malvaceae)

Description: The spreading stems of this 4–16" tall annual branch near the base. The palmate, 3–5 lobed, ¼–¾" wide leaves are on slender, ½–1½" stalks, and they are covered with stellate hairs that can be easily observed with a 10X hand lens. The ¼" long, pale pink, lavender, or white flowers are produced in leaf axils. The gray, dried, tiny fruit has 9–13 wrinkled, wedge-shaped segments, each with 1 seed.

Flowering Season: March to May

Habitat/Range: Small-Flowered Eremalche is found in Creosote Bush scrub and alkaline areas of the Mojave and Sonoran Deserts. Its range extends north to the White and Inyo Mountains, east to Arizona, and south to Baja California, Mexico.

Comments: This plant can be extremely abundant, in some years covering large open areas on the desert floor. The scientific name literally means "the slender, feeble, lonely mallow."

Tim Thomas

Desert Five-Spot

DESERT FIVE-SPOT
Eremalche rotundifolia (A. Gray) E. Greene
Mallow Family (Malvaceae)

Description: The erect, rough-hairy, 4–16" tall stems of this spectacular annual bear dark green, round, scalloped 1–2" long leaves on 1–4" stalks. The spherical flowers have 5 separate, pink, ¾–1¼" long petals, each with a dark purplish blotch on the inside.

Flowering Season: March to May

Habitat/Range: Desert Five-Spot occurs in Creosote Bush scrub below 3,600 feet in the eastern and northern Mojave Desert and west to the Barstow region. It is locally common in Death Valley. It also occurs in the Sonoran Desert.

Comments: Look for the larvae of the Large White Skipper *(Heliopetes ericetorum)*, which feed on Desert Five-Spot in the spring. They have white hairs and green stripes on a yellowish green background. The adult butterflies are on the wing from April to October.

MOJAVE SAND-VERBENA
Abronia pogonantha Heimeri
Four O'Clock Family (Nyctaginaceae)

Description: This low-growing, branched annual has hairy, sticky, pink stems that curve upward at the tips. The opposite, ovate, glutinous leaves are on ½–1" long petioles. The pink or white, ½–¾" long, tubular flowers occur in rounded clusters on 1–2" stalks, and each cluster has a series of ovate bracts beneath. The ¼" long, heart-shaped fruits have 2 wings.

Flowering Season: April to July

Habitat/Range: Mojave Sand-Verbena is locally common in sandy soil in Creosote Bush scrub, Joshua Tree woodland, and Pinyon-Juniper woodland below 5,000 feet in scattered locations throughout the Mojave Desert, but it is not common in the eastern Mojave. It is especially abundant near the Deep Creek Dam along the Mojave River. It also occupies the foothills of the southern Sierra Nevada Range, western Nevada, and the southern San Joaquin Valley.

Mojave Sand-Verbena

Desert Sand-Verbena

DESERT SAND-VERBENA
Abronia villosa S. Watson var. *villosa*
Four O'Clock Family (Nyctaginaceae)

Description: Desert Sand-Verbena is a sticky, hairy, trailing annual with branched 4–20" stems. The ½–1½" long leaves are triangular to round, opposite, and unequal at the base. The rounded, headlike flower clusters are on 1–3" stalks and have 15–35 pink, ½" long flowers and lanceolate bracts below. The triangular, ¼" long fruit has 3–4 wings and a hardened beak at the tip.

Flowering Season: March to June

Habitat/Range: This species is common in low, sandy valleys below 3,000 feet in Creosote Bush scrub, from the Mojave and Sonoran Deserts to northwestern Mexico.

Comments: Native Americans used the leaves and flowers of Desert Sand-Verbena as a poultice to reduce swellings and stop pain from burns.

Windmills

WINDMILLS
Allionia incarnata L.
Four O'Clock Family (Nyctaginaceae)

Description: This short-lived perennial has trailing, slender, glandular stems with forked branches. The opposite, unequal leaves are darker green on the upper surface and lighter below. The rose-colored, funnel-shaped, ½" long flowers are produced singly on ¼–1" stalks, and each has 3 partly fused, hairy bracts beneath. The oblong, compressed fruit has lengthwise glands and incurved margins, and it is less than ¼" long.

Flowering Season: April to June

Habitat/Range: Windmills occur in Creosote Bush scrub below 4,500 feet in the eastern and southern Mojave Desert and in the Sonoran Desert to Colorado, Texas, Mexico, and South America.

Comments: This genus was named in honor of Charles Allioni (1728–1804), a botanist and friend of Carl Linnaeus.

SPIDERLING
Boerhavia triqueta S. Watson
Four O'Clock Family (Nyctaginaceae)

Description: This annual is less than 24" tall, with slender stems that have sticky areas between the nodes. The opposite, entire ½–1¼" long leaves are narrowly lanceolate with brownish dots. The tiny, bell-shaped flowers are pale pink to white, and the club-shaped fruit has wrinkles between the 3–5 sharp, longitudinal ribs.

Flowering Season: September to December

Habitat/Range: Spiderling is found in sandy washes and gravelly open areas below 5,500 feet in Creosote Bush scrub and Joshua Tree woodland in the southern Mojave Desert and the Sonoran Desert to Baja California, Mexico.

Comments: The similar Wright's Boerhavia *(Boerhavia wrightii)* has large, persistent bracts below the reddish flowers, and the leaves are wider than those of Spiderling.

Spiderling

Wishbone Bush

WISHBONE BUSH
Mirabilis californica A. Gray
Four O'Clock Family (Nyctaginaceae)

Description: The forked, 6–24" long stems of this trailing perennial are sometimes woody at the base. The ovate, glandular-hairy leaves are ½–1" long and are opposite on short petioles. The bell-shaped, pink to white, ½" long flowers generally open during the morning hours but often close in the afternoon heat or wind. Each flower has a whorl of 5 partly fused bracts beneath.

Flowering Season: March to June

Habitat/Range: Wishbone Bush is very common in dry, rocky, or sandy areas and washes below 3,000 feet. It is found along the western edges of the Mojave Desert to Baja California, Mexico.

Comments: *Mirabilis bigelovei*, which occurs throughout the Mojave Desert, is very difficult to distinguish from *M. californica*. There is much overlap of ranges and morphological features, and they intergrade where their ranges overlap. The most recent taxonomic treatment merges both of these taxa as members of the same species, *M. laevis*.

Giant Four O'Clock

GIANT FOUR O'CLOCK
Mirabilis multiflora (Torrey) A. Gray var. *glandulosa* (Standley) J. F. Macrb.
Four O'Clock Family (Nyctaginaceae)

Description: This sprawling perennial has opposite, round to ovate leaves that are often glandular and hairy when young, becoming hairless with age. The funnel-shaped, 2½" long magenta flowers occur in groups of 6 in a cup formed by 5 partly fused bracts. The ¼–½" elliptic fruits are somewhat warty and gelatinous when wet.

Flowering Season: April to August

Habitat/Range: This variety of Giant Four O'Clock is found in the northern Mojave Desert in Inyo County, west to Colorado.

Comments: *Mirabilis multiflora* var. *pubescens* is distinguished from var. *glandulosa* by its smooth, nongelatinous, 10-ribbed fruits. It occurs in the eastern Mojave Desert and Sonoran Desert to northwestern Mexico.

STEPHEN INGRAM

BROAD-LEAVED GILIA
Gilia latifolia S. Watson
Phlox Family (Polemoniaceae)

Description: This fetid-smelling annual is one of the easiest *Gilia* species to identify. Its simple, broad, leathery, 1–3" long leaves are ovate to round with toothed margins. The 4–12" tall stem can be simple or branched, supporting a cluster of numerous, narrow, funnel-shaped flowers. The corolla is pale pink to tan on the outside and bright pink to red on the inside, and the stamens, which are of unequal lengths, barely protrude from the flower tube. The ¼" long capsule has 3 compartments and many reddish brown seeds.

Flowering Season: March to May

Habitat/Range: Broad-Leaved Gilia is fairly common in washes and on rocky hillsides below 2,000 feet in Creosote Bush scrub, especially in areas where desert varnish is evident.

Comments: The derivation of the genus name is unclear. Some sources say it was named for Felipe Luis Gil, a Spanish botanist,

Broad-Leaved Gilia

while others say it was for Filippo Luigi Gilli, an Italian astronomer who participated in publishing a botanical tome. These may be the same person, since they both lived from 1756–1821.

Desert Calico

DESERT CALICO
Loeseliastrum matthewsii (A. Gray) S. Tim-
brook
Phlox Family (Polemoniaceae)

Description: Desert Calico is a rounded, tufted, 1–6" tall annual with white stems. The alternate, ½–1½" long leaves have bristle-tipped teeth. The most common background color of the 2-lipped, ½–1" long flowers is rose-purple, but they also come in yellow or white. The erect upper lip has a white spot and arched maroon lines, while the lower lip has 3 teeth or notches. The 3-parted style and the stamens protrude from the corolla tube.

Flowering Season: April to June

Habitat/Range: Desert Calico is locally abundant in sandy and gravelly soils below 5,000 feet in Creosote Bush scrub and Joshua Tree woodland in the Mojave, Great Basin, and Sonoran Deserts to Sonora, Mexico.

Comments: This species was named in honor of Dr. W. Matthews, a physician who served in the United States Army post in Owens Valley in 1875.

Canaigre, Wild Rhubarb

CANAIGRE, WILD RHUBARB
Rumex hymenosepalus Torrey
Buckwheat Family (Polygonaceae)

Description: Wild Rhubarb is a conspicuous, 2–4' tall perennial with stout, reddish stems. The fleshy, oblong, 6–24" long leaves have curled margins and pointed tips. Each petiole clasps the stem, forming a papery sheath called the ochrea. Pink, 6-parted flowers are borne in a dense, 4–12" long cluster. The 3 outer flower lobes enlarge and become veiny, papery, and very conspicuous in the fruit.

Flowering Season: March to May

Habitat/Range: This species is common in dry sandy areas in Creosote Bush scrub and Joshua Tree woodland in the Mojave Desert and Western states to Baja California, Mexico.

Comments: Wild Rhubarb is toxic to humans and livestock if enough is eaten, but if the leaves are boiled first, they can be eaten like spinach. The early spring plants are especially nutritious, and present-day Hopi in Arizona still encourage the growth of this weedy species in their cornfields. The Navajo extracted orange dyes for basketry from this plant.

Sand-Cress

SAND-CRESS
Calyptridium monandrum Nutt.
Purslane Family (Portulacaceae)

Description: The 2–7" long, branched stems of this unusual, fleshy annual spread flat against the ground. The narrow, succulent, ¼–¾" leaves form a basal rosette, while the sparse stem leaves are smaller. The tiny flowers occur in short, flattened spikes on curved stalks. Each flower has 2 white-margined sepals and 3 white petals. The fruit is a flattened, ¼" long capsule with 5–10 tiny, shiny, black seeds.

Flowering Season: March to June

Habitat/Range: Sand-Cress is widely scattered in sandy open areas throughout the Mojave Desert and along desert edges, especially along the desert foothills of the Transverse Ranges. It is probably most common in coastal and inland valley areas of California to Sonora, Mexico.

Comments: Sand-Cress is known to be a fire follower and will sometimes be seen in great abundance on desert slopes of the mountains for the first few years after a burn.

PURPLE OWL'S CLOVER

Castilleja exserta (A. A. Heller) Chuang & Heckard ssp. *venusta* (A. A. Heller) Chuang & Heckard
Figwort Family (Scrophulariaceae)

Description: The erect, 4–18" tall stems of Purple Owl's Clover are reddish and hairy, with ½–2" long, narrow, linear, lobed leaves. The flowers are produced in a dense, 1–10" long, spikelike cluster with 1" linear, lobed, purple-tipped bracts. The ½–1" long calyx is split partway down the front, sides, and back, and the magenta, hairy, bilateral corolla, which is slightly longer than the calyx, has a hooked beak and orange-yellow lower lip.

Flowering Season: March to May

Habitat/Range: This subspecies is found in sandy soils and washes in Creosote Bush scrub and Joshua Tree woodland from 2,000 to 3,000 feet in the western and central Mojave Desert. Purple Owl's Clover can be locally common in years with good rainfall, covering vast open areas.

Purple Owl's Clover

Comments: The more widespread *Castilleja exerta* ssp. *exerta* occurs in grasslands in the Western states to northwest Mexico. It differs from ssp. *venusta* by having a white to light yellow lower lip.

Desert Bird's-Beak

DESERT BIRD'S-BEAK

Cordylanthus eremicus Munz ssp. *eremicus*
Figwort Family (Scrophulariaceae)

Description: This 4–32" tall, minutely hairy annual has foliage that is often tinged reddish. The sessile, threadlike leaves are 4–16" long and entire or with 2 linear lobes. The upper lobe of each ½–¾" long, pink and maroon-blotched flower is shaped like a bird's beak, enclosing the style and 4 anthers, and it often has a yellow tip. The bracts subtending the flowers have 3–7 fingerlike lobes.

Flowering Season: July to October

Habitat/Range: Desert Bird's-Beak occurs in dry, rocky soil from 5,000 to 9,000 feet in Pinyon-Juniper woodland in the mountains of the northern Mojave Desert, and at about 3,000 feet on the desert slope of the San Bernardino Mountains, near Cushenbury.

Comments: The uncommon Desert Bird's-Beak is on the California Native Plant Society's watch list.

Bigelow's Monkeyflower

TIM THOMAS

BIGELOW'S MONKEYFLOWER
Mimulus bigelovei (A. Gray) A. Gray
Figwort Family (Scrophulariaceae)

Description: This erect, 2–4" tall, glandular-hairy annual has sessile, entire, obovate, 1–1½" long leaves that abruptly narrow to a sharp, pointed tip. The magenta, 2-lipped, 1–1¼" long flowers have hairy, yellow, purple-dotted throats and hairy anthers. The calyx lobes are unequal and spreading, and the 2 unequal stigma lobes have a fringe of short hairs.

Flowering Season: March to June

Habitat/Range: Bigelow's Monkeyflower is common on slopes and along washes below 7,500 feet in Creosote Bush scrub, Joshua Tree woodland, Pinyon-Juniper woodland, and Sagebrush scrub in the Mojave Desert to Mono County.

Comments: Fremont Monkeyflower *(Mimulus fremontii)* is distinguished from Bigelow's Monkeyflower by its narrowly elliptic leaves, equal calyx lobes, and smaller flowers that lack hairs inside. It is found in shrubby areas in the southern Mojave Desert. The 2-parted stigma of a monkeyflower will fold together when touched. This is likely a natural response to pollination, preventing any more pollen from landing on the stigma.

Death Valley Monkeyflower, Rock Midget

DEATH VALLEY MONKEYFLOWER, ROCK MIDGET

Mimulus rupicola Cov. & A. L. Grant
Figwort Family (Scrophulariaceae)

Description: This delicate, appealing perennial is covered with fine hairs, some of them glandular. It can grow up to 6" tall, but it can begin flowering when less than 1" tall. It branches from the base and takes on a somewhat tufted appearance, with ovate, entire leaves that are about 1–3" long. The 2-lipped, rose to light pink 1–1¼" long corolla has glandular hairs inside the tube, and each lobe has a purple spot at base. The ⅝" long calyx has ridges, and the fruit is a 2-chambered, ⅛" long, curved capsule.

Flowering Season: March to May

Habitat/Range: Death Valley Monkeyflower grows in cracks and crevices of limestone from 1,000 to 5,000 feet in mountains of the northern Mojave Desert, including the Cottonwood, Grapevine, Last Chance, Funeral, and northern Panamint Ranges.

Comments: This uncommon species is on the California Native Plant Society's watch list. There are no immediate threats, since most of the populations are within Death Valley National Park.

White-Margined Beardtongue

LIMESTONE BEARDTONGUE
Penstemon calcareous Brandegee
Figwort Family (Scrophulariaceae)

Description: This 2–10" tall perennial is covered with a coarse, waxy powder and fine, short hairs, giving the foliage an ashy-gray appearance. The firm, entire, ½–1½" long leaves are on stalks at the base of the plant, but tend to be sessile up the stem. The bright pink, 2-lipped, ½–¾" long flowers have 4 stamens and a staminode that is densely covered with coarse golden hairs.

Flowering Season: April to May

Habitat/Range: Limestone Beardtongue occupies dry cracks and crevices in limestone from 3,500 to 6,000 feet in Creosote Bush scrub, Joshua Tree woodland, and Pinyon-Juniper woodland. Its range is restricted to the mountains surrounding Death Valley, including the Grapevine, Providence, and Last Chance Ranges.

Comments: The rare Limestone Beardtongue is found only in California. Many sources erroneously report its range as extending into Nevada.

WHITE-MARGINED BEARDTONGUE
Penstemon albomarginata M. E. Jones
Figwort Family (Scrophulariaceae)

Description: The hairless stems of this herbaceous perennial arise from a 1–4' taproot that is sunk deep into sandy soil. The ½–1¼" long, glossy, pale green leaves have entire margins and white edges, giving this plant its common name. The tubular, 2-lipped, pink to lavender flowers have spreading lobes and purple nectar guides, and the floor of the throat is hairy.

Flowering Season: March to May

Habitat/Range: In California, White-Margined Beardtongue is found only in the Mojave Desert in a 4-mile long wash and spreading basin near Pisgah Crater and Lavic Lake. There are 15 populations in southern Nevada, and it also occurs over a large plain extending west of the Hualapai Mountains in Arizona. It occurs in deep sand on flats, at bases of mountains, and in wash bottoms at elevations from 2,000 to 3,000 feet.

Comments: White-Margined Beardtongue is threatened by off-highway recreational and military vehicles. It is a federal species of concern.

STEPHEN INGRAM

Limestone Beardtongue

RT HAWKE

Pallid Box Thorn

PALLID BOX THORN

Lycium pallidum Miers var. *oligospermum* C. Hitchc.

Nightshade Family (Solanaceae)

Description: This thorny, hairless, 3–6' tall shrub has oblong, alternate, ½–2" long leaves. The drooping, narrowly bell-shaped, 5-parted flowers are produced on ½" stalks. The calyx lobes are at least half as long as the calyx tube, and the ½" long, lavender to white corolla has purplish veins. The fruit is a ¼–½" round, hard, greenish purple berry with 5–7 seeds.

Flowering Season: March to April

Habitat/Range: Pallid Box Thorn is found on rocky hillsides and washes below 2,500 feet in Creosote Bush scrub. It occurs from around Barstow to Death Valley, and it has also been found in the northern Sonoran Desert.

Comments: The genus name is derived from "Lycia," an ancient country in Asia Minor; the species name means "pale;" and the variety name means "several seeded."

STEPHEN INGRAM

Salt Cedar, Tamarisk

SALT CEDAR, TAMARISK
Tamarix ramosissima Ledeb.
Tamarisk Family (Tamaricaceae)

Description: Salt Cedar is a highly branched shrub or tree that grows to 25' tall. The twigs are reddish brown, and the green, sessile, scalelike leaves are on very slender green stems. The tiny, 5-parted, pink flowers are borne in masses of ½–3" long, fingerlike clusters. At the base of the ovary of each flower there is a nectar disk with rounded lobes that alternate with the placement of the stamens.

Flowering Season: April to August

Habitat/Range: Salt Cedar is common in washes, stream banks, and roadsides in much of the West.

Comments: Salt Cedar is native to eastern Asia and is an invasive weed in riparian areas throughout the Western states (see discussion in introduction). *Tamarix parviflora*, a native of the eastern Mediterranean region, can be distinguished by having 4-parted flowers. *Tamarix gallica*, a native of Africa introduced in Death Valley, has narrower leaves and long nectar disk lobes that are fused with the filaments.

RED AND ORANGE FLOWERS

JOHN REID

Desert Mallow, Apricot Mallow

In this section you will find flowers ranging from deep maroon to red, orange, and orange-yellow. Red and orange flower colors are produced by fat-soluble carotene compounds, such as the beta-carotenes you need in your diet. Reddish colors can also be due to the presence of water-soluble anthocyanin pigments located in the large central vacuole of plant cells. Red flowers often attract birds as pollinators, especially if they offer a large nectar reward.

Mojave Mound Cactus

MOJAVE MOUND CACTUS
Echinocereus triglochidiatus Engelm.
Cactus Family (Cactaceae)

Description: The Mojave Mound Cactus is named for the large circular mounds formed by clusters of rounded, light green stems. Some mounds can be 9' across with hundreds of stems, but most are smaller. Each stem is usually 4-8" tall with 10-12 ribs. The youngest reddish or yellowish spines appear on the stem tops, while older gray spines arise lower on the stems from areoles with cobwebby hairs. The 1-2 central spines are often twisted but not flattened. Narrow, scarlet, 2" long flowers with pink to light purple anthers are produced singly at areoles, followed by 1" long, oblong, reddish fruits with black seeds.

Flowering Season: April to June

Habitat/Range: Mojave Mound Cactus is found among rocks on slopes in Creosote Bush scrub, Joshua Tree woodland, and Pinyon-Juniper woodland, often on limestone. It occurs from the Inyo and White Mountains south to Riverside County, California, and east to Utah and Arizona.

Comments: The flowers of Mojave Mound Cactus remain open at night, while the flowers of its relative, the Hedge-Hog Cactus *(Echinocereus engelmannii),* close at night. Some botanists recognize var. *melanacanthus,* with shorter flowers and 1–3 spreading central spines. It is found in Joshua Tree National Park, Cushenberry Canyon in the San Bernardino Mountains, and Clark Mountain.

Pineapple Cactus, Devil Claw

STEPHEN INGRAM

PINEAPPLE CACTUS, DEVIL CLAW

Sclerocactus polyancistrus (Engelm. & J. Bigelow) Britton & Rose

Cactus Family (Cactaceae)

Description: The Pineapple Cactus is usually 12–16" high, with 13–17 vertical, nodular ribs. It is densely covered with gray, white, and red spines, and usually at least 1 spine is hooked at each areole. The central spines are smooth. On their first day of blooming, the flowers are a purple color as seen in the photograph, but they often turn red to pink by the third day.

Flowering Season: April to June

Habitat/Range: This species is found between 2,500 and 6,500 feet on gravelly and carbonate soils in Creosote Bush scrub and Pinyon-Juniper woodland. It occurs across the northern Mojave Desert to eastern Nevada, but it is most common in the central Mojave Desert around Barstow, Ridgecrest, and Opal Mountain. It has a widely scattered distribution and is almost never found growing in a dense colony.

Comments: The somewhat similar Barrel Cactus *(Ferocactus cylindraceous)* differs from the Pineapple Cactus in that the central spines have crosswise rings or ridges, its flowers are yellow, and it is a much larger plant. The Pineapple Cactus is susceptible to damage by insects and rodents, and it is also threatened from collection by horticulturalists, although it doesn't grow well in captivity. It is likely that mining of limestone areas near Victorville has made impacts on this species. Pineapple Cactus is on the California Native Plant Society's list 4, a watch list of species that could easily become vulnerable to extinction.

Linear-Leaved Stillingia

LINEAR-LEAVED STILLINGIA
Stillingia linearifolia S. Watson
Spurge Family (Euphorbiaceae)

Description: This erect, branched, 1–2' tall perennial with alternate, narrow, entire leaves bears separate male and female flowers in terminal spikes on the same plant. The male flowers have a 2-lobed calyx and 2 stamens, while female flowers have ovaries with 3 compartments and styles.

Flowering Season: March to May

Habitat/Range: Linear-Leaved Stillingia occurs in open, dry sites below 4,500 feet in Creosote Bush scrub in the central and eastern Mojave Desert.

Comments: A very similar species, Tooth-Leaf (*Stillingia paucidentata),* differs from Linear-Leaved Stillingia in that it has teeth on the leaf margin near the base. It seems to replace Linear-Leaved Stillingia in areas west of Barstow.

SCARLET MILKVETCH, SCARLET LOCOWEED
Astragalus coccineus Brandegee
Pea Family (Fabaceae)

Description: This clumped perennial is covered with dense white hairs, giving the entire plant a silvery cast. The 2–5" leaves are pinnately divided into 7–15 inversely lanceolate leaflets with pointed tips. The shimmering grayish foliage contrasts beautifully with the intense scarlet, "pea" flowers, which are produced in clusters of 3–10. The curved, compressed, 1–1½" long fruits have 1 compartment, and they are covered with long, silky hairs.

Flowering Season: March to June

Habitat/Range: Scarlet Milkvetch occupies gravelly and rocky soils from 2,000 to 7,000 feet in Pinyon-Juniper woodland in mountains of the northern and eastern Mojave Desert to northern Baja California, Mexico.

RT HAWKE
Scarlet Milkvetch, Scarlet Locoweed

Comments: The foliage of Newberry Milkvetch *(Astragalus newberryi)* resembles that of Scarlet Milkvetch, but the fruits of Newberry Milkvetch are only ½–1" long. Often the color of the dried flower remains can be used to distinguish these species.

MARIPOSA LILY

Calochortus kennedyi Porter var. *kennedyi*
Lily Family (Liliaceae)

Description: This perennial is usually 4–8"
tall. The linear, channeled leaves are up to 8"
long and can be seen coiled on the ground
before the flowering stalk appears. Each plant
usually produces 1–2 open, bell-shaped, ver-
milion flowers with 3 petals, each 1–2" long
with purplish spots and round, fringed glands
at the base. The anthers are purple. The lanceolate, striped, 1–3" long fruit has 3 compartments, each with 2 rows of seeds.

Flowering Season: April to June

Habitat/Range: Mariposa Lilies are found
between 2,000 and 6,500 feet in Creosote
Bush scrub, Joshua Tree woodland, and
Pinyon-Juniper woodland. They grow between
shrubs in rocky or gravelly areas with heavy
soil. Mariposa Lilies can appear with surprising density in years with heavy rainfall, making the landscape ablaze with color.

Comments: Mariposa Lilies from east of the
Panamint Mountains tend to have flowers
that are lighter orange than those of the western and southern Mojave Desert. Yellow-
flowered Mariposa Lilies from the Providence
and Clark mountains are *Calochortus kennedyi*
var. *munzii*.

Mariposa Lily

DESERT MALLOW, APRICOT MALLOW

Sphaeralcea ambigua A. Gray var. *ambigua*
Mallow Family (Malvaceae)

Description: This perennial subshrub is
densely covered with short, stellate, cream-
colored hairs. The thick, alternate, 3-lobed
leaves are 1–2" long and wide with somewhat
scalloped margins. The flowers have 5 separate orange-red petals and numerous stamens
that are fused by the filaments. The dry,
rounded fruit is comprised of 9–13 bumpy
segments, each with 2 seeds.

Flowering Season: March to June

Habitat/Range: Desert Mallow occurs on
sandy flats, rocky slopes, and canyons below
4,000 feet in Creosote Bush scrub and Joshua
Tree woodland. It is quite common in deserts
of the southwestern United States to Sonora,
Mexico.

Comments: A related variety with pink flowers (*Sphaeralcea ambigua* var. *rosacea*) is fea-
tured in the pink, rose, and magenta section of
this book.

JOHN REID

Desert Mallow, Apricot Mallow

STEPHEN INGRAM

California Poppy

CALIFORNIA POPPY
Eschscholzia californica Cham.
Poppy Family (Papaveraceae)

Description: This 6–24" hairless, herbaceous plant can be annual or perennial. The leaves are dissected several times into narrow, somewhat pointed segments. The 4-parted flowers open from erect buds, and the 1–2" petals vary in color and size, depending on the time of year. In the spring they are larger and orange, while later in the year they tend to be smaller and yellow. California Poppy is distinguished from other poppies by having 2 rims on the receptacle (the torus) at the base of the pistil.

Flowering Season: February to September

Habitat/Range: California Poppy occurs in the western Mojave Desert in grassy open areas. It is especially abundant near Lancaster, where the Antelope Valley Poppy Preserve has been established. It occurs in many plant communities throughout California to southern Washington, New Mexico, and Baja California, Mexico.

Comments: California Poppy is the California state flower. It was named for J. F. Eschscholtz, a Russian surgeon who traveled on expeditions to California in the early 1800s. Research is underway to determine if the wide variation in the life history of this species is genetically or environmentally determined.

Apache Plume

STEPHEN INGRAM

APACHE PLUME
Fallugia paradoxa (D. Don) Endl.
Rose Family (Rosaceae)

Description: This erect to sprawling, 1–5' tall shrub with grayish bark has rust-colored, flaky patches and short, white hairs. The alternate, ½" long leaves have 3–7 pinnate lobes with rolled-under margins. For much of the year, Apache Plume looks like a disheveled mass of branches with a few leaves, until it sends up long stalks with showy, white, 5-parted flowers. As the cluster of akenes from each flower matures, the styles enlarge and turn pinkish, feathery, and very ornate.

Flowering Season: May to June

Habitat/Range: Apache Plume is found on dry hillsides from 4,000 to 5,500 feet in Joshua Tree woodland and Pinyon-Juniper woodland in the mountains of the eastern Mojave Desert and throughout the Western states to Texas.

Comments: This genus was named for the 19th-century Italian botanist, Abbot V. Fallugi. It is widely used as a drought-tolerant ornamental in gardens in the southwestern United States.

Desert Paintbrush

DESERT PAINTBRUSH
Castilleja angustifolia (Nutt.) G. Don
Figwort Family (Scrophulariaceae)

Description: The grayish green stems of this herbaceous perennial are usually about 6–18" tall. The alternate, lanceolate, ½–1½" long leaves may be entire or have 1–2 pairs of narrow, spreading lobes. Leaves grade into lobed, scarlet-tipped flower bracts higher up the stem. The tubular, 2-lipped, ¾" long calyx is dark green with reddish margins, and it is split for approximately a third of its length. The cylindrical, 1" long corolla has a red-margined upper hood and a dark green lower lip, which is enclosed by the calyx.

Flowering Season: April to August

Habitat/Range: Desert Paintbrush is found on dry, brushy, or rocky hillsides from 2,000 to 9,000 feet in Joshua Tree woodland, Pinyon-Juniper woodland, Shadscale scrub, and Sagebrush scrub in the Mojave Desert and throughout many Western states.

Comments: Members of the genus *Castilleja* show variable degrees of root-parasitism. Some species have seeds that will sprout only if a suitable host is present, probably in response to a chemical given off by the root. The young seedlings sink rootlike projections called haustoria into the host tissues to absorb water and food. Plants grown in the greenhouse without a host are much less vigorous than plants in the field. The genus *Castilleja* was named after Domingo Castillejo, a professor of botany in Cadiz, Spain (1744–1793).

MOJAVE MONKEYFLOWER
Mimulus mohavensis Lemmon
Figwort Family (Scrophulariaceae)

Description: This purplish, 1–4" annual has glandular-hairy stems and opposite, elliptical, ½–1" long leaves. The radial, tubular flowers have an angled, purple, ½" long calyx with hairs along the veins, and the maroon corolla tube is around ¾" long. The petal lobes abruptly spread out flat, and the margins of the petal lobes are white to pinkish with a network of maroon veins.

Flowering Season: April to June

Habitat/Range: Mojave Monkeyflower grows on gravely slopes and washes from 2,000 to 3,000 feet in Creosote Bush scrub and Joshua Tree woodland. It occurs from northwest Victorville east of National Trails Highway to Barstow, Daggett, and south to Stoddard OHV Recreation Area and parts of the Ord Mountains in California.

Mojave Monkeyflower

Comments: This plant is threatened throughout its range by off-highway vehicles, mining, development, and grazing. Despite its restricted range and susceptibility, it currently has no legal protection.

Utah Penstemon, Utah Firecracker

UTAH PENSTEMON, UTAH FIRECRACKER
Penstemon utahensis Eastw.
Figwort Family (Scrophulariaceae)

Description: This erect, hairless perennial is usually 1–2' tall. The thick, opposite, entire leaves are often folded lengthwise. They have clasping bases and are up to 20" long near the base of the plant, decreasing in size up the stem. The 1" long, red, tubular to funnel-shaped flowers have upper lobes that spread backward.

Flowering Season: April to May

Habitat/Range: Utah Penstemon is found in rocky places from 4,000 to 5,500 feet in Shadscale scrub, Sagebrush scrub, and Pinyon-Juniper woodland in the New York and Kingston Mountains to southern Utah and northern Arizona.

Comments: Most red, tubular plant species tend to be pollinated by hummingbirds, and often the flowering season closely coincides with hummingbird migration.

WHITE TO CREAM FLOWERS

Rock Nettle, Sting-Bush

Since cream colors often grade into yellow, be sure to check the yellow flower section if you do not find the flower you are searching for here. White and cream-colored flowers appear to have no pigments, but in fact many have water-soluble flavonol compounds. White flowers (and flowers of other colors as well) often have ultraviolet markings that serve as nectar guides to orient visiting insects. White and cream-colored flowers that are open in the evening may be attractive to night-flying moths and sometimes bats.

Skunkbrush

SKUNKBRUSH
Rhus trilobata Torrey & A. Gray
Sumac Family (Anacardiaceae)

Description: The smooth, brownish branches of this deciduous, 2–6' tall, spreading shrub sometimes curve to the ground and root at the tips. The alternate, hairless leaves with 3 leaflets are on a common leaf stalk that is ½–1" long. The ¾–2" long terminal leaflet tapers at the base, where it attaches to the 2 smaller, lateral, 3-lobed leaflets. The small, cream-colored flowers, which appear before the leaves, are produced in ½–1" long clusters at branch ends. The fruit is a ¼" fleshy, red berry.

Flowering Season: March to April

Habitat/Range: Skunkbrush occurs in washes and on hillsides below 6,000 feet in many plant communities throughout California to Canada and northern Mexico. It is fairly common in the mountains of the eastern Mojave Desert.

Comments: The flexible stems of Skunkbrush were highly prized by Native Americans for basket making, and a lemonade-like drink was made from the fruits. Skunkbrush can easily be mistaken for Poison Oak *(Toxicodendron diversilobum)*, a member of the same plant family. However, the terminal leaflet of Poison Oak is on a stalk, while the terminal leaflet of Skunkbrush is sessile. Poison Oak is found in canyons and moist areas on desert slopes of the Transverse Ranges and elsewhere in California but is absent from most of the Mojave Desert.

Amsonia

AMSONIA
Amsonia tomentosa Torrey & Fremont
Dogbane Family (Apocynaceae)

Description: This milky-sapped perennial has numerous erect, herbaceous, 6–16" tall stems that sprout from a woody base. The alternate, green, ovate-lanceolate leaves are ¾–1½" long. White to light blue, 5-parted, tubular flowers with spreading lobes are produced in dense clusters at the tops of branches, followed by 1–3" long, narrow, 2-parted fruits.

Flowering Season: March to May

Habitat/Range: Amsonia occurs in dry soils and canyons from 1,000 to 4,000 feet in Creosote Bush scrub, Joshua Tree woodland, Blackbush scrub, and Pinyon-Juniper woodland in the mountains of the eastern and southern Mojave Desert, the north-facing slopes of the San Bernardino Mountains, and the Sonoran Desert to Utah.

Comments: The Paiute used Amsonia stem fibers to make cord, and a laxative was made from the milky juice.

Desert Milkweed

DESERT MILKWEED
Asclepias erosa Torrey
Milkweed Family (Asclepiadaceae)

Description: This 18–30" tall perennial has white-woolly stems and leaves that become green and hairless with age. The opposite, sessile, lanceolate leaves are 2–6" long and 1–3" wide, and they have a leathery texture. The margins of the leaves have minute, irregular teeth and a vein running parallel to the leaf margin. Numerous ¼" cream to greenish white flowers are produced in rounded, stalked umbels. These unusual flowers have filaments fused to form a central tube, and the anthers are also fused, forming a head with peculiar attachments called hoods and horns. The dry, brownish, 2–3" long, reflexed fruits split open lengthwise to release numerous seeds with long hairs.

Flowering Season: May to July

Habitat/Range: Desert Milkweed is found on dry slopes and in washes from 500 to 6,000 feet in Creosote Bush scrub, Joshua Tree woodland, and Pinyon-Juniper woodland in the Mojave Desert and in the Sonoran Desert to Baja California, Mexico.

Comments: Milkweeds are named for Asklepios, the Greek god of medicine. Herbalists and Native Americans employed various species of *Asclepias* as expectorants and purgatives and as remedies for lung problems. The pulp of the roots was used as a poultice on bruises, and seeds were ground and boiled as a remedy for sores and rattlesnake bites. The species name *erosa* means "chewed edges," referring to the jagged appearance of the leaf margins.

Narrow-Leaf Milkweed, Mexican Whorled Milkweed

NARROW-LEAF MILKWEED, MEXICAN WHORLED MILKWEED

Asclepias fascicularis Decne.
Milkweed Family (Asclepiadaceae)

Description: This hairless, erect, 20–30" tall perennial has linear to lanceolate leaves that are 1½–4" long and less than ½" wide. They occur in whorls of 3–6 on the stem and are often folded lengthwise. The small, greenish white flowers have reflexed petals and elevated hoods with thin, incurved horns. They are produced in rounded umbels at the tops of stems, followed by narrow, erect, ¼–½" long fruits that split open along 1 suture to release numerous, tufted seeds.

Flowering Season: June to August

Habitat/Range: Narrow-Leaf Milkweed is common around rivers and alkali seeps and springs in the Mojave Desert, as well as in valleys and foothills throughout the Western states.

Comments: This species is a food plant for Monarch butterflies *(Danaus plexippus),* which migrate from coastal wintering sites to deserts in the spring. The plant contains toxic compounds called cardiac glycosides, which the Monarchs store in their tissues, making them toxic to their predators. The Paiute used the fibers of Narrow-Leaf Milkweed to make cloth, rope, and nets. Young shoots were eaten like asparagus after the bitter, toxic compounds were boiled away. The milky juice, which contains latex, was boiled and sometimes mixed with deer fat to make chewing gum. Milkweeds also had many medicinal applications (see entry for Desert Milkweed).

RUSH MILKWEED, AJAMETE
Asclepias subulata Decne.
Milkweed Family (Asclepiadaceae)

Description: This greenish white, 2–5' tall perennial has rigid, rushlike stems, which give it a shrubby character. The opposite, sessile, threadlike leaves usually fall early, so plants appear mostly leafless. The cream-colored, ¼–½" long flowers are produced in rounded umbels at and near the branch tips. They have reflexed petals and hoods with horns. The slender, smooth, 2–4" long fruits contain smooth, tufted, ¼" seeds.

Flowering Season: April to December

Habitat/Range: Rush Milkweed is found along washes and in hot, sandy areas below 2,000 feet in Creosote Bush scrub in the eastern Mojave Desert and from the Colorado Desert to Baja California, Mexico.

Comments: The milky juice of Rush Milkweed contains good-quality latex rubber, although it is not used commercially.

Rush Milkweed, Ajamete

GRAVEL GHOST, PARACHUTE PLANT
Atrichoseris platyphylla A. Gray
Sunflower Family (Asteraceae)

Description: Branched, leafless, 1–5' high stems emerge from the flat basal rosette of this hairless annual. The round to oblong, 1–4" long, finely toothed basal leaves are grayish green above and purple on the undersurface. Stem leaves are reduced to triangular scales and are barely noticeable. The 1" flower heads have numerous, white, strap-shaped flowers and 2–4 rows of triangular, ¼" high phyllaries. The flowers have a vanilla odor.

Flowering Season: March to May

Habitat/Range: Gravel Ghost occurs in sandy washes and dark, rocky, and clay soils in Creosote Bush scrub in the eastern and northern Mojave Desert. It is especially common in open areas in Death Valley. It also occurs in the Colorado Desert east of Mecca.

Comments: The genus name is derived from the Greek word, *athrix,* which means "hairless." According to Jaeger, the common name of Parachute Plant was given because the spreading shroud of white flowers connecting at the nearly invisible stem is reminiscent of a parachute in the air.

JOHN REID

STEPHEN INGRAM

Gravel Ghost, Parachute Plant

Mule Fat

EMORY BACCHARIS

Baccharis emoryi A. Gray
Sunflower family (Asteraceae)

Description: This hairless, sticky, 3–12' tall shrub has erect, somewhat broomlike branches with longitudinal grooves. The ¾–1½" long lower leaves have a few teeth on the margins and 3 veins from the base, while the upper leaves are shorter, entire, and 1-veined. Male and female flowers are produced in large, loose clusters of narrow, cylindrical heads on separate plants. The ½" long white pappus is somewhat shiny and very noticeable.

Flowering Season: August to December

Habitat/Range: Emory Baccharis is widespread but not abundant, occurring along streams, seeps, and salt marshes below 3,000 feet in Creosote Bush scrub in the deserts and throughout southern California to Utah, Texas, and Baja California, Mexico.

Comments: A somewhat similar but more compact species, Desert Baccharis *(Baccharis sergiloides)* is usually around 2–6' tall. It is distinguished from *Baccharis emoryi* by having obovate, mostly entire leaves and a ⅛–¼" long pappus. It is found in washes and canyon bottoms throughout the Mojave Desert to Sonora and Baja California, Mexico.

MULE FAT

Baccharis salicifolia (Ruiz Lopez & Pavon) Pers.
Sunflower Family (Asteraceae)

Description: This sticky, erect, 3–12' tall shrub has alternate, sessile, linear to lanceolate leaves that are 2–6" long. They are somewhat sticky, with entire or slightly toothed margins, and 3 veins from the base, with the central vein more prominent than the lateral veins. The ¼" long male and female flower heads are produced in rounded clusters on separate plants, each with numerous, dull white, threadlike flowers and 4–5 rows of red-tinged, lanceolate phyllaries.

Flowering Season: July to November

Habitat/Range: Mule Fat is found along streams, seeps, and in canyon bottoms below 3,500 feet throughout the southwestern United States, including the deserts.

Comments: Mule Fat is not a willow, although it grows in the same habitat. Willows have only 1 vein from the leaf base, not 3, and willows never have the old dried clusters of phyllaries that persist on this shrub through the seasons. The Cahuilla prepared an eyewash by steeping Mule Fat leaves.

Emory Baccharis

WOOLLY BRICKELLIA
Brickellia incana A. Gray
Sunflower Family (Asteraceae)

Description: This dense, rounded, 1–3' tall shrub is covered with short, woolly, white hairs, making the entire plant look bleached white or light gray. The alternate, sessile, ovate leaves are up to 1" long with sawtoothed margins. The 1" long flower heads are produced in groups of 1–3 on branch ends, each with 8–12 whitish disk flowers and approximately 40 overlapping, hairy, 4-veined phyllaries.

Flowering Season: April to October

Habitat/Range: Woolly Brickellia is found on roadsides and in sandy washes and flats below 5,000 feet in Creosote Bush scrub, Shadscale scrub, and Joshua Tree woodland in the Mojave and northern Colorado Deserts.

Comments: The species name *incana* is the Latin word for "grayish" or "white woolly."

Woolly Brickellia

Long-Leaved Brickellia

LONG-LEAVED BRICKELLIA
Brickellia longifolia Wats.
Sunflower Family (Asteraceae)

Description: This hairless, 1–5' tall shrub has alternate, entire, shiny, linear leaves that are 1–4" long. There are about 3–5 disk flowers in each narrow, ¼" long head; these are arranged in small clusters. There are 10–12 overlapping, 3–4-veined phyllaries subtending each head, the outer ovate, and the inner lanceolate.

Flowering Season: April to May

Habitat/Range: Long-Leaved Brickellia occurs along dry stream banks and near springs from 3,000 to 5,000 feet in the northern and eastern Mojave Desert from the Panamint Mountains to Nevada.

Comments: This species is very difficult to distinguish from Inyo Bricklebush *(Brickellia multiflora)*, which tends to have wider, lanceolate leaves and up to 20 phyllaries below each head. It occurs in the mountains of Inyo County and Clark Mountain to Nevada.

Fremont Pincushion

FREMONT PINCUSHION
Chaenactis fremontii A. Gray
Sunflower Family (Asteraceae)

Description: This erect, hairless 4–12" tall annual has basal rosette leaves that wither by the time the flowers open. The alternate, somewhat fleshy, 1–2" long stem leaves are linear, or they may have 1–2 pairs of nearly linear lobes. The flower heads are produced singly or in small clusters on stalks up to 4" long. The ¼–½" heads have disk flowers but no ray flowers, with the outermost enlarged and nearly 2-lipped and the inner ones smaller with radial symmetry. Each head has 1 row of phyllaries with flattened, rigid, acute tips. The pappus consists of 4–5 membranous scales.

Flowering Season: March to May

Habitat/Range: Fremont Pincushion is very common in open sandy flats and mesas below 5,000 feet in Creosote Bush scrub and Joshua Tree woodland in the Mojave Desert and in the Colorado Desert to the Central Valley of California.

Comments: Another common species is *Chaenactis stevioides,* a nonfleshy annual with grayish, hairy leaves, cobwebby-hairy stem bases, twice-pinnately lobed leaves with short, thick segments and shorter, glandular-hairy phyllaries. Additionally, there is Pebble Pincushion *(C. carphoclinia),* with reddish, cylindrical, bristle-tipped phyllaries and leaves that are often 3–4 times pinnately lobed.

Hairy Daisy

HAIRY DAISY

Erigeron concinnus (Hook & Arn.) Torrey &
A. Gray
Sunflower family (Asteraceae)

Description: Numerous 3-12" tall stems arise
from the thickened, woody base of this
rounded perennial. The inversely narrow,
lanceolate to spoon-shaped, ¾-2½" long
leaves are mostly crowded near the base of the
plant. The ½" diameter flower heads have 40-
60 pink, blue, or white ¼-⅜" long ray flowers,
numerous yellow disk flowers, and numerous
phyllaries of equal lengths. There is an inner
papus of bristles and an outer papus of scales.

Flowering Season: April to July

Habitat/Range: Hairy Daisy occupies
crevices on dry, rocky slopes from 3,000 to
8,000 feet in Creosote Bush Scrub, Joshua
Tree woodland, and Pinyon-Juniper woodland, in the mountains of the eastern Mojave
Desert to Idaho, Wyoming, Colorado, and
New Mexico.

Comments: The species name refers to this
plant's resemblance to *Erica*, a member of the
heath family.

White Tidy-Tips

WHITE TIDY-TIPS
Layia glandulosa (Hook.) Hook. & Arn.
Sunflower Family (Asteraceae)

Description: This erect, 4–20" tall annual has branched, purplish stems with black glands. The thin, roughened basal leaves are toothed or lobed while the upper leaves are entire. Single flower heads are produced at the ends of branches, each with numerous ¼" long, yellow disk flowers, 10–14 white, 3-lobed ray flowers, and 1 row of ¼–½" long, glandular, hairy phyllaries. The hairy akenes are topped by a pappus of 10–15 narrow, bright white, flattened scales. This plant has a pleasant, spicy odor.

Flowering Season: March to June

Habitat/Range: White Tidy-Tips are found in sandy soil below 8,000 feet in many vegetation types in the Mojave and Sonoran Deserts and elsewhere in California, as well as throughout the western United States.

Comments: This genus was named for George Tradescant Lay, an early 19th-century naturalist aboard the *Blossom*, a ship that was assigned to follow and check up on the infamous *Bounty*. Lay later became a missionary to China. Tidy Tips *(Layia platyglossa)*, with yellow, white-tipped rays, occur on the western edge of the Mojave Desert.

Silver Lakes Daisy

SILVER LAKES DAISY
Machaeranthera arida Turner & Horne
Sunflower Family (Asteraceae)

Description: This glandular, roughened, 2–12" tall annual has a forked branching pattern. The 1–3" long, grayish, alternate lower leaves have spiny teeth on the margins, while the upper leaves are smaller and often entire. The heads are produced singly or in branched clusters, each with numerous yellow disk flowers, 25–35 whitish to pale blue ray flowers, and oblong, grainy-looking, ⅛" long phyllaries in 2–3 rows. The ray flower pappus consists of numerous bristles, but there is no pappus evident on disk flowers.

Flowering Season: March to June

Habitat/Range: Silver Lakes Daisy is found in very arid, open sandy and salty soils below 3,000 feet in Creosote Bush scrub, alkali sinks, and streambeds in the central and eastern Mojave Desert from the Barstow region to Arizona and Sonora, Mexico.

Comments: Most of the time this plant looks straggly and unattractive, but in years with abundant rain, this plant fills out and takes on an eye-catching, rounded, bushlike form.

STEPHEN INGRAM

Small Desert Star

SMALL DESERT STAR
Monoptilon bellidiforme A. Gray
Sunflower Family (Asteraceae)

Description: Several slender stems grow from the base of this low-growing annual. It is similar to but smaller than Desert Star *(Monoptilon bellioides)*, with wider, spoon-shaped or inversely lanceolate leaves. The ray flower corollas are less than ¼" long, and the pappus consists of a cup of tiny scales and 1 bristle with a feathery tip.

Flowering Season: March to June

Habitat/Range: Small Desert Star is found in sandy soil and washes from 2,000 to 4,000 feet in Creosote Bush scrub in the Mojave Desert and the northern Colorado Desert.

Comments: There are only 2 species of *Monoptilon* in the world; both occur in the Mojave Desert.

Desert Star

DESERT STAR
Monoptilon bellioides (A. Gray) H. M. Hall
Sunflower Family (Asteraceae)

Description: This 2–6" tall, cushionlike, stubbly-haired annual has entire, linear, ¼–½" long leaves, which occur in tufts below the flower heads. Each head has 1 row of equal, linear, firm phyllaries, numerous yellow disk flowers, and 12–20 white, ¼–½" long ray flowers. The pappus has up to 12 straight bristles and shorter, alternating, divided scales.

Flowering Season: February to May, and sometimes in September following summer rain

Habitat/Range: Desert Star is common on sandy and gravelly flats and washes below 3,000 feet in Creosote Bush scrub in the Mojave and Sonoran Deserts.

Comments: Desert Star is a true "belly-plant," since you have to get on your belly to see it.

JOHN REID

EMORY ROCK-DAISY
Perityle emoryi Torrey
Sunflower Family (Asteraceae)

Description: This brittle, 6–24" tall, glandular-hairy annual has 1–4" long, rounded, toothed or lobed leaves that are opposite near the base and alternate above. The flower heads have numerous tiny, yellow disk flowers and 8–12 white ray flowers. The boat-shaped, ¼" long phyllaries occur in 1–2 rows, and they are fringed with hairs at their tips.

Flowering Season: February to June

Habitat/Range: Emory Rock-Daisy is common among boulders, on slopes, and in washes below 3,000 feet in Creosote Bush scrub in the central, eastern, and southeastern Mojave Desert to the Sonoran Desert, coastal southern California, and the Channel Islands.

Comments: This plant was named in honor of Major W. H. Emory, who completed the Mexican Boundary Survey in 1855, resulting in the moving of the international boundary in southern Arizona and New Mexico to its present location. Other less common species of *Perityle* in the Mojave Desert are perennial and lack ray flowers.

Emory Rock-Daisy

Desert Chicory

DESERT CHICORY
Rafinesquia neomexicana A. Gray
Sunflower Family (Asteraceae)

Description: This hairless, 6–24" tall, milky-sapped annual often has weak, zigzag stems that grow up through shrubs for support and protection against herbivores. The 1½–4" long basal rosette leaves wither by the time the stem develops, and the smaller stem leaves are sessile, toothed, and alternate. The large, showy flower heads occur singly at the ends of branches. They have numerous white strap-shaped flowers that extend well beyond the pointed, ½–1" long phyllaries. The pappus consists of white, plumose bristles with tangled hairs.

Flowering Season: March to May

Habitat/Range: Desert Chicory occurs in sandy and gravelly soils in Creosote Bush scrub and Joshua Tree woodland in the Mojave and Sonoran Deserts to Texas and northern Mexico.

Comments: The rather weedy-looking California Chicory *(Rafinesquia californica)* differs from Desert Chicory with its stout, erect, self-supporting stems, inconspicuous flowers, and brownish pappus. It occasionally occurs on the deserts but is more common elsewhere in California to Utah and Baja California, Mexico.

Forget-Me-Not, *Cryptantha* species

Forget-Me-Not, *Cryptantha pterocarya*

Forget-Me-Not, *Cryptantha circumcissa*

JOHN REID

FORGET-ME-NOT

Cryptantha species
Borage Family (Boraginaceae)

Genus Description: Forget-Me-Nots generally have tiny, white, 5-parted flowers that often occur in coiled, spikelike clusters. Like many members of the Borage Family, they have rough hairs, and the ovary is divided into 4 parts called nutlets, each with 1 seed, although some of these may abort during development. There are numerous species of annual Forget-Me-Nots in the Mojave

Desert, and even the best of botanists can be confused when trying to identify them. Although many of the species are outwardly similar, they can often be distinguished by observing the magnified nutlets. The following table includes the distinguishing features, ranges, and habitat preferences of many of the annual Mojave Desert *Cryptantha* species.

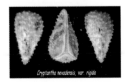

Cryptantha angustifolia

Cryptantha barbigera

Cryptantha circumcissa

Cryptantha maritima

Cryptantha nevadensis, var. rigida

Cryptantha pterocarya

Cryptantha recurvata

Cryptantha utahensis

Name & habitat	Vegetative features (calyx size in fruit)	Flower cluster & flowers	Fruits
C. angustifolia (widespread, <4,000 feet)	Lvs. narrow, linear, with bristly, pustulate, ashy-colored, flattened hairs	Long, dense, bractless spikes; fl. 1/16" wide; calyx 1/8" long	4 nutlets, 1 slightly larger; style longer than nutlets
C. barbigera (sandy to gravelly, <5,000 feet)	Lvs. narrowly lanceolate with dense, spreading, bristly hairs	Bractless spikes; fl. 1/16" wide; calyx 1/4–3/8" long	1–4 nutlets with strong vein pattern; style same length as nutlets
C. circumcissa (widespread, sandy to gravelly, <11,000 feet)	Plants cushionlike	Fl. 1/16" wide; calyx <1/4" long, connected below middle, detaching above connection	4 smooth, triangular nutlets with angled margins; style same length as nutlets
C. clokeyi (rare, only around Barstow)	Stem has stiff, flattened hairs; lvs. narrow with bristly hairs	Spikes dense above, sparser below; fl. 1/16" wide; calyx 1/4–3/8" long, narrow, bristly	4 shiny, whitish nutlets with translucent bumps; style longer than nutlets.
C. dumetorum (scattered, sandy to gravelly, <4,500 feet)	Stems very slender, sprawling or twining; narrow lvs. with short, stiff hairs with bulbous bases	Loose spikes; fl. <1/16" wide; calyx 1/8", with some hairs longer than sepal length	4 nutlets but smaller 3 abort; style shorter than nutlets
C. holoptera (eastern Mojave, gravelly to rocky, <2,000 feet)	Lvs. rough with short, straight, flattened hairs	Spikes with bracts; fl. 1/16" wide; calyx 1/8"long	4 dark, triangular nutlets with light bumps and winged margins; style longer than nutlets
C. maritima (widespread, sandy to gravelly, <4,000 feet)	Lvs. linear, rough, pustulate	Dense spikes with bracts; fl. < 1/16" wide; calyx 1/8" long, asymmetric, with tips coming together	1–2 nutlets, the larger smooth and shiny, the smaller dark and rough; style = length of smaller nutlet
C. micrantha (sandy, <7,500 feet)	Lower part of stem and rigid taproot with reddish to purplish dye	Dense spikes; fl. <1/16" wide; calyx 1/16" long	4 similar nutlets; style much longer than nutlets
C. muricata (widespread, gravelly, <5,000 feet)	Lvs. grayish, linear, with rough or bristly hairs, some with bulbous bases	Bractless spikes; fl. to 1/4" wide; calyx 1/8" long with tawny hairs & fused tips	4 glossy, veined nutlets with sharp edges; style longer than nutlets
C. nevadensis (widespread, sandy to gravelly, <6,000 feet)	Stem slender with short, stiff hairs; lvs. linear	Slender, congested spikes; fl. 1/16" wide; calyx to 1/2" long with hairy midribs and margins, tips bent back	4 narrowed nutlets with pointed tips
C. pterocarya (widespread, <6,000 feet)	Stems with short, stiff hairs; lvs. bristly	Bractless spikes; fl. <1/16" wide; calyx to 1/4" long	4 nutlets, 3 with lobed wings; style longer than nutlets
C. recurvata (uncommon in e. Mojave to ID, CO, NM, 2,500 to 6,500 feet)	Root with red dye.	Bractless spikes; fl. <1/16" wide; asymmetrical calyx 1/8" long, bent back, with thick, rough-hairy midvein	2 arched nutlets but smaller 1 aborts; style shorter than larger nutlet
C. utahensis (widespread, sandy to gravelly, <6,500 feet)	Stems with straight, flattened hairs; lvs. with short, stiff hairs; some of the lower lvs. pustular	Bractless spikes; fl. to 1/8" wide, fragrant; calyx to 1/8" long, often with short, stiff midvein hairs	1–2 nutlets with very sharp margins

Heliotrope

HELIOTROPE
Heliotropium curassavicum L.
Borage family (Boraginaceae)

Description: This fleshy, bluish, 4–24" tall perennial spreads from underground rootstocks to form matlike clumps. The inversely lanceolate, 1–3" long leaves are wedge shaped at the base. Numerous tiny, sessile flowers are produced in 2–4 coiled spikes at the ends of branches. Each white to purple, 5-parted, bell-shaped flower has a yellow center. The fruit consists of 4 smooth nutlets.

Flowering Season: March to October

Habitat/Range: Heliotrope is found in moist, sandy, alkaline springs and streams and moist roadside ditches below 7,000 feet in many plant communities throughout California to Utah and Arizona.

Comments: A related species, *Heliotropium convolvulaceum* var. *californicum,* occurs in the Mojave Desert east of Twentynine Palms. It is a non-fleshy annual with large, showy flowers that occur singly on short stalks in leaf axils.

Hairy-Leaved Comb-Bur

HAIRY-LEAVED COMB-BUR
Pectocarya penicillata
Borage Family (Boraginaceae)

Description: The numerous, slender, 1–10" long stems of this flat to erect annual have alternate, linear, bristly-haired leaves up to 1¼" long. The white, 5-parted flowers are very tiny and inconspicuous. As a flower ages and the fruit matures, the petals fall and the 4 nutlets enlarge to about ⅒" long. They spread to release the seeds while remaining attached at their bases to form a butterfly-shaped structure. Each nutlet has bristles at the enlarged end but is otherwise entire.

Flowering Season: March to May

Habitat/Range: Hairy-Leaved Comb-Bur is found on sandy and gravelly slopes, flats, and disturbed sites below 4,500 feet throughout many Western states to British Columbia, Canada, and Baja California, Mexico.

Comments: Several *Pectocarya* species that resemble Hairy-Leaved Comb-Bur can be distinguished by their nutlets. The linear nutlets of *P. recurvata* are toothed and strongly bent backward, while the lanceolate nutlets of *P. platycarpa* have very wide, toothed margins, and may be slightly bent backward. The toothed nutlet margins of *P. linearis* are wide at the apex and narrow near the base. *P. heterocarpa* has the upper nutlets in pairs, often with 2 that are somewhat entire with membranous margins and 2 with toothed margins.

Stiff-Stemmed Comb-Bur

STIFF-STEMMED COMB-BUR
Pectocarya setosa
Borage Family (Boraginaceae)

Description: This stiff, erect, 2–8" tall annual has alternate, linear, ¼–1" long leaves with pustulate hairs. The tiny, white, 5-parted flowers are short-lived and inconspicuous. The segments of the 4-parted fruits open and spread to release the seeds, leaving a butterfly-shaped structure with round, membranous margins with very thin hooked bristles.

Flowering Season: April to May

Habitat/Range: Stiff-Stemmed Comb-Bur grows in open areas from 500 to 7,500 feet in Creosote Bush Scrub, Joshua Tree woodland, and Pinyon-Juniper woodland in the Mojave Desert. It also occurs in the Colorado Deserts to Washington, Idaho, and Baja California, Mexico.

Comments: See descriptions of similar species under Hairy-Leaved Comb-Bur.

Parish's Popcorn Flower

PARISH'S POPCORN FLOWER
Plagiobothrys parishii Jtn.
Borage Family (Boraginaceae)

Description: The branched 2–12" stems of this prostrate annual are covered with short, spreading hairs. The bright green, narrow, linear leaves are ½–2" long and opposite on the lower stems. They have rough hairs with blistery bases on the undersurface. The white, ⅛–¼" wide flowers with yellow throats are produced abundantly along most of the stem length. The largest nutlet has a triangular scar, while the 3 smaller nutlets have a short linear scar.

Flowering Season: April to June

Habitat/Range: In the Mojave Desert, Parish's Popcorn Flower is confined to privately owned land at Rabbit Springs near Lucerne Valley. Other Mojave populations were known from Lovejoy Springs, Camp Cady, and Newberry Springs, but these have not been seen for many years and are believed to be extirpated. It is also reported in the Owens Valley, north of the Mojave.

Comments: Groundwater pumping has destroyed the habitat for Parish's Popcorn Flower in places where it has been extirpated. Potential future development in Lucerne Valley may adversely affect the groundwater levels, causing extinction of this population, yet it has not been listed as threatened or endangered.

SPECTACLE-POD
Dithyrea californica Harvey
Mustard Family (Brassicaceae)

Description: This 4–12" tall annual has stems that grow flat along the ground and curve upward at tips, although sometimes they may be erect. The leaves are somewhat thick, but not fleshy. The 1–6" long lower leaves are pinnately lobed, while the upper leaves are shorter and somewhat entire. The flowers are produced in dense clusters on upper stems. Each white, 4-parted flower is about ½" long, and the petals have 3 veins. The distinctive, flattened fruits have 2 round lobes, resembling eyeglasses.

Flowering Season: March to May

Habitat/Range: Spectacle-Pod is found in sandy soil and washes below 4,000 feet in Creosote Bush scrub in both the Mojave and Sonoran Deserts to Baja California, Mexico.

Comments: The genus name is Greek for "two shields", referring to the 2 lobes of the fruit.

STEPHEN INGRAM

Spectacle-Pod

Desert Alyssum, Bush Peppergrass

DESERT ALYSSUM, BUSH PEPPERGRASS
Lepidium fremontii S. Watson
Mustard Family (Brassicaceae)

Description: This 1–4' tall, grayish perennial has alternate, 1–4" long leaves that are either linear and entire or pinnately lobed with linear segments. Great masses of small, 4-parted flowers with white, clawed petals are produced in branched, leafy clusters, making this normally drab plant look white and suddenly conspicuous when in flower. The ¼" long, ovate, flattened fruits have a notch in the top.

Flowering Season: March to May

Habitat/Range: Desert Alyssum is common in sandy soil and rocky areas below 5,000 feet in Creosote Bush scrub and Joshua Tree woodland in both the Mojave and Sonoran Deserts.

Comments: Crushing the foliage will yield a smell similar to broccoli or cabbage, which are also in the Mustard Family. Native Americans ate the leaves and seeds.

Alkali Crucifer

ALKALI CRUCIFER
Thelypodium integrifolium (Nutt.) Endl.
Mustard Family (Brassicaceae)

Description: This stately, hairless, erect biennial generates a basal rosette of entire, elliptical, 3–12" leaves during the first growing season. During the second season the plant produces a 1½–6' tall stem, which branches into dense, stalked clusters of ¼–½" long, 4-parted, white to blue or pinkish flowers. Each flower is on a stalk above the receptacle, called a stipe. The narrow, ½–1" long fruits are somewhat cylindrical with swollen and constricted areas; these spread out horizontally from the stems.

Flowering Season: July to October

Habitat/Range: Alkali Crucifer occurs around alkali seeps and springs between 3,000 and 7,000 feet along the desert slopes of the San Bernardino Mountains, and in the western and northern Mojave Desert to Washington and Nevada.

Comments: The genus name is Greek for "female foot," referring to the flower stalks above the receptacle.

STEPHEN INGRAM

Fringe-Flowered Cactus

FRINGE-FLOWERED CACTUS

Escobaria vivipara (Nutt.) F. Buxb. var. *deserti*
(Engelm.) D. Hunt
Cactus Family (Cactaceae)

Description: The cylindrical stems of the Fringe-Flowered Cactus occur singly or sometimes in small clumps. Each stem has inconspicuous ribs and is 3–6" tall and up to 3½" wide. Each areole has fewer than 8 straight, white central spines with dark tips and 12–20 slender, straight, white radial spines that nearly conceal the stem surface. The straw-colored, yellow-green, or pinkish flowers are produced in a circular pattern at the tops of stems. The outer flower segments have fringed margins.

Flowering Season: April to May

Habitat/Range: This variety of Foxtail Cactus is found on limestone soil from 3,000 to 7,500 feet in the mountains of the eastern Mojave Desert.

Comments: The rare Foxtail Cactus *(Escobaria vivipara* var. *alversonii)* occurs on sandy to rocky granitic soil in the mountains of the eastern Mojave Desert. It has 8–10 central spines, 12–18 radial spines, and magenta to pink flowers. The Viviparous Foxtail Cactus *(E. vivipara* var. *rosea)* has more than 8 central spines, stems from 3–6" diameter, and magenta flowers. It is rare in the eastern Mojave Desert in California, but it is more widespread in Nevada and Arizona. It is threatened by horticultural collection.

JOHN REID

Frost Mat, Onyx Flower

FROST MAT, ONYX FLOWER

Achyronichia cooperi Torrey & A. Gray
Pink Family (Caryophyllaceae)

Description: Frost Mat is a flattened, branched, mat-forming annual with opposite, spatulate leaves up to ¾" long. The leaves in each pair are not equal, and they have ovate, fringed, white stipules. Clusters of 20–60 or more tiny white flowers are produced in leaf axils. Each flower has 5 sepals, no petals, and 2 style branches.

Flowering Season: January to May

Habitat/Range: Frost Mat is found in washes and on sandy flats and slopes below 3,000 feet in Creosote Bush scrub in both the Mojave and Sonoran Deserts to Baja California, Mexico.

Comments: Rixford Rockwort *(Scopulophila rixfordii)* is a very similar species that occurs on limestone in the northern Mojave Desert. It differs from Frost Mat in that it has 3 style branches, it is somewhat woody at the base, and it is erect. Some botanists believe that Rixford Rockwort and Frost Mat should be placed in the same genus.

JOHN REID

Brandegea

BRANDEGEA
Brandegea bigelovii (S. Wats.) Cogn.
Gourd Family (Cucurbitaceae)

Description: The stems of this hairless plant cling and climb over shrubs by means of unbranched tendrils. The alternate, rounded, palmately lobed leaves have white gland-dots on the upper surfaces. The tiny, cup-shaped flowers are white and very fragrant. Male flowers are produced in small clusters in leaf axils, with a single female flower on a slender stalk below at the same node. The dry, prickly fruit is around ¼" long.

Flowering Season: March to April, and sometimes following late summer rain

Habitat/Range: Brandegea is locally common in washes and canyons below 3,000 feet in Creosote Bush scrub. It occurs in the southern and southeastern Mojave Desert to Sonora and Baja California, Mexico.

Comments: There is some disagreement over the life history of this plant. The presence of a white, fleshy, 1" diameter taproot suggests that it is perennial, but a recent account claims that it is an annual that responds to spring rain. This genus was named in honor of Townsend Brandegee (1843–1925) and Mary Katherine Brandegee (1844–1920). Townsend came to California after studying botany under Professor William Brewer at Yale. He married Mary Katherine Layne Curran, who was the curator of botany for the California Academy of Sciences. Their honeymoon was spent hiking and botanizing from San Diego to San Francisco.

Dodder on Smoke Tree

DODDER
Cuscuta denticulata Engelm.
Dodder Family (Cuscutaceae)

Description: This slender, parasitic, annual vine twines around the stems of its host, sending tiny rootlets (haustoria) into host tissues to absorb water and nutrients. Its own root system is short-lived. The hairless stems are a yellowish to orange color with minute, scale-like leaves. Small, spikelike clusters of tiny, 5-parted, bell-shaped flowers are produced in leaf axils. The rounded, minutely toothed calyx lobes overlap and enclose the corolla tube. The lobes of the corolla are bent backwards, and the corolla tube length is less than its width. Both the calyx and corolla have fine teeth on the margins, and both have an artistic vein pattern that can be seen with a 10X hand lens. The fruit is a cone-shaped capsule.

Flowering Season: May to October

Habitat/Range: Dodder is parasitic on numerous shrub species, such as Creosote Bush *(Larrea tridentata)* and Cheesebush *(Hymenoclea salsola).* It occurs below 4,000 feet in Creosote Bush scrub and Joshua Tree woodland in the Mojave Desert and in the Sonoran Desert to Baja California, Mexico.

Comments: *Cuscuta indecora* differs from *C. denticulata* in that the corolla is erect with incurved tips, and the fruit is rounded at the top. The calyx lobes are not overlapping, and they are only about half of the length of the corolla tube. Although it is not as common in the Mojave Desert, *C. indecora* is widespread, occurring across the United States to Mexico, the Caribbean, and South America.

Rattlesnake Weed, White-Margin Sandmat

RATTLESNAKE WEED, WHITE-MARGIN SANDMAT

Chamaesyce albomarginata (Torrey & A. Gray)
Small
Spurge Family (Euphorbiaceae)

Description: Rattlesnake Weed is a hairless perennial with prostrate stems and milky sap. The round to oblong, opposite, ¼" long leaves have tiny, triangular, fringed stipules that are fused, forming a line across the stem at the nodes. Each flower cluster looks like a single flower but is in fact 1 female flower and 15–30 male flowers surrounded by 5 fused bracts. Each bract has a narrow, oblong gland with a conspicuous white appendage.

Flowering Season: April to November

Habitat/Range: This species occurs on dry slopes, flats, and roadsides below 7,500 feet in Creosote Bush scrub, Joshua Tree woodland, and Pinyon-Juniper woodland in the Mojave Desert and in the Sonoran Desert, and other habitats throughout the American Southwest.

Comments: Native Americans applied the milky juice of Rattlesnake Weed to rattlesnake bites, hence its common name. *Chamaesyce micromera* is an annual with triangular ciliate stipules fused below but not above; 2–5 male flowers; round, reddish, ¼" glands; no gland appendages; and very tiny bracts.

Yuma Spurge, Bristle-Lobed Sandmat

YUMA SPURGE, BRISTLE-LOBED SANDMAT
Chamaesyce setiloba (Torrey & A. Gray) Small
Spurge Family (Euphorbiaceae)

Description: Yuma Spurge is an annual with hairy, prostrate stems and opposite, ¹⁄₁₀–¼" leaves with separate, threadlike stipules. Each flower cluster has 3–7 male flowers and 1 female flower with 3 style branches. The bracts have oblong glands with white, 3–5-lobed gland appendages.

Flowering Season: January to December

Habitat/Range: Yuma Spurge is found in sandy soil below 4,500 feet in the Mojave and Sonoran Deserts to Texas and Mexico.

Comments: See descriptions of similar species under Rattlesnake Weed.

LANE MOUNTAIN MILKVETCH
Astragalus jaegerianus Per.
Pea Family (Fabaceae)

Description: This straggly milkvetch is often difficult to see, since it blends in with the shrubs through which it clambers. Its thin, 1–2½' long stems bear pinnately divided, 1–2" long leaves with 9–15 linear to oblong leaflets. Sparse clusters of 9–15 flowers are produced in leaf axils. Each "pea" flower is lavender when very young but soon turns to a cream color with purplish veins. The fruits are pendulous, speckled, 2-chambered pods with a fleshy to leathery texture.

Flowering Season: April to June

Habitat/Range: Lane Mountain Milkvetch grows on sandy, gravelly, and granitic soils from 3,000 to 4,000 feet in Creosote Bush scrub and Joshua Tree woodland. It is widely scattered within its limited range in the central Mojave Desert, including Coolgardie Mesa, Superior Valley, Montana Mine, and areas around Fort Irwin.

Comments: This species is listed as federally endangered due to threats from mining, grazing, and vehicles. Recent intensive surveys

STEPHEN INGRAM

Lane Mountain Milkvetch

have shown that the southward expansion of Fort Irwin will substantially reduce its already limited distribution.

Wild Licorice

WILD LICORICE
Glycyrrhiza lepidota Pursh
Pea Family (Fabaceae)

Description: This erect, perennial herb grows up to 40" tall, often forming dense patches. The pinnately divided, gland-dotted leaves have 9–19 lanceolate leaflets, and the foliage has a sticky coating. Cream-colored, ½" long, "pea" flowers occur in dense spikes in leaf axils, followed by dry, ½" fruits with hooked prickles.

Flowering Season: May to July

Habitat/Range: Wild Licorice has a scattered distribution in moist sites below 4,500 feet along drainage courses in the Mojave Desert and desert slopes of the San Bernardino Mountains and throughout the western United States to Canada and Mexico. It is especially common along the Mojave River.

Comments: *Glycyrrhiza glabra* is a cultivated relative of Wild Licorice. Its rootstocks are the source of licorice for sweets, plug tobacco, cough syrups, and other medications, and it is used in brewing stout beer.

Honey Mesquite

STEPHEN INGRAM

HONEY MESQUITE
Prosopis glandulosa Torrey var. *torreyana* (L. Benson) M. Johnston
Pea Family (Fabaceae)

Description: This deciduous shrub or small tree with arched branches can grow to over 20' tall. It has alternate, bright green, pinnately divided leaves with 1 or 2 pairs of opposite primary leaflets, each with 18–36 linear secondary leaflets that are up to 1" long. There are two ¼–1½" spines at each node. The small, cream-colored flowers are produced in dense, slender, 2–4" long spikes, followed by 3–8" long pods that are somewhat constricted between the seeds.

Flowering Season: April to June

Habitat/Range: Honey Mesquite is common in washes, alkali seeps, dunes, and flats below 5,000 feet in the Mojave and Sonoran Deserts to the upper San Joaquin Valley, Texas, Louisiana, and Mexico.

Comments: The taproot of Honey Mesquite can reach depths of 100'. Native Americans throughout the southwestern United States relied on Honey Mesquite pods as a food source and for shade and firewood. Fresh green pods were roasted over hot stones or eaten raw as snacks. Hardened mounds of mashed pods were stored, and caches of whole, dried pods have been found in caves. The traditional methods of using pods yielded high nutritional and caloric value for the amount of time spent processing. However, most modern humans do not find the taste enjoyable.

Screw Bean, Tornillo

SCREW BEAN, TORNILLO

Prosopis pubescens Benth.
Pea Family (Fabaceae)

Description: Screw Bean is a shrub or small tree that grows up to 30' tall. The alternate, pinnately divided leaves have 2 or 4 opposite primary leaflets, each with 10–16 oblong, hairy secondary leaflets that are up to ½" long. The paired, spiny stipules are whitish and stout. The small flowers occur in 1½–3" long, spikelike clusters in leaf axils, followed by coiled, ¾–1½" long fruits.

Flowering Season: May to July

Habitat/Range: Screw Bean occurs in canyons and washes below 4,000 feet in Creosote Bush scrub in the Mojave and Sonoran Deserts and throughout the southwestern United States and northern Mexico.

Comments: Since Screw Bean is restricted to sites with surface water, it is not as common as its close relative, Honey Mesquite *(Prosopis glandulosa)*. Screw Bean pods were highly prized and used for barter by Mojave Desert tribes. The pods were fermented in pits lined with Arrow-Weed *(Pluchea sericea)*, after which they were stored or ground into meal. The flavor is rather sweet, but teeth can be broken on the stonelike seeds!

YERBA SANTA
Eriodictyon trichocalyx A. A. Heller var. *trichocalyx*
Waterleaf Family (Hydrophyllaceae)

Yerba Santa

Description: This erect, evergreen, 1–6' tall shrub has spreading, gummy branches. The alternate, lanceolate, 2–5" long leaves are dark green and sticky on the upper surface, and grayish green with fine hairs and a netted vein pattern on the lower surface. They have entire to toothed, somewhat inrolled margins, and they are on ¼– ½" long stalks. Open, curved clusters of white, ¼–½" long, funnel-shaped, 5-parted flowers with 2 styles are produced on the ends of branches. The fruit is a tiny capsule with 4–8 dark brown seeds.

Flowering Season: May to August

Habitat/Range: Yerba Santa occurs on dry, rocky hillsides below 8,000 feet in Joshua Tree woodland and Pinyon-Juniper woodland along desert slopes of the San Gabriel and San Bernardino Mountains and in other habitats in southern California to Baja California, Mexico.

Comments: *Yerba Santa* means "holy herb" in Spanish. This plant is high in flavonoids, and a tea made from the leaves is a very effective decongestant and allergy reliever. *Eriodictyon angustifolium* is a very similar species with narrower, linear leaves. It is found in the eastern Mojave Desert.

Ives Phacelia

IVES PHACELIA
Phacelia ivesiana Torrey
Waterleaf Family (Hydrophyllaceae)

Description: This 2–10" tall, glandular-hairy annual has stems that tend to branch at the base and spread to form a widened crown. The ½–1½" long lower leaves are pinnately divided to the midrib into entire or toothed oblong segments; the upper leaves are smaller. The 1–1½" long, narrow, funnel-shaped flowers are white with a yellowish tube.

Flowering Season: March to June

Habitat/Range: Ives Phacelia is found in dry sandy soil and dunes below 3,000 feet in Creosote Bush scrub from the eastern Mojave Desert near Kelso to Colorado, Wyoming, and Arizona.

Comments: Ives Phacelia was at one time considered for listing by the California Native Plant Society but was determined to be too common. This species was named for Joseph Christmas Ives (1828–1868), the first white explorer of the Grand Canyon.

Round-Leaf Phacelia

ROUND-LEAF PHACELIA
Phacelia rotundifolia A. Gray
Waterleaf Family (Hydrophyllaceae)

Description: This low, glandular annual is covered with short, stiff hairs. The ½–1½" long, round, toothed leaves are on stalks longer than the blades. Narrow, bell-shaped, ¼" long flowers can vary in color from purplish to white or pink, and they have pale yellow tubes. The capsules are less than ¼" long with 50–100 tiny, pitted seeds.

Flowering Season: April to June

Habitat/Range: Round-Leaf Phacelia is most often found wedged in crevices and on rocky cliff faces below 6,000 feet in Creosote Bush scrub, Joshua Tree woodlands, and Pinyon-Juniper woodland. Its range includes both the Mojave and Sonoran Deserts.

Comments: See comment under Fremont Phacelia.

DESERT LILY
Hesperocallis undulata A. Gray
Lily Family (Liliaceae)

Description: This 1–6' tall perennial arises from a deep, underground bulb. Narrow bluish green leaves up to 20" long form a basal rosette, while smaller leaves may be found up the stem. It's easy to distinguish this plant by the obvious wavy leaf margins; there is no other desert plant with leaves like this. Elongated, showy flower clusters occur at the ends of unbranched stems. Each funnel-shaped flower has long, golden anthers and 6 white, waxy, 1½" segments, each with a silvery green strand on the back. The fruit is a ½–¾" long capsule with 3 compartments.

Flowering Season: March to May

Habitat/Range: Desert Lilies are found on sandy flats and dunes below 2,500 feet in Creosote Bush Scrub in the eastern and central Mojave Desert to the Colorado Desert.

Comments: The genus name, *Hesperocallis*, literally means "western beauty" in Greek.

Desert Lily

Parry's Nolina, Parry's Beargrass

PARRY'S NOLINA, PARRY'S BEARGRASS
Nolina parryi S. Watson
Lily Family (Liliaceae)

Description: Parry's Nolina is somewhat shrublike, with 65–200 long, concave, grayish green, sawtooth-margined leaves in dense rosettes atop a 12–16" thick, 3–6' tall trunk. Masses of ¼", cream-colored, 6-parted flowers are produced in very large, dense, branched clusters on 3–5' tall stalks, followed by ½" long and ½" wide capsules with 3 compartments.

Flowering Season: April to June

Habitat/Range: Parry's Nolina occurs from 3,500 and 6,000 feet in Joshua Tree woodland and Pinyon-Juniper woodland on desert slopes of the eastern San Bernardino Mountains and also in the Kingston, Eagle, and Little San Bernardino Mountain Ranges in the Mojave Desert. It is also found in the Sonoran Desert.

Comments: The genus *Nolina* was named for P. C. Nolin, a French agricultural writer in the mid-1700s. This species was named for Dr. Charles C. Parry, who served as a surgeon and naturalist for the Pacific Railway Survey, Mexican Boundary Survey, and Northwest Geologic Expedition. Many of the specimens he collected were sent to Torrey and Gray, and many were named for Parry. Bigelow's Nolina *(Nolina bigelovii)*, a trunkless species with flat, rigid leaves and brown fibers peeling from the margins, is found in dry canyons below 3,000 feet in the Sheephole and Eagle Mountains in the Mojave Desert.

Banana Yucca, Fleshy-Fruited Yucca, Spanish Bayonet

BANANA YUCCA, FLESHY-FRUITED YUCCA, SPANISH BAYONET
Yucca baccata Torrey
Lily Family (Liliaceae)

Description: This trunkless plant has rosettes of stiff, concave, 1–3' leaves with spiny tips and coarse fibers clinging to the margins. The light bluish green color is obvious from a distance, distinguishing this from the yellowish green Mojave Yucca. Clusters of flowers are nestled down in the leaves on short, leafless stalks. Each fleshy, waxy flower has 6, 2–4" segments that are cream-colored inside and reddish brown outside. The fruit is a fleshy, 6" long capsule.

Flowering Season: April to June

Habitat/Range: Banana Yucca is found on dry hillsides from 2,000 to 5,000 feet in Joshua Tree woodland and Pinyon-Juniper woodland in the eastern Mojave Desert to Texas.

Comments: Yuccas were a very important source of food and fibers for native people of the Mojave Desert. The fruits of Banana Yucca were made into flour or prepared and eaten like dried apples. Fibers from the leaves of all *Yucca* species were woven into baskets and sandals. The mashed roots have soaplike compounds (saponins) and were used for bathing and ritual shampooing before weddings.

Joshua Tree

STEPHEN INGRAM

JOSHUA TREE
Yucca brevifolia Engelm.
Lily Family (Liliaceae)

Description: This monocot has a trunk of fibrous tissue that can grow to over 30' tall. The trunk grows straight until insects or its own flowers destroy the growing tip; at this point, branching occurs, usually when the plant is between 3–9' tall. Older trees are usually branched sufficiently to form a rounded crown. The narrow, rigid, 8–14" long leaves are spine-tipped with tiny teeth on the margins, and they are coated with a thick waxy layer to retard water loss. Older leaves are bent downward, preventing some animals from climbing the trunk. Dense, 12–20" long clusters of cream-colored, 6-parted, 1½–3" long flowers are produced at branch tips, followed by oblong, 3-chambered, 2–4" long capsules.

Flowering Season: March to May

Habitat/Range: Joshua Tree occurs at elevations between 2,000 and 6,000 feet throughout the Mojave Desert. It is the dominant species of Joshua Tree woodland vegetation.

Comments: Joshua Tree leaves, which lack the fibrous margins of many *Yuccas*, resemble short versions of those of Our Lord's Candle *(Yucca whipplei)*, to which the Joshua Tree is most closely related. Many botanists recognize *Yucca brevifolia* var. *jaegeriana*, which occurs in the eastern Mojave Desert and has 4" long leaves and narrower trunks that branch lower to the ground. Var. *herbertii* in the western Mojave Desert has underground rhizomes, which form clones of short trunks in clusters up to 30' in diameter.

Mojave Yucca

TIM THOMAS

MOJAVE YUCCA
Yucca shidigera K. E. Ortgies
Lily Family (Liliaceae)

Description: Mojave Yucca has rosettes of stiff, 1–5' long, spine-tipped leaves on short 3–15' trunks. The leaves are unmistakable with their yellowish green color, shredding marginal fibers, and white bases. The waxy, cream-colored flowers with 6 incurved segments are produced in heavy, branched, 2–4' clusters on leafless stalks. The fruit is a fibrous 2–3" capsule.

Flowering Season: April to May

Habitat/Range: Mojave Yucca occurs on dry, rocky slopes and flats below 5,000 feet in Creosote Bush scrub, Joshua Tree woodland, and Blackbush scrub in the southern and eastern Mojave Desert. It also occurs in the northern Sonoran Desert and coastal areas of southern California to Baja, California, Mexico.

Comments: Since the fruits are small, Mojave Yucca was not as important a food source for Native Americans as were other *Yucca* species. The flowers have a pleasant flavor if the soapy-tasting, green ovary is removed. This species was an important source of fibers for sandals and other textiles, and torches were made from the dried leaves. Several varieties of Martin's Giant Skipper butterfly *(Megathymus coloradensis)* lay eggs on sucker shoots of various *Yucca* species. The larvae bore into the tissues, sometimes breaking the underground rhizome and separating the cloned *yucca* from its parent plant.

JOHN REID

Our Lord's Candle

OUR LORD'S CANDLE

Yucca whipplei Torrey ssp. *caespitosa* (Jones)
Haines
Lily Family (Liliaceae)

Description: This plant produces numerous basal rosettes of spreading, daggerlike, 3-edged leaves with saw-toothed margins. Each rosette sends up a 3–6' flower stalk; these stalks and the individual rosette from which they grew dry up and die after flowering. The flower stalk produces branched clusters of waxy, cream-colored, 6-parted flowers that are each approximately 1¼" long and somewhat spherical. The dry, 3-chambered fruit is similar to that of the Joshua Tree, to which Our Lord's Candle is most closely related.

Flowering Season: April to May

Habitat/Range: This subspecies occurs from 2,000 to 4,000 feet in Joshua Tree woodland and Pinyon-Juniper woodland along the desert slopes of the San Bernardino and San Gabriel Mountains, and along the western edge of the Mojave Desert. Other subspecies of Our Lord's Candle are found in chaparral and coastal sage scrub of southern California to Baja California, Mexico.

Comments: All of the *Yucca* species are pollinated by Yucca moths in the genus *Tegiticula* (also called *Pronuba*). The female moth gathers pollen and rolls it into a ball. She makes a hole in the pistil of a *Yucca* flower, deposits her eggs, and tamps the pollen ball into the hole, effectively pollinating the flower. Her larvae consume some of the *Yucca* seeds as the fruit develops, but some seeds escape predation, enabling the plant to sexually reproduce. This is a necessary tradeoff for the plant, as none of the seeds would have developed without the moth's activities. The similar Bogus Yucca moth, in the genus *Prodoxus*, eats *Yucca* flowers but not seeds, and it is not able to pollinate the plant. The shiny, bluish black California Solitary bee *(Xylocopa californica)* often nests in dead *Yucca whipplei* stalks in the winter.

Death Camas, Desert Zygadene

JOHN REID

DEATH CAMAS, DESERT ZYGADENE

Zigadenus brevibracteatus (M. E. Jones) H. M. Hall

Lily Family (Liliaceae)

Description: This perennial has an underground bulb from which numerous rosette leaves and nearly leafless, 12–20" tall flowering stems arise. The narrow, 4–10" long leaves have rough margins and are folded lengthwise. The cream-colored, ¼" long flowers with 6 equal segments are produced in an open, branched, 4–14" flower cluster. The fruit is an oblong, ½–¾" long capsule with numerous seeds.

Flowering Season: April to May

Habitat/Range: Death Camas is found in sandy areas from 2,000 to 5,000 feet in Creosote Bush scrub and Joshua Tree woodland in the western and southern Mojave Desert and in the Colorado Desert to San Luis Obispo County.

Comments: Many, if not all, species of *Zigadenus* have highly toxic alkaloid compounds that affect humans and livestock.

Rock Nettle, Sting-Bush

ROCK NETTLE, STING-BUSH

Eucnide urens (A. Gray) C. Parry
Loasa Family (Loasaceae)

Description: Numerous, clumped, 1–3' tall stems grow from the woody base of this perennial. The alternate, oval, toothed, 1–2" long leaves have long, sharp, stinging hairs that can deliver a painful blister. The cream-colored, 5-parted, 1–2" long flowers are produced on bracted stalks in leaf axils. They have numerous stamens, 5 stigma lobes, and an inferior ovary with tiny seeds.

Flowering Season: April to June

Habitat/Range: Rock Nettle is found in rocky areas and washes below 4,000 feet in Creosote Bush scrub. It ranges from Red Rock Canyon State Park to Utah, Arizona, and Baja California, Mexico. It is very common in the Death Valley region.

Comments: The rash caused by this plant is not an allergic reaction but due to irritation by toxins released from the sharp, tubular leaf hairs when they are bumped. Surgeon and botanist Dr. John M. Bigelow collected the type specimen of Rock Nettle on his survey of the Colorado River in the mid-1800s.

Canyon Petalonyx, Smooth Sandpaper Plant

CANYON PETALONYX, SMOOTH SANDPAPER PLANT

Petalonyx nitidus Wats.
Loasa Family (Loasaceae)

Description: This 1–2' tall shrub has dark green, ½–1¾" long leaves that are on leaf stalks up to ¼" long. They are shiny and ovate with irregularly toothed margins, and they are more or less the same size throughout the plant body. The ¼–½" long, cream-colored flowers with protruding stamens are produced in dense 1½–2" long clusters on the ends of branches, followed by tiny 5-ribbed fruits.

Flowering Season: May to July

Habitat/Range: This species is found on rocky slopes and in canyons and washes from 3,000 to 6,500 feet in Creosote Bush scrub, Joshua Tree woodland, and Pinyon-Juniper woodland on the desert slopes of the San Bernardino Mountains and in the mountains of the eastern and northern Mojave Desert, especially in the Kingston Range and in Death Valley.

Comments: The type specimen of Canyon Petalonyx was collected in southern Nevada by George M. Wheeler, who conducted expeditions for the United States Corps of Engineers in the mid- to late 1800s.

DEATH VALLEY SANDPAPER PLANT

Petalonyx thurberi ssp. *gilmanii* (Munz) Davis & Thompson
Loasa Family (Loasaceae)

Description: This branched, 1–3½' tall shrub has soft, spreading hairs, giving the younger leaves and stems a feltlike texture. The sessile, triangular to heart-shaped leaves are larger near the base of the plant and reduced upwards. The 5-parted, white to cream-colored flowers, which are less than ¼" long, occur in narrow, dense, ½–1¾" clusters at the ends of branches. Oddly, the stamens appear to be placed outside of the petals, which are fused along the upper part of their narrow, clawed bases.

Flowering Season: May to June and September to November

Habitat/Range: Death Valley Sandpaper Plant occurs on sand dunes and in washes below 3,500 feet in Creosote Bush scrub. It is known from only 20 occurrences in Death Valley National Park and is listed in the Cali-

Death Valley Sandpaper Plant

fornia Native Plant Society's *Inventory of Rare and Endangered Plants of California.*

Comments: The more widespread Sandpaper Plant *(Petalonyx thurberi* A. Gray ssp. *thurberi)* is similar but with short, stiff, down-turned hairs, which give it a sandpapery texture and bleached grayish green appearance. Sandpaper Plant is fairly common in open, sandy or gravelly places below 4,000 feet in Creosote Bush scrub in both the Mojave and Colorado Deserts to northern Mexico.

CARPET-WEED

Mollugo cerviana (L.) Ser.
Carpet-Weed Family (Molluginaceae)

Description: This tiny, slender-stemmed, 1–6" tall summer annual is often overlooked. It has 5–10 linear leaves in a whorl at each node. The minute, inconspicuous flowers are produced in whorls on threadlike stalks in leaf axils. Each flower has 5 sepals, which are white on the inside, and 3 stigmas. The fruit is a tiny, round capsule with brown, net-veined seeds.

Flowering Season: September to October in the Mojave Desert, following summer rainfall

Habitat/Range: Carpet-Weed is uncommon in sandy areas below 5,000 feet in Creosote Bush scrub and Joshua Tree woodland in the Mojave Desert and in scattered locations in the Western states and Mexico.

Comments: There is some speculation that Carpet-Weed is an introduction from the Old

Carpet-Weed

World. However, it lacks traits common to most introduced species. It doesn't have a weedy habit, it almost always grows in undisturbed places, and it is responsive to summer, and not winter, rainfall.

SMALL-FLOWERED ABRONIA
Tripterocalyx micranthus (Torrey) Hook.
Four O'Clock Family (Nyctaginaceae)

Small-Flowered Abronia

Description: A thick, heavy taproot anchors this glandular-sticky perennial to loose sand. The opposite, entire, narrowly ovate leaves have blades about ½–2" long, and some of the leaf stalks are longer than the blades. The white, tubular, ¼–¾" long flowers with abruptly spreading triangular lobes are produced in heads with 5–10 leafy green bracts below. The fruit has 3 membranous, net-veined wings.

Flowering Season: April to May

Habitat/Range: Small-Flowered Abronia is found on sand dunes from 2,500 to 7,500 feet in the southeastern Mojave Desert, as at Kelso Dunes, to Montana, South Dakota, and New Mexico.

Comments: This genus was segregated from the genus *Abronia* (the Sand Verbenas), in part because it has membranous, not thick, fruit wings, and the receptacle has thick, peglike flower stalks, which are lacking in *Abronia*.

SPINY MENODORA
Menodora spinescens A. Gray
Olive Family (Oleaceae)

Spiny Menodora

Description: The angled branches of this rounded, 1–3' tall shrub become very spiny with age. The linear, entire, somewhat fleshy, ¼–½" long leaves are mostly alternate and sometimes clustered at the node. The white, ½" flowers are produced singly or in clusters on short stalks in leaf axils, and the ¼" long capsules have round, pitted, dark brown seeds.

Flowering Season: April to May

Habitat/Range: Spiny Menodora occurs on dry slopes and flats between 3,000 to 6,500 feet in Shadscale scrub, Blackbush scrub, and Joshua Tree woodland in the eastern Mojave Desert, the north slope of the San Bernardino Mountains, and the southern Sierra Nevada Range. It is also found in Joshua Tree National Park.

Comments: The genus name was derived from Greek words meaning "force" and "spear," probably in reference to the strong, spiny branches.

JOHN REID

Booth's Primrose

BOOTH'S PRIMROSE
Camissonia boothii (Douglas) Raven ssp. *desertorum* (Munz) Raven
Evening Primrose Family (Onagraceae)

Description: This erect, 4–14" tall annual with shiny and peeling stems bears lanceolate, ½–1½" long, red-tinged leaves, which decrease in size up the stem. A rosette of leaves is usually present early in the season. Clusters of white, 4-parted flowers are produced on pendant stem tips. The sessile, nonwoody fruits curve downward. They are enlarged at the base and taper toward the tip, with 1 row of seeds in each of the 4 chambers.

Flowering Season: March to June

Habitat/Range: This subspecies of Booth's Primrose is found in loose soil and open areas from 1,300 to 6,000 feet in Creosote Bush scrub and Joshua Tree woodland in the Mojave Desert. Several other subspecies occur throughout the western United States to Mexico.

Comments: *Camissonia boothii* ssp. *condensata* is generally 2–8" tall with woody fruits that bend outward. It is found in the Mojave and Sonoran Deserts to northwestern Mexico.

Brown-Eyed Primrose

BROWN-EYED PRIMROSE
Camissonia claviformis (Torrey & Fremont)
Raven ssp. *claviformis*
Evening Primrose Family (Onagraceae)

Description: This annual has a well-developed rosette of purple spotted, pinnate leaves with large lateral leaflets. Flower clusters are produced at the tips of drooping, 4–24" stalks. The 4-parted flowers have white or yellowish petals with dark spots near the inner base, giving the plant its common name. The straight, stalked fruit is over ⅛" wide and has 2 rows of unwinged seeds per chamber.

Flowering Season: March and May

Habitat/Range: This subspecies of Brown-Eyed Primrose is common in sandy soils and washes below 4,000 feet in Creosote Bush scrub and Joshua Tree woodland in the Mojave Desert. Numerous other subspecies are found in many other habitats throughout the western United States. Brown-Eyed Primrose is probably one of the most common and widespread spring wildflowers of both the Mojave and Sonoran Deserts.

Comments: The large, striped larvae of the White-Lined Sphinx moth *(Hyles lineata)* devours all parts of this plant and other plants in this family. There are colossal population outbreaks, where swarms of these hungry creatures migrate through the desert, consuming vast quantities of plant material and stripping foliage bare.

STEPHEN INGRAM

Eureka Dunes Evening Primrose

EUREKA DUNES EVENING PRIMROSE
Oenothera californica (S. Watson) S. Watson ssp. *eurekensis* (Munz & Roos) Klein
Evening Primrose Family (Onagraceae)

Description: This 6–24" tall, grayish green perennial has both flattened, dense, white hairs and wavy, spreading hairs. It has a deep, fleshy rootstock for anchorage, and the old fruiting stem tips are able to sprout after being buried by sand. The crowded, ½–1½" long, triangular to ovate leaves may have toothed or entire margins. The 4-parted white flowers have separate petals up to 1" long, which often fade pink as the flower ages. The inferior ovary develops into a very narrow, 1–2" long capsule with numerous seeds.

Flowering Season: April to June

Habitat/Range: This plant is found only on sands dunes in Eureka Valley in Death Valley National Park.

Comments: This subspecies is listed as state rare and federally endangered. It has been impacted by dune recreation but is now recovering. *Oenothera californica* ssp. *avita* and ssp. *california* are more widespread.

Prickly Poppy

PRICKLY POPPY
Argemone corymbosa E. Greene
Poppy Family (Papaveraceae)

Description: This bristly, erect, 16–32" tall annual has orange, milky juice. The alternate, 3–6" long, pinnately toothed or lobed leaves have stiff hairs on the veins and margins, especially on the lower surface. White flowers with 4 or 6 separate petals and 100–120 yellow stamens are produced singly on the ends of stems, followed by 1–1¼" long, ovate capsules with numerous, tiny, dark brown seeds.

Flowering Season: April to May

Habitat/Range: Prickly Poppy is very common along roadsides and in dry, sandy areas and valley bottoms below 3,500 feet in Cre-osote Bush scrub throughout the Mojave Desert.

Comments: Roasted Prickly Poppy seeds were eaten by the Kawaiisu to induce vomiting and as a laxative, and they used mashed seeds as a treatment for wounds and head lice. Chicalote *(Argemone munita)* has yellow sap, 150–250 stamens, and stiff hairs along veins on both the upper and lower leaf surfaces. It is scattered in mountains and on rocky slopes and ridges above 4,000 feet in the Mojave Desert but is more widespread elsewhere.

Pygmy Poppy

PYGMY POPPY
Canbya candida C. Parry
Poppy Family (Papaveraceae)

Description: This 1" tall, tufted, hairless annual has linear to oblong, fleshy basal leaves with entire margins. Very short, leafless stems each bear a single flower with 6 separate, white, ovate petals and 6–9 stamens. The 3 sepals fall off before the flower opens. The fruit is a tiny, ovate capsule with minute, shiny brown seeds.

Flowering Season: April to May

Habitat/Range: Pygmy Poppy occurs on sandy soil from 2,000 to 4,000 feet in Creosote Bush scrub, Saltbush scrub, Joshua Tree woodland, and Pinyon-Juniper woodland. It seems to prefer sandy washes as they empty out from the mountains onto the desert floor. It has a limited distribution in the western Mojave Desert from Hesperia and Victorville, east to the Lancaster area, and north to Kramer, Calico, and Walker Pass.

Comments: Development and the invasion of non-native species are threats to this rare species. However, it is not in immediate danger of extinction and is not currently listed as threatened or endangered.

Desert Plantain

TIM THOMAS

DESERT PLANTAIN
Plantago ovata Forsskal
Plantain Family (Plantaginaceae)

Description: Desert Plantain is an erect, 2–10" tall annual that is covered with silky, flattened hairs. The narrow, linear, 1–7" long leaves occur in a clump at the base of the plant. Numerous, papery, 4-parted flowers and bracts are produced in dense, woolly, cylindrical, ½–1½" long spikes at the tops of the leafless stems. The small, ovate capsules open by lids to release shiny yellowish red seeds.

Flowering Season: March to April in the Mojave Desert

Habitat/Range: Desert Plantain is found on gravelly or sandy flats and slopes below 4,000 feet in Creosote Bush scrub and Joshua Tree woodland in the Mojave Desert and throughout the Western states to Baja California, Mexico.

Comments: There is speculation that Desert Plantain is an introduced weed from the Mediterranean region. If so, the introduction likely occurred very long ago. This species is very widespread and does not behave like a weed. Furthermore, it is very closely related to another widespread species, *Plantago erecta*, possibly indicating that there has been ample time since the suspected introduction for these to evolve into separate species.

Evening Snow

EVENING SNOW
Linanthus dichotomus Benth.
Phlox Family (Polemoniaceae)

Description: The shiny, brownish, wiry stems of this hairless, 2–8" tall annual have a forked branching pattern and bear 1–2 pairs of opposite leaves with 3–7 linear, palmate lobes. The white, funnel-shaped, 1¼" long flowers are open in the evening and early morning. The hairless sepals have spreading, green tips, and the back of each petal has a light brown to purple area along 1 edge.

Flowering Season: April to June

Habitat/Range: Evening Snow is found in the Mojave Desert in sandy or gravelly sites below 5,000 feet, growing between shrubs in Creosote Bush scrub and Joshua Tree woodland. It is more widespread in other areas of California and throughout the western United States.

Comments: *Linanthus bigelovei* is a similar species with smaller flowers and longer, wider, entire leaves.

Parry's Linanthus, Sandblossoms

PARRY'S LINANTHUS, SANDBLOSSOMS

Linanthus parryae (A. Gray) E. Greene
Phlox Family (Polemoniaceae)

Description: This 1–4" tall, nearly stemless annual has crowded, tufted, glandular-hairy leaves with 3–7 linear, palmate lobes. Congested clumps of sessile, 5-parted, funnel-shaped flowers often obscure the leaves. The ½" long flowers can be either white or blue (see another photo in blue flower section) and they have maroon, kidney-shaped arches on the throat below each petal lobe. The fruit is a 3-chambered capsule, and the seeds have a white outer membrane.

Flowering Season: March to May

Habitat/Range: Parry's Linanthus occurs over large sandy expanses below 3,500 feet in Creosote Bush scrub and Joshua Tree woodland in the western Mojave Desert.

Comments: A single gene determines flower color in this species. Some populations are predominantly blue or white, but most have varying amounts of both colors. Recent research shows that a natural selection process is likely involved in maintaining both colors. In dry years, the blue flowers seem to have an advantage, producing more seeds than white-flowered plants, but in wet years the reverse is true. The mechanism of this selection process is not yet known.

STEPHEN INGRAM

Schott Gilia, Little Sunbonnets

SCHOTT GILIA, LITTLE SUNBONNETS

Loeseliastrum schottii (Torrey) S. Timbrook
Phlox Family (Polemoniaceae)

Description: This tufted, 1–4" tall annual has ½–1½" long, linear leaves with comb-toothed margins and bristle-tipped teeth. The white to yellow, pink, or pale lavender, ¼–½" long corolla is weakly bilateral, with a 3-lobed upper lip and 2-lobed lower lip. The stamens are shorter than the upper lip, and they have yellow pollen. The pointed sepals are up to half as long as the corolla tube.

Flowering Season: March to June

Habitat/Range: Schott Gilia is found in gravelly and sandy soil in washes and valleys below 5,000 feet in Creosote Bush scrub and Joshua Tree woodland in the Mojave Desert to the San Joaquin Valley and Mexico.

Comments: This species was named in honor of Arthur Schott, a naturalist of the Mexican Boundary Survey in the mid-1800s.

Flat-Topped Buckwheat, Skeleton Weed

FLAT-TOPPED BUCKWHEAT, SKELETON WEED

Eriogonum deflexum Torrey var. *deflexum*
Buckwheat Family (Polygonaceae)

Description: This 4–28" tall annual has 1 or a few slender, erect, hairless flowering stems from a basal rosette. The ½–1" long, heart-shaped to kidney-shaped leaf blades have dense white wool on the undersurfaces, and they are on ½–2" long leaf stalks. The spreading flower cluster has 3 triangular bracts at the branching points. The broad, flat-topped crown can be up to 2' across on larger plants. The tiny white to pink flowers are produced within ¹⁄₁₀" long involucres with 5 tiny teeth at the tip; these often hang down from the horizontal branches. As the plant ages, the stems turn dark reddish brown or black. These conspicuous dried stems often persist for several seasons, giving the plant the common name of Skeleton Weed.

Flowering Season: May to October

Habitat/Range: Flat-Topped Buckwheat is widespread in sandy and gravelly soil below 6,000 feet in both the Mojave and Colorado Deserts to Baja California, Mexico.

Comments: *Eriogonum deflexum* var. *rectum* is a less common variety with a narrow, upright crown and erect involucres. Var. *barbatum*, with inflated stems, is found from 3,000 to 9,500 feet on north slopes of the Transverse Ranges and in scattered desert mountain ranges to southern Nevada.

JOHN REID

California Buckwheat

CALIFORNIA BUCKWHEAT
Eriogonum fasciculatum Benth. var. *polifolium*
(A. DC.) Torrey & A. Gray
Buckwheat Family (Polygonaceae)

Description: The branched stems of this 1–3'
tall shrub have alternate clusters (fascicles) of
¼–¾" long, sessile, oblong to linear leaves.
These leaves are covered with dense, short
hairs, and their margins roll under slightly.
The dense, round, headlike flower clusters are
produced on leafless 1–4" stalks with leafy
bracts below. The fuzzy, whitish, 6-parted
flowers become pink with age, and as they dry
they turn a rich, burnt-orange color. These
dried flower clumps often persist until the
next flowering season.

Flowering Season: April to November

Habitat/Range: This variety is very common
on dry hillsides and in canyons and washes
below 7,000 feet in Sagebrush scrub, Joshua
Tree woodland, and Pinyon-Juniper woodland

in the Mojave Desert to Inyo County and in
the Sonoran Desert. Other varieties occur
throughout California to northwestern Mexico.

Comments: California Buckwheat is a food
plant for the Mormon Metalmark butterfly
(Apodemia mormo mormo), which flies from
April to June and August to September in the
northern and eastern Mojave Desert. Various
species of *Eriogonum* were used by many groups
of Native Americans. Seeds were gathered and
stored in the fall for later consumption, tea
made from the flowers was used as an eyewash, and a drink made from the leaves cured
headache and stomachache. Buckwheat teas
were used for gargling and douching, as astrin-
gents, and as a remedy for kidney problems and
excessive menstrual bleeding.

Punctured Bract

TIM THOMAS

PUNCTURED BRACT
Oxytheca perfoliata Torrey & A. Gray
Buckwheat Family (Polygonaceae)

Description: The slender, 4–12" long, green and reddish stems of this annual have forked, horizontal branches. The inversely lanceolate, ½–2½" long leaves occur in a basal cluster, and they have hairs along the margins. The upper nodes each have 3 bracts that are fused into a ½–1" wide, angled, funnel-shaped structure with short, fleshy to spiny tips in the corners.

Flowering Season: April to July

Habitat/Range: Punctured Bract is common in sandy or gravelly soil from 2,500 to 6,000 feet in Creosote Bush scrub, Joshua Tree woodland, and Pinyon-Juniper woodland in the Mojave Desert north to Lassen County.

Comments: The larvae of the Small Blue butterfly *(Philotes speciosa)* feed only on the short, fleshy bract tips of Punctured Bract. The apple green, white-haired larvae curl up around the stem inside of the bracts when they are not eating. The genus name is derived from the Greek words that mean "sharp box," referring to the spiny, angled, fused bracts.

Linear-Leaved Cambess

LINEAR-LEAVED CAMBESS
Oligomeris linifolia (M. Vahl) J. F. Macbr.
Mignonette Family (Resedaceae)

Description: Linear-Leaved Cambess is a somewhat fleshy, branching annual with erect, 4–12" tall stems. The entire, linear, ½–1½" long leaves are sessile in alternate bundles. The flowers are produced in 1–4" long spikes on the upper stems. Each tiny flower has 4 sepals, 2 white petals, and a triangular bract below.

Flowering Season: March to July

Habitat/Range: This species occurs in alkali flats and Creosote Bush scrub in deserts and on sea bluffs throughout the American Southwest to California's Channel Islands and Baja California, Mexico. It is also found in Eurasia.

Comments: Linear-Leaved Cambess is often common in areas with desert varnish. The genus name literally means "few parts" in Greek, referring to the flower structure.

Desert Almond

DESERT ALMOND
Prunus fasciculata (Torrey) A. Gray var. *fasciculata*
Rose Family (Rosaceae)

Description: Desert Almond is a rounded, deciduous, 3–6' tall shrub with very angled and somewhat spiny branchlets. The narrow, entire, ¼–½" long leaves are alternate and bundled into very small, budlike branches. Inconspicuous, white, sessile flowers occur singly or in groups of 2–3 along the branches. The immature fruit resembles a tiny, fuzzy, green peach, but when mature, the 1-seeded, ½" long fruit is brownish and fibrous.

Flowering Season: March to May

Habitat/Range: Desert Almond is found in dry canyons and washes from 2,500 to 6,000 feet in Creosote Bush scrub, Joshua Tree woodland, and Pinyon-Juniper woodland along the north bases of the Transverse Ranges and in mountains throughout the Mojave Desert and in the Colorado Desert.

Comments: The weblike tents of the Tent Caterpillar moth (*Malacosoma* species) are often found in profusion on Desert Almond in the spring. The larger, least active caterpillars often occupy the center of the web, while smaller ones move about along the tent margins. A related tent moth species causes much damage to peaches and plums (which are also members of the genus *Prunus*) in the eastern United States.

Bitterbrush, Antelope Bush

BITTERBRUSH, ANTELOPE BUSH
Purshia tridentata (Pursh) DC. var. *glandulosa*
(Curran) M. E. Jones
Rose Family (Rosaceae)

Description: This highly branched, evergreen shrub has somewhat sticky, alternate, ¼–½" long leaves with 3–5 pinnate lobes, inrolled margins, and sunken glands on the upper surface. Cream-colored, 5-parted, ¼" flowers are often produced in profusion, making the plant very fragrant. As the akene develops, the feathery style enlarges to nearly 1" long.

Flowering Season: April to June

Habitat/Range: Bitterbrush is found on slopes between 2,500 to 8,000 feet in Joshua Tree woodland and Pinyon-Juniper woodland. It grows on the north-facing slopes of the Transverse Ranges and in various other mountain ranges throughout the Mojave Desert.

Comments: *Purshia tridentata* var. *tridentata* is a dominant plant of the Great Basin, with a range extending from many states west of the Rockies to northern Mexico. The Owens Valley Paiute used Bitterbrush for firewood, fiber, violet dye, and many medicinal treatments. The Behr's Hairstreak butterfly *(Satyrium behrii behrii)* uses Bitterbrush as a food plant. This genus is named for Frederick Traugott Pursh, botanic garden curator and author of the first flora of North America, *Flora Americae Septentrionalis*, which included many collections from the Lewis and Clark expedition. He had a competitive, turbulent relationship with Thomas Nuttall and other botanists of the early 1800s, so it seems fitting that Bitterbrush should be named for him.

Yerba Mansa

GHOST-FLOWER
Mohavea confertiflora (Benth.) A. A. Heller
Figwort Family (Scrophulariaceae)

Description: This hairy, erect, 4–16" tall annual has alternate, lanceolate, ½–2½" long leaves on short stalks. The showy, cream-colored flowers are over 1" long and are sessile in upper leaf axils. They are 2-lipped with a swollen base and constricted throat, and the lower lip has maroon spots. The fruit is a rounded, ½" capsule with dark, tiny seeds.

Flowering Season: March to April

Habitat/Range: Ghost-Flower grows in washes and in gravelly and sandy areas below 3,000 feet in Creosote Bush scrub. It is primarily a Sonoran Desert species, but it occurs in the southern Mojave Desert at Sheephole Pass, the Bristol Mountains, Rattlesnake Canyon, and near Cleghorn Pass and also in the eastern Mojave in the Whipple Mountains.

Comments: There are striking similarities in color, size, and growth form between this species and Sand Blazing Star *(Mentzelia involucrata),* and to a lesser degree, Rock Nettle *(Eucnide urens).* This could possibly be an example of convergent evolution where similar features were favored as plants evolved in the same environment. Further study is needed.

YERBA MANSA
Anemopsis californica (Nutt.) Hook.
Lizard's-Tail Family (Saururaceae)

Description: This 6–20" tall perennial spreads by creeping, woody rhizomes. The oblong to elliptic, 4–6" long basal leaves are on long stalks, while the stem leaves are sessile, ovate, and sparse. The terminal, stalked flower cluster has 5–8, 1" long, white bracts that may be mistaken for petals. Individual greenish flowers appear in a cone-shaped spike above the bracts. The dried, rusty-brown flower clusters persist for a long time after flowering season.

Flowering Season: March to September

Habitat/Range: Yerba Mansa is common in moist, alkaline soil around seeps, springs, and playas in the Mojave Desert to Texas and Mexico.

Comments: *Yerba Mansa* means "gentle herb" in Spanish. This plant had many medicinal uses in Native American culture. The bark was boiled and the liquid imbibed as a cure for ulcers and chest infections or used as a wash for wounds.

Ghost-Flower

Jimson Weed, Thorn-Apple, Sacred Datura

JIMSON WEED, THORN-APPLE, SACRED DATURA
Datura wrightii Regel
Nightshade family (Solanaceae)

Description: This conspicuous, 2–5' tall perennial has up to 8" long, dark green, ovate leaves with smooth or slightly lobed edges. The 6–8" long, white, trumpet-shaped flowers open in the morning and evening. Each flower has 5 winglike ribs toward the base of the calyx. The round, drooping fruits are at least 1" long, are covered with prickles, and contain flat, tan seeds.

Habitat/Range: Jimson Weed is commonly found in sandy soils, roadsides, and disturbed places below 7,000 feet throughout the Mojave Desert and southwestern United States to New Mexico and Texas.

Comments: This plant contains several toxic alkaloid compounds. Symptoms of ingestion include extreme thirst, visual disturbances, nausea, fever and delirium, incoherency, and even respiratory arrest and death. The amounts of toxic alkaloids vary, so taking any amount of the plant material can be very dangerous. However, these same compounds, when concentration is strictly controlled, are very useful in modern pharmaceuticals. Important constituents include scopolamine, a motion sickness medication, and atropine, which counteracts muscle spasms. Native Americans used this plant in several rituals. Livestock don't eat Jimson Weed, but it is a small part of the diet of Merriam's Kangaroo rats, although it is not known if they suffer from any toxic effects. The common name may have been derived from the name of a related species, Jamestown Weed *(Datura stramonium)*, which is native to Mexico and also found on the east coast of the United States. The only species that may be confused with this one is *Datura discolor,* a much smaller annual with hairy flowers and ribbed calyx. It grows on the eastern margins of the Mojave Desert but is much more common in the Sonoran Desert to northwestern Mexico. Jimson Weed is pollinated by large hawkmoths.

STEPHEN INGRAM

Cooper's Box Thorn, Peach Thorn

COOPER'S BOX THORN, PEACH THORN
Lycium cooperi A. Gray
Nightshade Family (Solanaceae)

Description: This thorny, 3–5' tall shrub has sturdy, rigid stems and pinkish brown bark, which ages to a brownish black color and then peels. The alternate, inversely lanceolate, ½–1¼" long leaves often occur in tight clusters. They fall off in late summer, and the plant remains leafless until the next spring. The narrowly funnel-shaped, white to greenish, ½" long flowers are produced singly or in groups of 2–3 in leaf axils. The lobes of the bowl-shaped calyx are at least ⅛" long. The ½–⅜" egg-shaped fruits are green and dry, with a horizontal constriction near the top.

Flowering Season: March to May

Habitat/Range: Cooper's Box Thorn is found on dry slopes and in washes below 5,000 feet in Creosote Bush scrub, Joshua Tree woodland, Blackbush scrub, and Pinyon-Juniper woodland in the Mojave and Colorado Deserts.

Comments: This species was named for Dr. J. G. Cooper, a geologist with the United States Geological Survey in California, who collected plants in the Mojave Desert from Cajon Pass to Camp Cady in 1861.

JOHN REID

Coyote Tobacco

COYOTE TOBACCO
Nicotiana obtusifolia Martens & Galeotti
Nightshade Family (Solanaceae)

Description: This sticky, glandular, perennial herb develops clumps of erect, 8–36" stems. The dark green, triangular to ovate, lower leaves are up to 6" long, while upper leaves are smaller. Flowers occur in a loose cluster on the upper stems. Each dingy white, ½–1" long, funnel-shaped flower has a narrow throat and petal lobes that spread abruptly. The fruit is a dry, ¼–½" long, 2-chambered capsule with numerous seeds.

Flowering Season: March to June

Habitat/Range: Coyote Tobacco is found on ledges and in crevices in rocky canyons below 4,000 feet in Creosote Bush scrub and Joshua Tree woodland. It occurs in the Mojave and Colorado Deserts to Texas and Mexico. It is especially common on basalt and desert varnish.

Comments: Coyote Tobacco was dried and smoked for rituals and pleasure by various groups of Native Americans, although Indian Tobacco *(Nicotiana quadrivalvis)* was preferred. The Paiute mixed it with Mistletoe and stuffed it into the inflated stems of Desert Trumpet *(Eriogonum inflatum),* using them as pipes. This genus was named for Jean Nicot, who introduced tobacco to France in the mid-1500s. He was the French Ambassador to Portugal and the author of one of the first French dictionaries.

Indian Tobacco

INDIAN TOBACCO
Nicotiana quadrivalvis Pursh
Nightshade Family (Solanaceae)

Description: This sticky, glandular, 1–6' tall annual has a foul odor, similar to the fresh leaves of cultivated tobacco. The leaves are 1½–6" long, the upper shorter and sessile, and the lower longer on short stalks. The cream-colored flowers are produced in loose, branched, bracted clusters. The narrow 1–2" long tubular corollas have petals that abruptly flare to 1–2" wide where the lobes spread at the tips. The dried, 2-chambered fruits are around ¾" long.

Flowering Season: May to October

Habitat/Range: Indian Tobacco is uncommon in well-drained washes below 5,000 feet in the Mojave Desert to Washington and the eastern United States.

Comments: Native Americans preferred to smoke the dried leaves of this plant above any of the other native tobacco species.

YELLOW FLOWERS

Desert Sunflower

*This section includes flowers that are light yellow
to deep, golden yellow. Cream-colored flowers
grade into yellow, so be sure to check the white to
cream-colored section if you cannot find the flower
you are looking for here. Yellow flower colors are
produced by water-soluble pigments called
flavonols (derived from the Latin word for yellow)
and fat-soluble carotenes, also found in many
yellow fruits and vegetables.*

Goldenhead

GOLDENHEAD
Acamptopappus sphaerocephalus (A. Gray) A. Gray
Sunflower Family (Asteraceae)

Description: This rounded, mostly hairless 1–3' tall shrub has slender, rigid, somewhat furrowed stems. The sessile, ¼–¾" long, narrowly spoon-shaped leaves have short, pointed tips. In addition, the leaves are alternate, sometimes forming bundles due to partial development of axillary buds. The ¼–⅜" long flower heads are produced singly at ends of branchlets, each with 13–27 yellow disk flowers and 4 rows of rounded, whitish, green-tipped phyllaries. The pappus consists of 30–40 silvery, flattened scales and bristles of various widths that are swollen toward the tips.

Flowering Season: May to June

Habitat/Range: Goldenhead is found on gravelly slopes, flats, and washes below 4,500 feet in Creosote Bush scrub and Joshua Tree woodland in the central, northern, and eastern Mojave Desert and the western edge of the Colorado Desert.

Comments: The genus name literally means "stiff, unbending paper," likely referring to the phyllary texture. Shockley's Goldenhead *(Acamptopappus shockleyi)* has large flower heads with both disk and ray flowers. It is found on flats and in washes from 3,000 to 6,200 feet in the eastern Mojave Desert to the White and Inyo Mountains and southern Nevada. It may hybridize with Goldenhead in areas where they both occur.

COOPER'S DYSSODIA, COOPER'S GLANDWEED
Adenophyllum cooperi (A. Gray) Strother
Sunflower Family (Asteraceae)

Description: The stout, ridged stems of this 1–2' tall perennial grow from a woody base. The toothed, alternate, ovate leaves are less than 1" long. Each flower head has 7–13 ray flowers, numerous disk flowers, and 3 rows of ½" phyllaries, the outer ones comparatively shorter. The pappus consists of 15–20 scales, each dissected into 5–9 bristles. The phyllaries, foliage, and stems have conspicuous, translucent oil glands that yield an oily, turpentine-like odor.

Habitat/Range: Cooper's Dyssodia is found on open slopes and sandy washes from 2,000 to 5,000 feet in Creosote Bush scrub and Joshua Tree woodland from Victorville to Arizona, Nevada, and the northeastern Sonoran Desert. It is fairly common in the eastern Mojave Desert and on the north-facing slopes and bases of the San Bernardino Mountains.

Comments: The genus name means "gland leaf." A similar species, *Adenophyllum porophylloides,* occurs on dry, rocky hillsides in the Sonoran Desert but can occasionally be found in the southern Mojave Desert. It has pinnately divided leaves, opposite lower leaves, and shorter phyllaries than Cooper's Dyssodia.

Cooper's Dyssodia, Cooper's Glandweed

SCALE-BUD
Anisocoma acaulis Torrey & A. Gray
Sunflower Family (Asteraceae)

Description: This milky-sapped annual generates 1 to several leafless, 2–8" tall flower stalks from a basal rosette of pinnately toothed or divided leaves. The 1" cylindrical flower heads are produced singly, each with numerous pale yellow, strap-shaped flowers. The flattened, serial phyllaries have red tips and papery margins. The inner phyllaries are long and narrow, grading to short and round outermost layers. The pappus is composed of 10–12 bright white, feathery bristles in 2 unequal rows.

Flowering Season: April to June

Habitat/Range: Scale-Bud is found in sandy soil in Creosote Bush scrub, Joshua Tree woodland, and Pinyon-Juniper woodland from 2,000 to 7,800 feet in the Mojave Desert to southwestern Kern County and in the Sonoran Desert to Baja California, Mexico.

Comments: The genus name means "unequal clumps of hair," referring to the 2 unequal rows of pappus bristles.

Scale-Bud

STEPHEN INGRAM

Desert Marigold

DESERT MARIGOLD
Baileya multiradiata A. Gray var. *multiradiata*
Sunflower Family (Asteraceae)

Description: This 8–20" tall, short-lived perennial has white-woolly stems that branch from a taproot. The 1–4" long, spatulate to oblong, pinnately lobed leaves occur on the lower half of the stem and in a basal rosette. The 4–12" long, stout, leafless flower stalks bear ½–1½" heads with numerous, yellow, hairy, gland-dotted disk flowers and 50–60 bright yellow ray flowers that are arranged in several rows. The strap-shaped corollas of the ray flowers dry and bend back as the flowers age. The fruit is a cylindrical akene with no pappus.

Flowering Season: April to July, and again in October if summer showers have occurred

Habitat/Range: Desert Marigold is common in sandy and rocky flats, washes, and hillsides from 2,000 to 5,000 feet in Creosote Bush scrub and Joshua Tree woodland. It occurs mostly in the eastern Mojave Desert but has been reported as far west as Terrace Spring on the eastern end of the San Bernardino Mountains. Its range extends to Texas and northern Mexico.

Comments: Woolly Marigold *(Bailey pleniradiata)* is distinguished from Desert Marigold by having leafy flower stalks; the basal leaves wither by the time the flowers open. There are 20–60 ray flowers, and the akenes have prominent, angled ribs.

STEPHEN INGRAM

Lax-Flower, Colorado Desert Marigold

LAX-FLOWER, COLORADO DESERT MARIGOLD
Baileya pauciradiata A. Gray
Sunflower Family (Asteraceae)

Description: This 4–20" tall branched annual is covered with soft, woolly hair. The 1½–5½" long stem leaves are entire and linear to lanceolate, while the 1–4" long basal leaves have 2–5 pairs of short, pinnate lobes. The basal leaves wither before the flowers open. The ¼–½" flower heads are produced in loose clusters with distinct, woolly phyllaries below. Each head has numerous disk flowers and 4–8 light yellow ray flowers, which become papery and bend backward as they age. No pappus is present on the pale akenes.

Flowering Season: February to June, and also in October following summer rain

Habitat/Range: Lax-Flower occurs on very loose, sandy soil and dunes below 3,500 feet in Creosote Bush scrub in the eastern Mojave Desert. It is more common in the Sonoran Desert to Mexico.

Comments: The genus name honors Jacob Whitman Bailey (1811-1857), a pioneer of microscopic technique and professor of geology and chemistry at West Point. His son, William Whitman Bailey, was a professor of botany at Brown University.

Sweetbush

TIM THOMAS

SWEETBUSH
Bebbia juncea (Benth.) E. Greene var. *aspera* E. Greene
Sunflower Family (Asteraceae)

Description: This 2–5' tall, rounded, broom like shrub has slender, brittle stems, which are covered with short hairs with swollen bases, making it rough to the touch. It often appears leafless, since the linear leaves fall early when drought stressed. The entire plant has a strong odor. The ¼–½" hemispheric flower heads are produced on ½–2½" stalks. They have numerous yellow disk flowers and lanceolate phyllaries in several rows. The receptacle has chaffy bracts, and the pappus consists of 15–20 bristles.

Flowering Season: April through July

Habitat/Range: Sweetbush occurs on gravelly slopes and in rocky washes below 4,000 feet in Creosote Bush scrub. It is found mostly in the eastern Mojave Desert, but collections have been made as far west as Twentynine Palms. It is also found throughout southern California to Baja California, Mexico, and throughout the Sonoran Desert to New Mexico and Sonora, Mexico.

Comments: Sweetbush is a favorite food of the Desert tortoise. The genus name is in honor of Michael Schuck Bebb (1833–1895), who was a resident of San Bernardino and an authority on willows of North America.

Yellow Tack-Stem

JOHN REID

YELLOW TACK-STEM
Calycoseris parryi A. Gray
Sunflower Family (Asteraceae)

Description: This 2–6" tall, branched annual has milky sap throughout. The pinnately divided, 1–5" long leaves occur at the base of the plant and along the stem. The stalked, 1–1½" flower heads have yellow, straplike flowers and numerous, narrow phyllaries with membranous edges and dark reddish, tack-shaped glands. The tapered, beaked akenes are topped with a pappus of white, slender bristles.

Flowering Season: March to May

Habitat/Range: Yellow Tack-Stem is found on slopes and in washes below 6,000 feet in Creosote Bush scrub, Joshua Tree woodland, and Pinyon-Juniper woodland in the Mojave and Sonoran Deserts to Utah and Arizona.

Comments: This plant is often confused with Desert Dandelion *(Malacothrix glabrata)*, which does not have tack-shaped glands or beaked akenes. White Tack-Stem *(Calycoseris wrightii)* is a white-flowered species with tack-shaped glands that is occasionally found in the Mojave Desert but is very common in the Sonoran Desert.

Rubber Rabbitbrush

RUBBER RABBITBRUSH
Chrysothamnus nauseosus (Pallas) Britton ssp. *mohavensis* (E. Greene) H. M. Hall & Clements
Sunflower Family (Asteraceae)

Description: Rubber Rabbitbrush is a 2–8' tall, highly variable shrub with numerous, parallel, erect yet flexible branches. The stems are coated with a fine layer of dense wool, giving the plant a light bluish or grayish cast. Leaves, when present, are alternate, narrowly linear, and ½–1" long. Many small heads of 5 yellow disk flowers are produced in crowded, rounded or elongated clusters. Below each head are erect, hairless, angled phyllaries that are in distinct, vertically aligned rows. The phyllary angles form ribs, which are glandular toward the tips. The pappus is comprised of numerous thin bristles.

Flowering Season: September to October

Habitat/Range: This shrub is common on roadsides and disturbed areas below 7,800 feet in Creosote Bush scrub, Joshua Tree woodland, and Pinyon-Juniper woodland throughout the Mojave Desert to eastern Nevada and central California. It is also found in 4 locations in the Santa Monica Mountains, which may be relict populations from the xerothermic period of the middle Holocene.

Comments: This plant was investigated as a potential source of rubber during World War II, since good-quality latex can be extracted from stems. The idea was discarded when it was estimated that the yield would be very small for the effort and expenditure required for extraction. Native Americans made a tea from the leaves or roots for stomachaches and colds, and root extract was used to make chewing gum. Many insects visit Rubber Rabbitbrush during flowering season. You may notice the chubby, purplish black, clear-winged Cactus fly *(Volucella mexicana),* a frequent visitor. Its larvae feed on decaying cacti, especially Prickly Pear and Cholla.

Black-Banded Rabbitbrush

BLACK-BANDED RABBITBRUSH

Chrysothamnus paniculatus (A. Gray) H. M. Hall

Sunflower Family (Asteraceae)

Description: The erect, loosely branched stems of this hairless, resinous, 2–5' tall shrub often have irregular, distinct, black, gummy bands. The alternate, light green, ½–1½" long leaves are cylindrical, each narrowing abruptly to a pointed tip. Heads with 5–8 yellow disk flowers are grouped into large, branched, dense clusters. The ¼" long phyllaries are in 4–5 rows, and the pappus consists of numerous brownish white, soft, thin bristles.

Flowering Season: June to December

Habitat/Range: Black-Banded Rabbitbrush inhabits dry washes with subsurface water from 1,300 to 5,200 feet in Creosote Bush scrub throughout the Mojave Desert and along the western and northern borders of the Colorado Desert.

Comments: The black, gummy stem bands found on many branches are possibly from a smut fungus infection or insect attack.

Bigelow's Coreopsis, Bigelow's Tickseed

BIGELOW'S COREOPSIS, BIGELOW'S TICKSEED

Coreopsis bigelovii (A. Gray) H.M.Hall
Sunflower Family (Asteraceae)

Description: This 4-12" tall, hairless, slender-stemmed annual has 1-3" long, basal, pinnate leaves with linear lobes. The leafless stems bear individual heads with 20-50 disk flowers and 5-10 ray flowers. The 4-7 outer phyllaries are ¼- ½" long and linear, while the 4-8 inner phyllaries are longer and oval to oblong. Each flattened, oblong disk akene has hair along the margins and a pappus consisting of 2 tiny, bright white scales, while ray akenes lack both hairs and pappus.

Flowering Season: March to May

Habitat/Range: Bigelow's Coreopsis is common on dry, gravelly slopes under 6,000 feet in Creosote Bush scrub, Joshua Tree woodland, and Pinyon-Juniper woodland. It occurs in the central, eastern, and northern Mojave Desert to northern California, and in southern California to the Santa Monica Mountains.

Comments: Leafy-Stemmed Coreopsis *(Coreopsis calliopsidea)* is similar to Bigelow's Coreopsis, but it occurs primarily in the western Mojave Desert to northern California. It has alternate stem leaves in addition to basal leaves and outer phyllaries that are triangular to ovate. The genus name means "resembling a tick" in Greek, referring to the akene shape.

Acton Encelia

STEPHEN INGRAM

ACTON ENCELIA
Encelia actoni Elmer
Sunflower Family (Asteraceae)

Description: Acton Encelia is a rounded, 1½–4' tall shrub that produces slender branches from the base. The bark of older stems is cracked while the younger stems are yellow-green and covered with velvety hairs. The entire, ovate to triangular, 1–2" long leaves have short, soft hairs giving them a silvery, whitish appearance. Flower heads have numerous disk flowers and 15–25 ray flowers, each with ½–1" long, shallowly toothed, strap-shaped corollas. The ovate phyllaries are in 2–3 rows. The akenes have no pappus and are surrounded by receptacle chaff.

Flowering Season: March to July

Habitat/Range: Acton Encelia can be found on rocky slopes, open areas, and roadsides below 5,000 feet in Creosote Bush scrub. It is widespread in the western and southern Mojave Desert to the western Transverse Ranges, White and Inyo Mountains, San Joaquin Valley, and Baja California, Mexico.

Comments: This genus was named in honor of Christoph Entzelt (1517–1583), a Lutheran clergyman who wrote about medicinal uses of plants. The type specimen was collected in Acton in the western Mojave Desert. *Encelia virginensis* is similar to *E. actoni*, but it occurs primarily in the eastern Mojave Desert. The flower heads are smaller, and the greener leaves have some longer hairs in addition to short, soft hairs.

Brittlebush, Incienso

BRITTLEBUSH, INCIENSO
Encelia farinosa Torrey & A. Gray
Sunflower Family (Asteraceae)

Description: The white stems of this aromatic, rounded, 1–5' tall shrub ooze golden resin when broken. The alternate, ovate, 1–4" long leaves have short, dense, white-silvery hairs and mostly entire margins. The 1" wide flower heads are produced in branched clusters on long, leafless stalks that rise above the leaves, forming a rounded, yellow arch over the silvery ball of foliage. Each flower head has numerous disk flowers and 11–21 ray flowers with ½" long, strap-shaped corollas. The ¼" long, flattened akenes have silky hairs on the margins, but no pappus is present.

Flowering Season: March to May in the Mojave Desert

Habitat/Range: Brittlebush grows on rocky slopes and fans below 3,000 feet in Creosote Bush scrub. It occurs in the Death Valley region and eastern Mojave Desert, as well as around the Sheephole Mountains and Twentynine Palms, but it is more common in the Sonoran Desert to Baja California and Sonora, Mexico. It is not well-adapted to the cooler temperatures of the western and north-ern Mojave Desert, although the California Department of Transportation has hydroseeded it along some highways there for erosion control.

Comments: Fossilized pack rat midden data indicate the presence of Brittlebush in the southern Mojave Desert by 9,500 years ago. This species is readily drought-deciduous, and it will lose all of its leaves under extreme drought conditions. The new leaves produced following rain are bluish green and hairless. As the soil dries out, the larger leaves fall. The smaller leaves that are retained become thicker and develop hairs, which reflect up to 70% of the incoming solar radiation, effectively cooling the plant and decreasing evaporation from the leaf surfaces. Spanish missionaries used the gold resin from woody stems as incense, and the Cahuilla heated the resin and rubbed it on the chest to reduce pain. A boiled decoction of flowers, stems, and leaves was placed on a tooth to relieve toothache. This species is often cultivated as an ornamental for drought-tolerant landscapes.

Rayless Encelia, Green Brittlebush

RAYLESS ENCELIA, GREEN BRITTLEBUSH
Encelia frutescens (A. Gray) A. Gray
Sunflower Family (Asteraceae)

Description: The whitish stems of this rounded, 3–5' tall shrub are rough to the touch. The dark green, ovate, 1" long leaves have blisterlike swellings at the base of the coarse leaf hairs. Single ½–1" flower heads with numerous yellow disk flowers and no ray flowers are produced on leafless stalks. The akenes are black and flattened, and they have silky hairs along their margins.

Flowering Season: February to May in the Mojave Desert; in the lower Sonoran Desert these plants bloom in response to summer rain

Habitat/Range: Rayless Encelia is often found in washes and on rocky flats and slopes in Creosote Bush scrub in the eastern and southern Mojave Desert and in the Sonoran Desert to Baja California and Sonora, Mexico.

Comments: This plant is able to maintain low levels of photosynthesis with very low water availability, but if the water reserves are too low, the leaves drop. It is also capable of photosynthesis at quite high temperatures (to 104 degrees F), but it evaporates a lot of water in the process. In the hottest, driest parts of its range in the lower Sonoran Desert, these characteristics restrict the plant to desert wash habitats, where soil moisture may be more reliable.

Panamint Daisy

STEPHEN INGRAM

PANAMINT DAISY

Enceliopsis covillei (Nelson) S. F. Blake
Sunflower Family (Asteraceae)

Description: This stately perennial can grow to heights of over 40", branching from the woody base. The silvery, 3-veined, diamond-shaped leaves with winged petioles are tufted at the bases of branches. The 3½–5" diameter flower heads with numerous yellow disk and ray flowers are produced on 12–20" long stalks. Each head is subtended by a ¾" tall involucre of lanceolate phyllaries. The akenes are nearly ½" long with a pappus of 2 short scales.

Flowering Season: March to June

Habitat/Range: Panamint Daisy is found only on rocky slopes and in canyons from 1,300 to 4,000 feet on the western side of the Panamint Mountains.

Comments: Although not legally protected as an endangered or threatened species, the Panamint Daisy has a very limited distribution and has been threatened from mining, grazing, and horticultural collecting. It has been adopted as the official logo for the California Native Plant Society.

TIM THOMAS

Naked-Stemmed Daisy

NAKED-STEMMED DAISY
Enceliopsis nudicaulis (A. Gray) Nelson var. *nudicaulis*
Sunflower Family (Asteraceae)

Description: This 4–16" tall perennial has mostly leafless stems from a woody base. The dull, gray-green, ovate leaves are around 1–2½" long, and they have tufts of woolly hairs in the leaf axils. The flower heads are produced on 6–18" long, gray-fuzzy stalks. Each 1½–3½" diameter head has numerous disk flowers and 21 ray flowers, subtended by 3 rows of narrowly lanceolate, gray-fuzzy phyllaries. The akenes are slightly over ¼" long, and they are covered with silky hairs.

Flowering Season: April to May

Habitat/Range: Naked-Stemmed Daisy occupies rocky slopes and canyons from 3,000 to 6,000 feet in the mountains of the eastern and northern Mojave Desert to the White and Inyo ranges, Utah, Idaho, and northern Arizona. It often occurs on volcanic or carbonate soils.

Comments: This uncommon plant is on the California Native Plant Society's watch list. It is rare in California but somewhat widespread elsewhere, and it is not in danger of extinction at this time. More information is needed on the closely related Ash Meadows Daisy (*Enceliopsis nudicaulis* var. *corrugata*), which is state-listed as critically endangered in Nevada and is known in California from only 2 locations near Teakettle Junction.

Cooper's Goldenbush

STEPHEN INGRAM

COOPER'S GOLDENBUSH
Ericameria cooperi (A. Gray) H. M. Hall var.
cooperi
Sunflower Family (Asteraceae)

Description: This 1–2' tall, gummy-textured shrub has many erect branches from the base. The young, active shoots have long, slender, alternate leaves that are approximately ½" long, but as they age, the axillary buds become active and dense clumps of ¼" leaves develop. Clusters of stalked, ¼" flower heads are produced abundantly over the top portion of the plant. Each head has 4–7 disk flowers and 0–2 ray flowers. Between 9–15 short-haired phyllaries occur in 3–4 rows; the outer phyllaries are ovate and the inner phyllaries are oblong. The pappus consists of soft, white bristles, and the nearly cylindrical akenes have silky hairs.

Flowering Season: March to June

Habitat/Range: Cooper's Goldenbush is common on dry flats and mesas from 2,000 to 6,000 feet, mostly in Joshua Tree woodland; it is usually absent in the lowest, hottest, driest areas of the desert. It occurs from Antelope Valley and the Little San Bernardino Mountains to Mono County and Nevada.

Comments: In a study in the Owens Valley, Cooper's Goldenbush plants were not clumped but had a random distribution pattern, likely due to competition for water. They have shallow root systems that could overlap and compete for water that is limited in surface soil layers. In the same study, Rabbitbrush plants had deep taproots that could access deeper, more reliable water sources. They were less affected by competition from neighboring plants, allowing them to have a clumped distribution pattern. This species was named for J. G. Cooper, a United States Geological Survey geologist (see information under Cooper's Box Thorn in white to cream flowers section).

STEPHEN INGRAM

Cliff Goldenbush

CLIFF GOLDENBUSH
Ericameria cuneata (A. Gray) McClatchie var.
spathulata (A. Gray) H. M. Hall
Sunflower Family (Asteraceae)

Description: This 4–20" tall, spreading, gland-dotted shrub has crowded, green-glossy, spoon-shaped leaves that are up to 1" long with entire margins. They stay on the plant all year, but change to a duller grayish green in the very cold months. Flower heads consist of 7–15 disk flowers and 0–3 ray flowers. The linear to oblong phyllaries are in 4–6 rows, forming a ¼" high involucre. The akenes have dense, flattened hairs with a sparse, brownish pappus.

Flowering Season: September to November

Habitat/Range: Cliff Goldenbush grows in granitic rock cracks and crags between 2,600 and 6,000 feet in Joshua Tree woodland and Pinyon-Juniper woodland. It can be found across the Mojave Desert and parts of southern California to the eastern Sierra Nevada and northwestern Mexico.

Comments: It is curious that this plant is almost never found in regular soil. It could be restricted to rocks because it is unable to compete with other shrubs, or it may be escaping herbivores.

Interior Goldenbush, Linear-Leaved Goldenbush, Stenotopsis

INTERIOR GOLDENBUSH, LINEAR-LEAVED GOLDENBUSH, STENOTOPSIS

Ericameria linearifolia (DC.) Urb. & J. Wussow
Sunflower Family (Asteraceae)

Description: The resinous, erect twigs of this highly branched, 1–5' tall shrub bear crowded, bundled, alternate leaves that are linear, cylindrical, and ½–2" long. The ¼–¾" wide flower heads are produced at the ends of nearly leafless flower stalks. Each head has numerous disk flowers and 13–18 ray flowers. The lanceolate phyllaries with stalked glands, a green center, and fringed margins occur in 2–3 rows. The flattened, silky-haired akene has 6–8 veins and a white pappus.

Flowering Season: March to May

Habitat/Range: Interior Goldenbush is common on dry hillsides below 6,500 feet in Creosote Bush scrub, Joshua Tree woodland, and Pinyon-Juniper woodland. It occurs through-out the Mojave but is far more common in the western and southern Mojave Desert. Its range extends to the south Coast Ranges and Baja California, Mexico.

Comments: If there are California Junipers nearby, a light tapping of the Interior Goldenbush might scare up perched Juniper Hairstreak butterflies *(Mitoura siva juniperaria).* The larvae feed on the Juniper, and the adults suck nectar from the Goldenbush. Interior Goldenbush can be mistaken for the similar Turpentine-Brush *(Ericameria laricifolius),* which has much narrower leaves, fewer than 11 ray flowers, and flower heads smaller than ¼" wide. It occurs from 3,000 to 6,000 feet in the mountains of the eastern Mojave Desert.

Barstow Woolly Sunflower

TIM THOMAS

BARSTOW WOOLLY SUNFLOWER
Eriophyllum mohavense (I. M. Johnston) Jepson
Sunflower Family (Asteraceae)

Description: This ½–1" tall, tufted annual is covered with long, woolly hairs. The spoon-shaped leaves may have 3 pointed teeth near the wider tip. The stalked flower heads have 3–4 disk flowers and 3–4 linear, concave phyllaries. The pappus consists of 12–14 oblong scales.

Flowering Season: April to May

Habitat/Range: This rare species occurs in open loamy, gravelly, or clay soil from 1,500 to 3,000 feet in Creosote Bush scrub and Saltbush scrub. Its known range stretches from the northeastern edge of Edwards Air Force Base to Kramer Hills, Boron, the Harper Dry Lake area, Opal Mountain, and Cuddeback Lake.

Comments: Barstow Woolly Sunflower is threatened in nearly its entire range by vehicles, grazing, military activities, and energy development. Although the criteria for listing this species are met, it has not yet been given legal protection. An inadequately small portion of its range is included in a Bureau of Land Management area of critical environmental concern.

Pringle's Woolly Daisy

PRINGLE'S WOOLLY DAISY
Eriophyllum pringlei A. Gray
Sunflower Family (Asteraceae)

Description: This ½–3" tall, tufted annual is branched from the base. The spoon-shaped, woolly leaves usually have 3 rounded lobes near the tip, and the margins curl under. The unstalked, ⅛–¼" flower heads are produced in small clusters in the leaf axils and at the branch tips. Each head has 10–25 tiny disk flowers with 6–8 phyllaries below; there are no ray flowers. The tiny akenes have some long, flattened hairs, and the pappus scales have a shredded appearance.

Flowering Season: April to June

Habitat/Range: Pringle's Woolly Daisy is found in open, sandy areas from 1,000 to 7,000 feet in Creosote Bush scrub, Joshua Tree woodland, and Sagebrush scrub in both the Mojave and Sonoran Deserts.

Comments: This species was named for Cyrus Guernsey Pringle (1838–1911), a Quaker who was imprisoned for being a conscientious objector during the Civil War. After being released, he returned home and developed improvements to several varieties of crop plants. Asa Gray of Harvard sent him on numerous plant collection trips to the Western states and Mexico, where he collected about 500,000 specimens, many new to science.

Wallace's Woolly Daisy

WALLACE'S WOOLLY DAISY
Eriophyllum wallacei (A. Gray) A. Gray
Sunflower Family (Asteraceae)

Description: Wallace's Woolly Daisy is a tufted, woolly, 1–3" tall annual with spoon-shaped, entire, ¼–¾" long leaves. The flower heads are produced singly on ½–1" long stalks. Each head consists of numerous yellow disk flowers, 5–10 yellow ray flowers (often 8), and 5–10 pointed, overlapping, ¼" phyllaries. The tiny, club-shaped akenes are usually nearly hairless, and the pappus is less than ¹⁄₁₆" long.

Habitat/Range: This species is very common in sandy soil below 6,000 feet in Creosote Bush scrub, Joshua Tree woodland, and Pinyon-Juniper woodland. It occurs in both the Mojave and Sonoran Deserts to Mono County and mountains of southern California to northern Baja California, Mexico.

Comments: This plant may be confused with its larger relative, *Eriophyllum ambiguum*, which has longer flower stalks and tends to occur on steep, rocky slopes. Also see comment for the similar False Woolly Daisy *(Syntrichopappus fremontii)*. The genus name for this plant and the 2 preceding species literally means "hairy leaf." This species is named for William A. Wallace, who made extensive plant collections in the Los Angeles area in the mid-1800s.

Desert Sunflower

DESERT SUNFLOWER
Geraea canescens A. Gray
Sunflower Family (Asteraceae)

Description: Desert Sunflower usually behaves as an annual, although it sometimes lives more than 1 season. It branches from the base, producing leafy stems up to 2' high. The alternate, ½–4" long, slightly roughened leaves are elliptic with entire or toothed margins. The lower leaves have winged petioles, while the upper leaves are sessile. The 1–3" wide flower heads are produced in loose, branched clusters, each head with numerous disk flowers and 10–21 golden yellow ray flowers. The narrow, white-fringed phyllaries are in 2–3 rows, forming a ¼–½" high involucre. The flattened, wedge-shaped, ¼" long akenes of the disk flowers are black with long, white hairs on the margins.

Flowering Season: February to May, and also in October to November following summer rain

Habitat/Range: This species grows in sandy flats below 3,000 feet in Creosote Bush scrub. It is very conspicuous on roadsides in the central and eastern Mojave Desert, especially around the Barstow area. Its range extends to the Colorado Desert and Sonora and Baja California, Mexico.

Comments: The root word of the genus name means "old," probably in reference to the long white hairs of the disk flower akenes. Desert Sunflower has been known to hybridize occasionally with *Encelia farinosa.*

Sticky Snakeweed, Matchweed

STICKY SNAKEWEED, MATCHWEED
Gutierrezia microcephala (DC.) A. Gray
Sunflower Family (Asteraceae)

Description: This 8–24" tall perennial has a gummy, fibrous texture. It is highly branched, with upward-curving, furrowed stems that are yellow to greenish above and brown and somewhat woody near the base. The linear, dark gray-green leaves are entire and have gland dots. Numerous skinny, cylindrical flower heads are produced in clusters of 5–6 on upper branches. Each head has 4–6 phyllaries, 1–2 disk flowers, and 1–2 ray flowers with ⅛" long, strap-shaped corollas.

Flowering Season: July to October

Habitat/Range: Sticky Snakeweed is common on roadsides and in disturbed and open, sandy areas below 7,500 feet in Saltbush scrub, Creosote Bush scrub, and Joshua Tree woodland throughout the Mojave Desert and in the Sonoran Desert to Colorado and central Mexico.

Comments: Native Americans used the leaves for a hot poultice for sprained muscles, and they were sometimes brewed into a tea taken for colds. However, the leaves contain saponins, which taste soapy and are somewhat toxic. Livestock avoid it, and it spreads rapidly in overgrazed and other disturbed areas. A common related species, *Gutierrezia sarothrae*, differs from Sticky Snakeweed in that it is a smaller plant with larger, globular heads with 8–21 phyllaries and more numerous disk and ray flowers. This genus was named for the Spanish nobleman P. Gutierrez.

Red Rock Tarplant

STEPHEN INGRAM

RED ROCK TARPLANT
Hemizonia arida Keck
Sunflower Family (Asteraceae)

Description: This 1–3' tall branched annual has a bristly feel due to its sparse, short, stiff hairs. The lower leaves are inversely lanceolate and hairless with toothed margins, while upper leaves are entire with bristly hairs. Flat-topped clusters of flower heads are produced at the tops of stems. Each ¼" head has 18–25 yellow disk flowers and 5–10 pale yellow ray flowers. The bristly, glandular phyllaries halfway enclose the akenes of the ray flowers.

Flowering Season: May and November

Habitat/Range: Red Rock Tarplant occurs on clay and volcanic soils in washes from 1,000 to 3,000 feet. It is known from only 10 sites in the western Mojave Desert in the vicinity of Red Rock Canyon State Park.

Comments: Off-highway vehicles posed a threat to Red Rock Tarplant, but roads have now been closed to protect substantial portions of the populations. A similar species with entire lower leaves, Mojave Tarplant *(Hemizonia mohavensis)*, was presumed to be extinct until rediscovered in the foothills of the San Jacinto Mountains in 1994 by Oscar Clarke and Andrew Sanders of the UC Riverside Herbarium. It had not been seen since the type specimen was collected in 1933 from what is now the Mojave Forks Dam. Since its rediscovery it has been found growing in Short Canyon near Ridgecrest in the northern Mojave. It is hairy and sticky, with 5 ray flowers, 8 disk flowers, and 5–9 disk pappus scales. It is listed as state endangered.

Alkali Goldenbush

ALKALI GOLDENBUSH

Isocoma acradenia (E. Greene) E. Greene var.
acradenia
Sunflower Family (Asteraceae)

Description: The brittle, ascending stems of this 1–2½' tall, rounded shrub are shiny, hairless, and densely branched. The resinous, gland-dotted, oblong leaves are ½–2" long with entire or few-toothed margins. The flower heads are clustered tightly in groups of 4–5, each with 6–12 yellow disk flowers, no ray flowers, and 22–28 firm phyllaries in 3–4 rows. The cylindrical corolla tube of each flower expands abruptly near the throat, which is a diagnostic characteristic of this genus. The blunt phyllary tips appear swollen and wartlike due to conspicuous resin pockets.

Flowering Season: August to November

Habitat/Range: Alkali Goldenbush inhabits alkaline soils below 3,000 feet in the southwestern Mojave Desert and the base of the San Bernardino Mountains to Nevada and Arizona.

Comments: The Cahuilla drank tea from the boiled roots of this species to cure colds, and hot rocks were dropped into the tea to create a vapor that the patient inhaled. It was also used as a poultice, as well as an insect repellant on horses. Some look-alike species have poisons that can cause liver damage. *Isocoma acradenia* var. *bracteosa* in the northwestern Mojave Desert tends to have toothed leaves that get smaller toward the stem tips, 10–17 flowers, and 25–36 phyllaries per head. *I. acradenia* var. *eremophila* has 15–25 flowers per head, fewer than 28 phyllaries with widely rounded tips, and leaf margins with 4–6 soft-pointed teeth per side. It occurs in both the Mojave and Sonoran Deserts.

Goldfields

GOLDFIELDS
Lasthenia californica Lindley
Sunflower Family (Asteraceae)

Description: This silky-haired annual is less than 16" tall. The slender stems are either simple or branched from the base, with opposite, linear, hairy leaves that are ¼–2½" long. The hemispheric flower heads, which often nod in bud, have numerous disk flowers, 6–13 ray flowers, and 4–13 separate, hairy phyllaries.

Flowering Season: February to June

Habitat/Range: Goldfields inhabit open sandy areas below 3,000 feet in Creosote Bush scrub in the western, southern, and central Mojave Desert to Oregon and Baja California, Mexico.

Comments: Goldfields often show up in profusion after winter rain, turning entire landscapes yellow. Lasthenia, for whom this genus was named, was supposedly a female student of Plato.

GREENBROOM
Lepidospartum latisquamum Wats.
Sunflower Family (Asteraceae)

Description: Greenbroom is a spreading, green, 3–6' tall shrub with striped stems and fuzzy branches. The threadlike, alternate, sessile leaves are ¾–1¼" long. The flowers are produced in branched clusters of 3–5 heads on upper stems. Each head has 4–5 disk flowers and 3–5, ¼" inner phyllaries, which grade into bracts below. The 5-veined, ¼" long akenes have long, white hairs between the veins and a pappus of numerous white to tan bristles.

Flowering Season: July and August

Habitat/Range: Greenbroom has a spotty distribution in the Mojave Desert. There are populations in the northern Mojave, such as at Willow Creek near the Last Chance Mountains, and it also occurs on the north slope of the San Gabriel Mountains, as in Piñon Hills. There don't seem to be many records from the southeastern or central Mojave, although its reported range extends to Nevada and Arizona. This is a far more common species near the coast from northern California to Baja California, Mexico.

Greenbroom

Scale-Broom

MICHAEL HONER

SCALE-BROOM

Lepidospartum squamatum (A. Gray) A. Gray
Sunflower Family (Asteraceae)

Description: The erect, broomlike stems of this 3–6' tall shrub have alternate, entire, scalelike leaves that are less than ½" long. The flower heads are produced in loose clusters at the stem tips. Each head has 9–17 disk flowers and many hairless, overlapping phyllaries in 3–4 rows, forming a ¼" high involucre. There are no ray flowers present. The anthers protrude from the flower tubes, and the pappus consists of numerous thin bristles.

Flowering Season: August to October

Habitat/Range: Scale-Broom is found in washes, stream terraces, and canyon bottoms below 5,000 feet in both the Mojave and Sonoran Deserts, and in adjacent coastal and inland areas from the Central Valley to Baja California, Mexico.

Comments: This is the plant that ate Corona! A washwith Scale-Broom in Corona, California, was filled with dirt to make a level pad on which numerous homes were built. This plant lives in washes, so it is accustomed to being flooded and buried. It responded to burial as usual, sending up shoots that penetrated through concrete foundations of garages, living rooms, sidewalks, and driveways, causing millions of dollars' worth of damage. Newer laws require Scale-Broom surveys before construction.

JOHN REID

Desert Dandelion

DESERT DANDELION
Malacothrix glabrata A. Gray
Sunflower Family (Asteraceae)

Description: Desert Dandelion is a mostly hairless 2–16" tall, annual. Most of the leaves are in a basal rosette, which withers by the time the flowers open; these and the sparser stem leaves have teeth or deep, linear lobes. The stalked flower heads have numerous ½–1" long, lemon yellow, straplike flowers, sometimes with an orange-tinged spot near the center of the cluster. The hairless, overlapping phyllaries are up to ¾" long. The small akenes have veins and a pappus of teeth and bristles.

Flowering Season: March to June

Habitat/Range: This species is one of the most common spring annuals on roadsides, vacant lots, sandy flats, and washes below 6,000 feet in Creosote Bush scrub, Joshua Tree woodland, and Saltbush scrub. It seems to be very tolerant of disturbance. It occurs in both the Mojave and Sonoran Deserts and in adjacent cismontane valleys from San Diego County to Santa Barbara County and Idaho.

Comments: Related species in the Mojave Desert include *Malacothrix californica*, which has hairs on the basal leaves and no stem leaves, *M. sonchoides* with fleshy basal leaves with toothed lobes, and Snake's Head *(M. coulteri)* with distinctive, rounded phyllaries.

Chinch-Weed

CHINCH-WEED
Pectis papposa Harvey & A. Gray var. *papposa*
Sunflower Family (Asteraceae)

Description: This gland-dotted, ½–8" tall, mound-forming or spreading annual has a pungent, spicy odor. The opposite, narrow, sessile leaves are ½–1½" long, and they have bristly hairs on the margins, especially along the winged base. Numerous ¼–½" flower heads are produced in dense, branched clusters. Each head has 6–14 disk flowers and 8 ray flowers. There is 1 row of 8 green phyllaries, each with a gland near the tip and glands along the margins. The akenes are small and cylindrical, and the disk akenes have a pappus of bristles, while the pappus on the ray akenes forms a low crown of small scales.

Flowering Season: September to November, following summer rains

Habitat/Range: Chinch-Weed is found on dry flats and rocky slopes below 5,000 feet in Creosote Bush scrub and Joshua Tree woodland. It is rare in the western Mojave Desert, but it is more common in the central and eastern Mojave. It occurs in all of the deserts of North America.

Comments: The major essential oil of Chinch-Weed is cumin oil. It has been suggested as a commercial source, since the plant grows rapidly and thrives in hot weather.

Pygmy-Cedar

TIM THOMAS

PYGMY-CEDAR
Peucephyllum schottii A. Gray
Sunflower Family (Asteraceae)

Description: This evergreen shrub or small tree superficially resembles a conifer, with its dense, shiny green, needlelike leaves that are less than 1" long. Solitary flower heads are produced on ⅓–1" stalks, each with 12–21 pale yellow, ½" long disk flowers. Each head has one row of 9–18 thick, pointed, ¼–½" long phyllaries that are gland dotted near the tips. The tiny, blackish akenes have a pappus of fine bristles.

Flowering Season: May to December

Habitat/Range: Pygmy-Cedar can be found on rocky outcrops, canyons, upper alluvial fans, and sometimes road-cuts below 3,000 feet in Creosote Bush scrub. It occurs in both the Mojave and Colorado Deserts to northwestern Mexico.

Comments: Studies in Death Valley have shown that Pygmy-Cedar is not able to handle drought stress as well as its neighbors Creosote Bush *(Larrea tridentata)* and Desert Holly *(Atriplex hymenelytra)*. This restricts the plant to areas where there is less evaporation or more runoff water available, such as in gullies and between rocks. Fossilized pack rat midden data show that this plant probably occupied its present range beginning about 10,000 years ago. Individuals of Pygmy-Cedar can live at least 100 years, as shown by repeat photography. This species was named for Arthur Schott, a naturalist of the Mexican Boundary Survey.

Mealy Rosette, Annual Turtleback

MEALY ROSETTE, ANNUAL TURTLEBACK
Psathyrotes annua (Nutt.) A. Gray
Sunflower Family (Asteraceae)

Description: This grayish green, very compact annual has an odor of vinegar combined with sweet perfume. The alternate, rounded, ⅓–⅔" long leaves usually have teeth toward the tip. The ¼" flower heads are produced on short stalks in leaf axils. Each head has 13–16 disk flowers and 2 rows of short phyllaries. The tiny, weakly 10-ribbed akene has a pappus of 35–50 coarse, reddish brown bristles.

Flowering Season: June to October

Habitat/Range: Mealy Rosette occupies sandy or rocky and sometimes alkaline soil below 6,000 feet in Saltbush scrub and Creosote Bush scrub. It occurs in the western, northern, and eastern Mojave Desert and on the low northeastern slopes of the San Bernardino Mountains to Mono County and Utah.

Comments: See comments for Turtleback *(Psathyrotes ramosissima).*

TIM THOMAS

Turtleback, Velvet Rosette

TURTLEBACK, VELVET ROSETTE
Psathyrotes ramosissima (Torrey) A. Gray
Sunflower Family (Asteraceae)

Description: This gray, dome-shaped, 2–6" tall annual is very compact and has a strong resinous or turpentine odor. The young stems are covered with soft white hair, but the older stems are smooth and hairless. The thick, velvety, ¼–¾" long leaf blades have irregular, rounded teeth, prominent veins, and long leaf stalks. The flower heads are produced on short stalks in leaf axils. Each head has 16–32 small, yellow to purplish disk flowers subtended by 2 rows of ¼" phyllaries. The tiny akenes have numerous brownish pappus bristles in 3–4 rows.

Flowering Season: March to June

Habitat/Range: Turtleback is found on sandy flats and in washes below 3,000 feet in Creosote Bush scrub in the northern, eastern, and southern Mojave, such as at Ibex Pass, Fort Irwin, Baker, and Death Valley. It is much more common from Twentynine Palms south through the Sonoran Desert to northwestern Mexico.

Comments: Both Turtleback and Mealy Rosettes had numerous medicinal uses to local Native Americans. They were used as a tea for intestinal and urinary tract disorders, as a dressing on snakebites, as an eyewash, and as a cure for toothache.

Paper Daisy

PAPER DAISY
Psilotrophe cooperi (A. Gray) E. Greene
Sunflower Family (Asteraceae)

Description: Paper Daisy is an 8–24" tall, often nearly spherical perennial with many branched, white-woolly stems arising from a woody base. The alternate, linear 1–2" long leaves have a fuzzy coating that wears off as the leaves age. The showy flower heads are produced on 1–3" stalks. Each head has up to 25 protruding disk flowers and 4–8 wide, ovate, ¼–¾" long ray flowers with 3 teeth at the tips. These fold back and become very papery with age, clinging to the plant until the akenes are shed. The tiny, hairless akenes bear a pappus of short scales.

Flowering Season: April to June, and in late fall following summer rain

Habitat/Range: Paper Daisy occupies alluvial slopes and rocky flats from 2,000 to 5,000 feet in Creosote Bush scrub and Joshua Tree woodland in the eastern Mojave Desert and in the northern Colorado Desert to New Mexico and northern Mexico.

Comments: Paper Daisy will quickly drop its leaves with the onset of drought. This species is named in honor of Dr. James Graham Cooper (1830–1902), who worked as a geologist for the Geological Survey of California. He collected Mojave Desert plants in the early 1860s, and several species have been named after him.

California Butterweed

CALIFORNIA BUTTERWEED

Senecio flaccidus Less. var. *monoensis* (E. Greene) B. Turner & T. Barkley
Sunflower Family (Asteraceae)

Description: This 1–3' tall, hairless, green perennial has furrowed, arching stems from a strong taproot. The alternate, 1–4" long leaves are linear and entire or pinnately divided into linear segments, and bundles of younger leaves may occur in leaf axils. There are 3–10 flower heads produced in a loose cluster on the upper stems. Each head has numerous disk flowers and 8 ray flowers with ½–1" long, strap-shaped corollas. There are 13 or 21 lanceolate phyllaries in an even inner row, and there is also an outer row of very short, spreading, conspicuous phyllaries, which is characteristic of many *Senecio* species. The soft-hairy, cylindrical akenes are less than ¼" long, and they have a pappus of thin bristles.

Flowering Season: March to May, and in the fall following summer rain

Habitat/Range: This variety of California Butterweed occurs in washes in Creosote Bush scrub, Joshua Tree woodland, and Pinyon-Juniper woodland in the Mojave Desert and in the northern Colorado Desert to Mono County, Utah, Arizona, Texas, and northwestern Mexico.

Comments: *Senecio flaccidus* var. *douglassii* is taller and shrubbier with whitish hairs. It is found in inland valleys and coastal drainages of California to Baja California, Mexico. It seems to be replaced by var. *monoensis* in the deserts, except on desert slopes of the Transverse Ranges. Black, shiny, solitary bees are often seen in the evening resting in the foliage of California Butterweed on the north slopes of the San Gabriel Mountains.

Mojave Butterweed

MOJAVE BUTTERWEED
Senecio mohavensis A. Gray
Sunflower Family (Asteraceae)

Description: This branched, hairless annual is usually 8–16" tall. The green, 1–3½" long, lobed or toothed leaves are distributed alternately along the entire length of the purplish stems, and the upper leaves have clasping bases. Loose clusters of ½" flower heads are produced atop the stems, each with numerous disk flowers and sometimes a few inconspicuous ray flowers. There is 1 main row of 8 or 13 linear, ¼" long phyllaries with pointed green tips, and there may also be some very short, outer phyllaries. The tiny, cylindrical akenes have soft, short, white hairs.

Flowering Season: March to May

Habitat/Range: Mojave Butterweed usually occupies shady areas under shrubs and among boulders on rocky slopes below 3,000 feet in the eastern and southern Mojave Desert and in the Sonoran Desert to northwestern Mexico.

Comments: This species is indistinguishable from *Senecio flava* from the Middle East. Both species are self-fertilizing, and the mucilaginous seeds remain viable for 15 years. It has been suggested that Mojave Butterweed might have been introduced from that region fairly recently by bird-dispersed seeds. If so, it is curious that our species has an endemic Tephritid fly that feeds on the flowers, since recently introduced plants are usually not hosts to endemic insects.

False Woolly Daisy

FALSE WOOLLY DAISY
Syntrichopappus fremontii A. Gray
Sunflower Family (Asteraceae)

Description: This 1–4" tall, branched annual is covered with short hairs. The linear to spoon-shaped, ¼–¾" long leaves may have 3 teeth near the tip. Flower heads have several yellow disk flowers, 5 ray flowers, and 5 hardened, boat-shaped phyllaries with dry, thin margins that partly enclose the ray akenes. The strap-shaped corollas of the ray flowers are strongly 3-lobed or toothed. The small, hairy akene has a pappus of 30–40 bright white bristles that are united at the base.

Habitat/Range: This plant grows in sandy or gravelly soil between 2,500 and 7,500 feet in Creosote Bush scrub and Joshua Tree woodland in the northern, eastern, and southern Mojave Desert.

Comments: False Woolly Daisy is commonly confused with Wallace's Woolly Daisy *(Eriophyllum wallacei)*. However, Wallace's Woolly Daisy usually has 8–10 ray flowers, which are not strongly lobed, and the pappus, if present, consists of 6–10 oblong scales that are less than ¹⁄₁₆" long. It is usually found in low, sandy areas, while False Woolly Daisy is often above the desert floor.

Cotton-Thorn

TIM THOMAS

COTTON-THORN

Tetradymia axillaris Nelson var. *longispina*
(M. E. Jones) Strother
Sunflower Family (Asteraceae)

Description: The stems of this spiny, 2–5' tall shrub have an even, white, woolly coating. The alternate primary leaves develop into straight, ½–2" long spines, and clusters of shorter, green, linear leaves are produced in the leaf axils due to the partial development of the axillary buds. These clustered leaves are up to ½" long, and they may be hairy when very young but quickly become hairless as they mature. Clusters of 1–3 flower heads are produced on hairy stalks in the leaf axils. Each head consists of 5–7 pale yellow, ¼–⅜" long disk flowers and 5 narrowly ovate, hairy, ¼" long phyllaries. The densely hairy akene is less than ¼" long, and it has a pappus of approximately 25 slender scales.

Flowering Season: May to August

Habitat/Range: Cotton-Thorn occurs on dry slopes and flats from 3,500 to 7,000 feet in the southwestern Mojave Desert and the eastern slopes of the Sierra Nevada Range to Oregon, Nevada, and Utah.

Comments: Mojave Horsebrush *(Tetradymia stenolepis)* has silvery, hairy leaves, straight spines, and a striped appearance below the spines because of uneven distribution of the white, fuzzy coating. It is found in scattered locations on dry slopes and flats from 2,000 to 5,000 feet in Creosote Bush scrub and Joshua Tree woodland throughout much of the Mojave Desert. *T. spinosa* has hairless leaves and curved spines. *T. canescens* is a silvery, spineless shrub of the Transverse Ranges, desert mountains, and Great Basin Desert.

Thymophylla

THYMOPHYLLA
Thymophylla pentachaeta (DC.) Small var.
belenidium (DC.) Strother
Sunflower Family (Asteraceae)

Description: This 6–12" tall, gland-dotted perennial has very slender stems that are somewhat woody at the base. The opposite, ½–1¼" long leaves are pinnately divided into 3–5 stiff, spine-tipped, linear lobes. The ¼" flower heads are produced singly on 1–2" stalks. Each head has numerous disk flowers, 13 ray flowers, 2 rows of ¼" long inner phyllaries, and an outer row of a few short, triangular phyllaries. The tiny akene has a pappus of 10 scales, each divided into 3 awns.

Flowering Season: April to June

Habitat/Range: Thymophylla is found on dry, gravelly benches and slopes, often on limestone soils, from 3,000 to 5,600 feet in Creosote Bush scrub and Joshua Tree woodland. It occurs mostly in the eastern Mojave Desert, as in the New York Mountains and Ivanpah Valley, but there is also a population in the northwestern Mojave Desert at Dove Spring in Kern County. Its range extends to Texas and northern Mexico.

Comments: Thymophylla, especially when blooming during the first year, is sometimes confused with Chinch-Weed *(Pectis papposa)*. However, Chinch-Weed blooms in the fall, has simple leaves, and never develops woody tissue.

YELLOW-HEADS

Trichoptilium incisum A. Gray
Sunflower Family (Asteraceae)

Description: This 2–10" tall annual has fuzzy, forked stems. The ½–1¼" long, inversely lanceolate, toothed leaves with winged petioles are densest at the base of the plant and along the lower stems. The rounded flower heads occur singly on 1–4" long, glandular-hairy stalks. Each hemispheric head has numerous yellow disk flowers with 2 rows of lancolate, glandular-hairy, ¼" long phyllaries. The tiny akenes have a pappus of 5 divided scales.

Flowering Season: February to May, and sometimes October to November following summer rain

Habitat/Range: Yellow-Heads are found on rocky slopes or desert pavement below 2,200 feet in Creosote Bush scrub in the southern Mojave Desert, as in the Sheephole Mountains, but they are more common in the Colorado Desert. Their range extends to southern Nevada, western Arizona, and Baja California, Mexico.

Comments: The flowers of this species look like yellow versions of Pincushions (*Chaenactis* species), to which they are closely related.

Yellow-Heads

Trixis

TRIXIS

Trixis californica Kellogg var. *californica*
Sunflower Family (Asteraceae)

Description: This erect, leafy, 1–3' tall shrub has white, brittle stems. The lanceolate, alternate, bright green leaves are 1–4" long with entire to minutely toothed margins. The ½–1" tall flower heads are produced in somewhat flat, branched, leafy-bracted clusters. Each head bears numerous disk flowers with 2-lipped, yellow corollas and 8–10 green, pointed phyllaries. The narrow akenes have a pappus of white to beige bristles.

Flowering Season: February to April

Habitat/Range: Trixis occurs on rocky slopes, canyons, and washes below 3,000 feet in Creosote Bush scrub in the southern Mojave Desert as in the Sheephole Mountains. It is more common in the Sonoran Desert to western Texas and northern Mexico.

Comments: Native Americans in the Sonoran Desert smoked the leaves of this plant like tobacco, and a tea was made from the roots to aid in childbirth.

Devil's Lettuce, Checker Fiddleneck

DEVIL'S LETTUCE, CHECKER FIDDLENECK

Amsinckia tessellata A. Gray
Borage Family (Boraginaceae)

Description: This erect, bristly, 8–24" tall annual has alternate, entire, nearly linear leaves. The stiff leaf hairs have bulbous bases that can be seen with a hand lens. The 5-parted, ⅓–⅔" long, yellow to orange flowers occur in a 2–5" long, coiled spike at the top of the stem. Each corolla is less than ¼" wide, and the flower tubes are cylindrical. Some of the calyx lobes are fused, so there appears to be 3–4 lobes instead of 5; the lobes have white hairs on the margins.

Flowering Season: March to May

Habitat/Range: Devil's Lettuce is common throughout both the Mojave and Sonoran Deserts. Its range extends to eastern Washington and Baja California, Mexico. Although it is present in nondesert areas of southern California, it is very uncommon there.

Comments: Rancher's Fireweed *(Amsinckia menziesii)* is a similar species, which differs from Devil's Lettuce by having 5 distinct calyx lobes rather than 3–4. It grows on coastal plains and in inland valleys from San Diego County, California, to Washington and Utah. It is occasionally found in the Mojave Desert, especially along the desert margins.

Yellow Pepper-Grass

YELLOW PEPPER-GRASS

Lepidium flavum Torrey var. *flavum*
Mustard Family (Brassicaceae)

Description: This 2–16" tall, hairless, yellow-green annual often grows flat on the ground with stem tips upturned. The pinnately lobed, 1–2" long, spoon-shaped leaves are in a basal rosette, with smaller, toothed leaves toward the stem tip. The tiny flowers have 4 separate, bright yellow petals, 4 greenish yellow sepals, and 6 stamens. The flattened, ovate fruit has 2 winglike projections near the notch at the top.

Flowering Season: March to May

Habitat/Range: Yellow Pepper-Grass occurs in alkaline flats, playas, puddles, and washes below 4,500 feet in Creosote Bush scrub and Joshua Tree woodland in the western, central, and northern Mojave Desert. It is especially abundant in Death Valley, Lucerne Valley, and around Lancaster. It is less common in the Sonoran Desert. Its range extends to Nevada and Baja California, Mexico.

Comments: This plant has a spicy flavor and odor similar to many members of the Mustard Family, especially Watercress.

STEPHEN INGRAM

Beadpod, Bladderpod

BEADPOD, BLADDERPOD
Lesquerella tenella Nelson
Mustard Family (Brassicaceae)

Description: This annual has several ascending, branched, 4–24" long stems with both basal and stem leaves. The 1–2½" long basal leaves are entire or coarsely toothed or lobed, while the stem leaves are shorter and linear to inversely lanceolate. The showy, bright yellow flowers are produced in 3–8" long clusters on the upper stems. Each flower has 4 sepals and 4 rounded, ¼–½" long petals that taper to a clawlike base. The plump, spherical, ⅛" fruits are on ½" long, S-shaped stalks, and the reddish brown, flattened seeds have a narrow wing on the margin. The entire plant, including the fruit, is densely covered with stellate hairs.

Flowering Season: March to May

Habitat/Range: Beadpod grows in sandy areas below 3,500 feet in the eastern Mojave Desert and northeastern Colorado Desert. Its range extends to New Mexico and northern Sonora and Baja California, Mexico.

Comments: This genus was named in honor of Charles Leo Lesquereux (1806–1889). He was the leading authority on American botanical fossils, and he authored several important articles on mosses.

Panamint Plume, Tall Prince's Plume

PANAMINT PLUME, TALL PRINCE'S PLUME
Stanleya elata Jones.
Mustard Family (Brassicaceae)

Description: This erect, 2–5' tall, short-lived perennial has stalked, leathery, ovate, 4–8" long leaves that taper at both ends. The flowers are produced in a dense terminal cluster that can be up to 20" long. Each light yellow, hairless, ½" long flower has 4 reflexed sepals and 4 clawed petals with wide bases. The narrow, spreading, 2–4" long fruits are on ½" long stalks.

Flowering Season: May to July

Habitat/Range: Panamint Plume occurs among rocks in desert washes and on slopes between 4,000 and 6,500 feet in Joshua Tree woodland and Pinyon-Juniper woodland in the mountains of the northern Mojave Desert and the White Mountains.

Comments: This genus was named in honor of Lord Edward Smith Stanley (1773–1849), who was the 13th Earl of Derby, an ornithologist, and a president of the Linnaean Society. Also see comments under Prince's Plume.

Prince's Plume

PRINCE'S PLUME
Stanleya pinnata (Pursh) Britton
Mustard Family (Brassicaceae)

Description: Prince's Plume is a 16–60" tall perennial from a thick, branched, woody base. The hairless, 2–6" long lower leaves have deep pinnate lobes, while the upper leaves are shorter and mostly entire. Showy yellow flowers are produced in 4–12" long clusters on upper stems. Each ½–¾" long flower has 4 sepals, 4 petals, and 6 stamens. The petals taper into claws with dense, long, wavy hairs on the inside surfaces.

Flowering Season: April to September

Habitat/Range: Prince's Plume is found in washes and on slopes from 1,000 to 7,500 feet in Creosote Bush scrub, Joshua Tree woodland, and Pinyon-Juniper woodland throughout the Mojave Desert and many Western states.

Comments: Prince's Plume and Panamint Plume tend to grow on soils rich in selenium and may accumulate this nutrient up to 46 parts per million, making them toxic to livestock and humans. The Paiute and Shoshone consumed young stems and leaves, but the plants had to be repeatedly boiled, rinsed, and squeezed, and the first cooking water was discarded. The plants were then dried and boiled again later when needed, effectively reducing the toxins to a safe level. Livestock seem to avoid consuming this plant.

Panamint Butterfly Bush

STEPHEN INGRAM

PANAMINT BUTTERFLY BUSH

Buddleja utahensis Cov.
Buddleja Family (Buddlejaceae)

Description: This 1–2' tall, grayish green, densely branched shrub is covered with branched and stellate hairs. The thick, linear, ½–1¼" long leaves have wavy, rolled-under margins. The male and female flowers are produced on separate plants in dense, rounded clusters in leaf axils on upper stems. Each cream-colored, 4-lobed flower is less than ¼" long.

Flowering Season: May to October

Habitat/Range: Panamint Butterfly Bush is found on rocky, carbonate soils from 2,500 to 4,500 feet in the eastern Mojave Desert to Nevada and Utah. It is relatively rare in California, occurring in few places, including the Panamint Mountains, the Kingston Range, and the Grapevine Mountains.

Comments: The Panamint Butterfly Bush was considered for listing as threatened or endangered, but it was rejected when found to be too common.

WENDELL MINNICH

Cotton-Top

COTTON-TOP
Echinocactus polycephalus Engelm. & J. Bigelow
var. *polycephalus*
Cactus Family (Cactaceae)

Description: The Cotton-Top may resemble a small barrel cactus, but unlike the single barrel, the stems occur in clumps of 10–30. Each 1–2' tall stem has 10–21 ribs and is usually 8–14" in diameter. There are 3–4 central spines that are fuzzy when young, but as they mature they become red or gray, flattened, 2–3" long, and develop crosswise markings. There are also 6–8 similar but shorter radial spines. The 1–2" long, yellow flowers are produced at the top of the stems, and they are surrounded by woolly fibers. The ¾–1½" long, densely woolly fruits contain angled seeds.

Flowering Season: March to May

Habitat/Range: Cotton-Top commonly occupies rocky slopes and ridges from 2,000 to 5,000 feet in Creosote Bush scrub from the central and northern Mojave Desert and Sonoran Desert to northwestern Sonora, Mexico.

Comments: Native Americans ate the seeds, applied baked and ground-up plants to burns, and used the thick spines as needles and boring tools. Although this species is not particularly showy, several members of its genus are extremely attractive and sought after for horticultural collections.

California Barrel Cactus, Visnaga

CALIFORNIA BARREL CACTUS, VISNAGA
Ferocactus cylindraceus (Engelm.) Orc. var. *cylindraceus*
Cactus Family (Cactaceae)

Description: The massive, unbranched, globular or columnar stem of the Barrel Cactus stands 2–9' tall and is usually 12–16" thick. It has 18–27 longitudinal ribs that are almost obscured by the dense spines. There are 10–18 spines at each areole, varying from straw-colored to red while young and then graying with age. Around 4–7 of these are central spines, with crosswise rings or markings; these are 3–8" long and curved. The showy, 1–2½" long, yellow flowers are produced in a circle at the top of the barrel. The green, 1¼" long fruits have pitted seeds.

Flowering Season: April to May

Habitat/Range: California Barrel Cactus occurs on fractured, rocky soils and upper alluvial and gravelly slopes, canyon walls, and wash margins in Creosote Bush scrub. Its range is the eastern and southern Mojave Desert and the Sonoran Desert to Baja California, Mexico.

Comments: Winter temperatures limit the northern and elevational distributions of this species, so it tends to grow only on south-facing slopes, tilting its body to the south in the northern parts of its range. This plant is highly adapted to drought and heat. After rain, special "rain roots" are produced, which increase water uptake while it is available, but these roots die after the soil water reaches a critical low level. The plant has crassulacean acid metabolism (CAM photosynthesis), which allows it to open its stomates to take in carbon dioxide at night to minimize transpirational water loss. It has succulent stems for water storage and stem ribs that allow the stem to expand and contract with water availability; the plant can lose up to 80% of water stored in the stem and still remain alive! Seedlings, however, are not as drought tolerant due to their high surface area to volume ratio; losing over 80% of their stored water usually kills them. Even though the mature stems contain a lot of water, it is a myth that a thirsty desert traveler can drink clear water from a barrel cactus, as depicted in some Western movies. The interior of the stem is juicy but very pulpy, and it contains very bitter alkaloid compounds.

STEPHEN INGRAM

Buckhorn Cholla, Staghorn Cholla

BUCKHORN CHOLLA, STAGHORN CHOLLA

Opuntia acanthocarpa Engelm. & J. Bigelow
var. *coloradensis* L. Benson
Cactus Family (Cactaceae)

Description: One trunklike stem forks repeatedly to form this 3–6' tall, spreading, treelike cactus. The cylindrical joints are 6–12" long with conspicuous, ½–1¼" long protrusions (tubercles) that are flattened sideways and are more than twice as long as they are broad. Each areole has 12–21 brownish spines with tan sheaths. The 2" wide flowers have numerous yellow to orange petals and purple to reddish filaments with dull yellow anthers. The bumpy, spiny, 1–1¼" long fruit contains tan seeds.

Flowering Season: May to June

Habitat/Range: Buckhorn Cholla grows on sandy and gravelly slopes and flats from 2,000 to 4,000 feet in Creosote Bush scrub and Joshua Tree woodland in the eastern Mojave Desert and Sonoran Desert to northwestern Mexico.

Comments: Touching the stamens of most cactus flowers causes a thigmotropic response; that is, the stamens move in response to touch. This may facilitate pollen dispersal by coating the visiting insects with pollen. Buckhorn Cholla might be confused with Silver Cholla *(Opuntia echinocarpa)*, but can be distinguished most reliably by flower color (Silver Cholla flowers are greenish) and also by tubercle length. The tubercles of Silver Cholla are less than twice as long as they are broad.

Pancake-Pear

STEPHEN INGRAM

PANCAKE-PEAR
Opuntia chlorotica Engelm. & J. Bigelow
Cactus Family (Cactaceae)

Description: The Pancake-Pear is unique among the flat-jointed cacti in that it grows up to 7½' tall, and it is quite obvious with its light yellowish green, circular, 5–8" pads. Each areole has numerous yellowish, ¼" long glochids and 3–6 straw-colored spines that are approximately 1–2" long and pointed downward. Large yellow blossoms are produced on the edges of pads, followed by 1½–2" rounded, spineless, rose-colored fruits, which linger on the plant long after their production.

Flowering Season: May or June

Habitat/Range: The Pancake-Pear occurs in rocky areas and canyons in Creosote Bush scrub, Joshua Tree woodland, and Pinyon-Juniper woodland in the eastern and southern Mojave Desert to the Sonoran Desert and Baja California, Mexico.

Comments: A study showed that the pads of Pancake-Pear were most likely to be facing north-south in winter and early spring in the Mojave Desert, when water is available and when the sun appears further south. Pads with this orientation had over 100% more light available for photosynthesis than pads oriented other directions. East-west facing pads had an advantage in the southern Sonoran Desert, where much of the rain falls in late summer when the sun is more directly overhead.

TIM THOMAS

Mojave Prickly-Pear, Old Man Cactus

MOJAVE PRICKLY-PEAR, OLD MAN CACTUS

Opuntia erinacea Engelm. & J. Bigelow var. *erinacea*

Cactus Family (Cactaceae)

Description: The clumped stems of this cactus are generally less than 1½' tall and 3" wide with flattened, 2–7" long, elliptical pads. The spine-bearing areoles are less than ½" apart, and each areole can have up to 24 spines, although there are usually 4–9. The central, longest spine is up to 5" long and surrounded by shorter spines. These numerous spines are white to grayish and bent downward, suggesting a bearded appearance and giving the plant one of its common names of Old Man Cactus. Yellow flowers with white filaments and green stigmas are produced on the upper edges of pads. The dry, short-spiny, 1–1½" long fruits contain ¼" cream-colored seeds.

Flowering Season: May to June

Habitat/Range: Mojave Prickly-Pear is found in dry, gravelly, and rocky areas from 1,500 to 8,000 feet in Creosote Bush scrub, Joshua Tree woodland, and Pinyon-Juniper woodland. It occurs on the north slopes of the San Bernardino Mountains and in mountains of the eastern and northern Mojave Desert to California's Mono County, Washington, New Mexico, and northwestern Mexico.

Comments: Mojave Prickly-Pear is found at relatively high elevations, suggesting that it may be somewhat hardy in cold temperatures. It is fairly closely related to *Opuntia polyantha,* a widespread, cold-tolerant species of the Rocky Mountain states that occurs in Canada, farther north than any other cactus species.

Club Cholla, Mat Cholla, Horse Crippler, Dead Cactus

CLUB CHOLLA, MAT CHOLLA, HORSE CRIPPLER, DEAD CACTUS
Opuntia parishii Orc.
Cactus Family (Cactaceae)

Description: The main stems of the densely spiny Club Cholla creep flat on the ground, forming mats that are 4–6" high and up to 6' across. The erect, club-shaped, terminal pads are narrow at the base and thicker at the apex. Each areole has 1 broad, 1½" central spine flanked by a ring of rounded spines that are nearly the same length. Shorter, slender spines and glochids surround these. Yellow flowers with 1" long petals and green filaments are produced atop the terminal pads, followed by club-shaped, yellowish green, 1½–3" long fruits with yellow glochids.

Flowering Season: May to June

Habitat/Range: Club Cholla is found in very dry, sandy, flat areas from 3,000 to 5,000 feet in Creosote Bush scrub and Joshua Tree woodland. It occurs in the southern and eastern Mojave Desert, from the Little San Bernardino Mountains to Clark Mountain, western Nevada, and southern Arizona.

Comments: This plant is often overlooked, not only because it grows low to the ground, but also because it looks dead most of the time. When conditions are favorable, the new growth will have reddish spines, but older growth looks dehydrated and lifeless. Keep a wary eye out for this species. It's called Horse Crippler for a reason! Repeat photography has shown that patches of this plant can live for over 80 years.

Mojave Stinkweed

MOJAVE STINKWEED
Cleomella obtusifolia Torrey & Fremont
Caper Family (Capparaceae)

Description: The branched stems of this hairy annual spread to form rounded, 3–6" tall mats. The compound leaves have 3 obovate, ¼–½" long leaflets. The dark yellow, 4-parted, ¼" long flowers are produced singly on ¼–½" stalks on younger plants and in dense clusters at the ends of branches of older plants. The sepals have hairs on the margins. The odd fruit looks like 2 cones stuck together on a long stalk.

Flowering Season: April to October

Habitat/Range: Mojave Stinkweed occurs in sandy and alkaline areas, roadsides, and the edges of playas below 4,000 feet in Creosote Bush scrub and Joshua Tree woodland throughout the Mojave Desert. It also is found in the Colorado Desert and Inyo County.

Comments: The Caper *(Capparis spinosa)* is the pungent-tasting, pickled flower bud of a related genus, possibly the only edible member of this family.

Bladderpod

BLADDERPOD
Isomeris arborea Nutt.
Caper Family (Capparaceae)

Description: This malodorous green shrub usually grows from 2–5' tall. The alternate, green leaves have 3 elliptic leaflets that are ½–2" long. The flowers are produced in clusters at the tops of branches. Each ½–¾" long flower has 4 partially fused green sepals, 4 bright yellow petals, and protruding stamens. The 1–2" long fruit is a smooth, leathery, inflated capsule on a stalklike receptacle.

Flowering Season: Flowers can be found on Bladderpod almost any time of year, even when there has been little rain.

Habitat/Range: Bladderpod is found on roadsides, washes, and flat areas below 4,000 feet in the western Mojave and Colorado Deserts to Baja California, Mexico.

Comments: Orange and black Harlequin bugs *(Murgantia histrionica)* are commonly found on this plant, and the yellow to orange eggs of Becker's White butterfly *(Pieris beckeri)* are often seen on the fruits and foliage. The nasty odor of Bladderpod indicates the presence of chemicals called secondary compounds, which it produces to discourage insects from eating it. Many plants produce such chemicals, some of which are unpalatable, and some are downright toxic. But some populations of insects, with their short generation times, are able to quickly evolve enzymes to break down the secondary compounds. To avoid being eaten, the plants must evolve to produce new compounds, leading to a type of arms race between plants and insects. The Harlequin bug and Becker's White butterfly are examples of insects that have evolved to tolerate the secondary compounds of this plant.

STEPHEN INGRAM

Mojave Spurge

MOJAVE SPURGE
Euphorbia incisa Engelm.
Spurge Family (Euphorbiaceae)

Description: Mojave Spurge is an erect perennial with hairless, 4–16" tall stems. The ¼–¾" long leaves are sessile and ovate, and they have pointed tips. What looks like 1 flower is actually a cluster of 1 female and several male flowers. Below each flower cluster are 5 small bracts, which are fused into a bell-shaped involucre. These have crescent-shaped, yellow glands with scalloped edges.

Flowering Season: March to May

Habitat/Range: Mojave Spurge is found on slopes and rocky places above 3,000 feet in Creosote Bush scrub, Joshua Tree woodland, and Pinyon-Juniper woodland in the mountains of the eastern Mojave Desert and the White and Inyo Ranges.

Comments: Juba II, King of Maretania and son-in-law of Antony and Cleopatra, named this genus for his Greek doctor, Euphorbus. Juba was supposedly delighted by the play on words this represented, since Euphorbus meant "well-fed": The plant being named *(Euphorbia resinifera)* was fat and succulent, and his doctor was corpulent!

Catclaw, Wait-a-Minute Bush

CATCLAW, WAIT-A-MINUTE BUSH

Acacia greggii A. Gray
Pea Family (Fabaceae)

Description: This plant can grow as a 3–6' shrub or as a tree up to 20' tall. The stems bear curved spines resembling cat claws, giving it its common name and entangling the unwary. The twice-pinnate leaves have 2–3 pairs of primary leaflets and 10 pairs of ¼" long secondary leaflets. Dense, cylindrical, 1½" long spikes of tiny, light yellow flowers are produced with the leaves on short branchlets, followed by narrow, flattened, ¼–¾" long pods that are constricted between the seeds.

Flowering Season: April to June

Habitat/Range: Catclaw is common in canyons and washes, as well as on rocky slopes and flats, below 6,000 feet in Creosote Bush scrub, Joshua Tree woodland, and Pinyon-Juniper woodland. It occurs in the eastern and southern Mojave Desert and the Sonoran Desert to Texas, Sonora, Mexico, and Baja California, Mexico.

Comments: This species is named in honor of Josiah Gregg (1806–1850), an unpopular frontier trader, author, gold seeker, and part-time naturalist who sent botanical specimens to George Engelmann, an eminent botanist from St. Louis, Missouri. Gregg died young after being stranded in a redwood forest during a wet winter.

Desert Rock-Pea

DESERT ROCK-PEA
Lotus rigidus (Benth.) E. Greene
Pea Family (Fabaceae)

Description: The erect, firm, branched stems of this 1–4' tall, somewhat straggly-looking perennial are woody at the base. The stem internodes are far longer than the sparse, pinnately divided leaves with 3–5 narrow leaflets, so the plant may seem to be nearly leafless. The yellow, ½–¾" long "pea" flowers are produced on 1–2½" stalks in umbel-like clusters of 1–3; these may become orange-tinged with age. The straight, hairless 1½" fruits are erect or spreading.

Flowering Season: March to May, even in the driest years

Habitat/Range: Desert Rock-Pea is found on dry slopes and in washes below 6,000 feet in Creosote Bush scrub, Joshua Tree woodland, and Pinyon-Juniper woodland. It occurs in the southern, eastern, and northern Mojave Desert to Inyo County and in the Sonoran Desert to Baja California, Mexico.

Comments: The roots of Desert Rock-Pea form nodules that house nitrogen-fixing bacteria.

STIFF-HAIRED LOTUS
Lotus strigosus (Nutt.) E. Greene
Pea Family (Fabaceae)

Description: Stiff-Haired Lotus is a prostrate, branching, somewhat fleshy annual with slender stems and stiff, flattened hairs. The pinnately divided, ½–1" long leaves have 4–9 obovate, alternate leaflets on a flattened rachis. The stalked flower clusters bear 1–3 yellow "pea" flowers that are less than ½" long. The ½–1½" long fruit is compressed and curved near the tip, and it has sparse, flattened hairs.

Flowering Season: March to June

Habitat/Range: Stiff-Haired Lotus is common on sandy flats, alluvial slopes, roadsides, and disturbed areas below 7,500 feet from central California to Baja California, Mexico. Its range includes both the Mojave and Sonoran Deserts.

Stiff-Haired Lotus

JOHN REID

Comments: *Lotus humistratus* is similar in appearance and habitat preference to Stiff-Haired Lotus, but the hairs on this common, fleshy annual are dense and not flattened. Flowers occur singly in leaf axils and are not on stalks.

Desert Senna, Spiny Senna

DESERT SENNA, SPINY SENNA

Senna armata (S. Watson) H. Irwin & Barneby
Pea Family (Fabaceae)

Description: This 2–5' tall, rounded shrub has yellow-green, hairless, furrowed stems. The pinnately divided leaves, with 2–4 pairs of opposite, ¼" leaflets, appear only after rain, so the plant is often leafless. The leaf axis elongates into a weak, green spine after the leaflets fall. The bright yellow, 5-parted, ⅓–½" long flowers are produced in 2–6" clusters at the branch ends and in groups of 1–2 in leaf axils. The spongy, lanceolate, 1–1¾" fruits split apart to release the few seeds they contain.

Flowering Season: April and May

Habitat/Range: Desert Senna is locally common in sandy and gravelly washes and in open areas below 3,000 feet in Creosote Bush scrub in both the Mojave and Sonoran Deserts.

Comments: Desert Senna is a host plant of the Cloudless Sulfur butterfly *(Phoebis sennae)*. It is bright yellow with brownish, circular spots and wavy lines on the underwings. The adults perch on the plant with closed wings during the flowering season.

White-Stemmed Stick-Leaf

WHITE-STEMMED STICK-LEAF
Mentzelia albicaulis Hook.
Loasa Family (Loasaceae)

Description: This highly variable, 2–16" tall, white-stemmed annual has a basal rosette of leaves with narrow, pinnate, pointed lobes. The upper leaves are usually smaller and entire to lobed. The bright yellow flowers are less than ½" long, and they have 5 separate, ovate petals with pointed tips. The narrow, tapered, ½–1" long fruit is straight, with 2–3 rows of seeds in the upper half. The seed surfaces have pointed bumps and sharp angles.

Flowering Season: March to June

Habitat/Range: White-Stemmed Stick-Leaf is common in a variety of habitats below 7,000 feet in both the Mojave and Sonoran Deserts to Colorado, British Columbia, and Baja California, Mexico.

Comments: Native Americans used the seeds of this plant to make a paste similar to peanut butter. The seeds may have also been used by the Kawaiisu to make pottery, although it is not certain whether they were mixed with clay before firing or if perhaps the pots were coated with the seed oil after firing. Many small-flowered, annual *Mentzelia* species occur in the Mojave Desert, and they are difficult to identify. *Mentzelia obscura* differs from *M. albicaulis* in that the seed surfaces have rounded bumps and rounded angles, and *M. affinis* has seeds with grooved angles that are in 1 row in the upper half of the fruit.

SAND BLAZING STAR
Mentzelia involucrata S. Watson
Loasa Family (Loasaceae)

Description: This erect, sandpaper-textured, branched annual grows to 18" tall. The basal rosette leaves are toothed or lobed, while the stem leaves are lanceolate and alternate. The ½–2½" long, funnel-shaped flowers have numerous stamens, 3 stigma lobes, and red-veined, cream-colored to yellowish petals that narrow to a point at the tip. There are 4–5 white, fringed bracts with green margins that surround the flower bases, hiding the sepals. The fruit is a tapered, ½–1" long capsule.

Flowering Season: February to April

Habitat/Range: Sand Blazing Star occurs on steep, rocky banks, slopes, and washes below 4,000 feet in Creosote Bush scrub in the southern Mojave, especially in the Sheephole and Bristol Mountains and at Twentynine Palms Marine Corps Base. It is rare in the mountains of the eastern Mojave Desert but

Sand Blazing Star

STEPHEN INGRAM

has been reported from Death Valley and the Argus and Panamint Mountains in the northern Mojave Desert. It seems to be most common in the Colorado Desert through Imperial County and to Baja California, Mexico.

Comments: Like all members of the Loasa family, the foliage of this plant has minutely barbed hairs that cling to cotton clothing like Velcro.

Blazing Star

BLAZING STAR
Mentzelia laevicaulis (Hook.) Torrey & A. Gray
Loasa Family (Loasaceae)

Description: This 8–40" tall, erect perennial branches from the upper stem. The 8–10" long, pinnately lobed lower leaves form a basal rosette, while the upper leaves are alternate and toothed. The bright yellow flowers, which open in early evening, have 5 separate petals that are 1¼–3¼" long. The cylindrical, 1½"-long fruit is located beneath the sepals and contains light brown, winged seeds.

Flowering Season: June to October

Habitat/Range: Blazing Star occurs on rocky and sandy hillsides, washes, and roadsides below 9,000 feet in a variety of vegetation types throughout the Western states to British Columbia, Canada.

Comments: This genus was named for Christian Mentzel (1622–1701), a German physician and botanist.

Golden Evening Primrose

STEPHEN INGRAM

GOLDEN EVENING PRIMROSE

Camissonia brevipes (A. Gray) Raven ssp. *brevipes*

Evening Primrose Family (Onagraceae)

Description: This annual produces 1–2' tall stems from a basal rosette. The 2–6" long, pinnate leaves have conspicuous red veins on the undersurfaces. Smaller, bractlike leaves may be found up the stem. Yellow, 4-parted flowers with ¼–¾" long petals are produced in nodding clusters; these open in the morning. The cylindrical, ¾–4" long, slender fruits contain 2 rows of tiny seeds in each compartment.

Flowering Season: March to May

Habitat/Range: Golden Evening Primrose occurs in washes and on dry slopes below 5,000 feet in Creosote Bush scrub and Joshua Tree woodland in both the Mojave and Sonoran Deserts to Inyo County.

Comments: Golden Evening Primrose has been known to hybridize occasionally with Brown-Eyed Primrose, a white-petaled species with flowers that open in the evening. The hybrids resemble Brown-Eyed Primrose in size, shape, and habit, but the petals are yellowish. Golden Evening Primrose has been used to study the effects of increased temperature and carbon dioxide on the photosynthetic rates of desert plants.

STEPHEN INGRAM

Mojave Sun Cup, Field Primrose

MOJAVE SUN CUP, FIELD PRIMROSE

Camissonia campestris (E. Greene) Raven
Evening Primrose Family (Onagraceae)

Description: This branched annual has very slender and somewhat curving, hairless stems with white, peeling epidermis. The alternate, 1" long leaves are linear to narrowly elliptic with fine-toothed margins. The yellow flowers have 4 separate petals, each with 1–2 red dots at the base, and the 4 sepals are reflexed in pairs. The stigma is positioned above the anthers, and the linear fruits are ¾–1½" long.

Flowering Season: March to May

Habitat/Range: Mojave Sun Cup is found in open, sandy areas below 3,000 feet in Creosote Bush scrub in the Mojave Desert and in interior southern California to San Diego County.

Comments: This genus was named in honor of Adelbert Ludwig von Chamisso (1781–1838), a botanist on the *Rurik,* which visited California in the early 1800s. He named the California Poppy *(Eschscholzia californica)* in honor of his good friend, Dr. Johann Friedrich Gustav von Eschscholtz.

Pale Primrose

PALE PRIMROSE
Camissonia pallida (Abrams) Raven ssp. *hallii*
(Davidson) Raven
Evening Primrose Family (Onagraceae)

Description: This low annual is grayish green, due to a coating of dense, flattened hairs. The entire, narrowly elliptic, ½–1¼" long leaves are mostly found at the base of the plant, forming a loose rosette. The yellow flowers have 8 stamens of unequal lengths and 4½" long petals that often have 1–3 red dots at the base. They open during the day. The narrow, 4-sided, sessile fruit is ½–1" long and has 1 row of brownish seeds per chamber.

Flowering Season: March to May

Habitat/Range: Pale Primrose is found in washes and on flats and slopes below 6,000 feet in Creosote Bush scrub to Pinyon-Juniper woodland on the north slopes of the San Bernardino Mountains, the southern Mojave Desert, and the northern Sonoran Desert.

Comments: The similar and more widespread *Camissonia pallida* ssp. *pallida* has smaller flowers with ¼" long petals. It occurs in both the Mojave and Sonoran Deserts to Inyo County and Baja California, Mexico.

Yellow Evening Primrose, Spring Evening Primrose

DESERT GOLD-POPPY
Eschscholzia glyptosperma E. Greene
Poppy Family (Papaveraceae)

Description: This slender, leafless, 8–12" tall annual has several leafless stems that grow from a basal rosette of dissected leaves with pointed lobes. Yellow-gold flowers with 4 separate, ½–1" long petals open from erect buds, and the sepals fall off when the flowers open. The receptacles lack the spreading rims seen in the California Poppy *(Eschscholzia californica)*. The ¼" long cylindrical capsules have numerous tiny, round, pitted seeds.

Flowering Season: March to May

Habitat/Range: Desert Gold-Poppy occurs on open flats and slopes below 5,000 feet in Creosote Bush scrub and Joshua Tree woodland in the Mojave Desert and in the Sonoran Desert.

Comments: Parish's Gold-Poppy *(Eschscholzia parishii)* and Little Gold-Poppy *(E. minutiflora)* both differ from Desert Gold-Poppy by having stem leaves in addition to basal leaves. Parish's Gold-Poppy has bright green to yellow-green leaves, round seeds, and ¼–1¼" long petals.

YELLOW EVENING PRIMROSE, SPRING EVENING PRIMROSE
Oenothera primaveris A. Gray
Evening Primrose Family (Onagraceae)

Description: This stemless, glandular annual grows from a deep taproot. The entire plant has coarse hairs, sometimes with blistered bases. The ½–5" long, pinnately lobed or toothed leaves are in a strong basal rosette, and they have petioles about the same length as the blades. Each 4-parted flower has ¼–1½" long, bright yellow petals, which fade to an orange or purplish color as they age. The ovate capsules are ½–1" long, square in cross section, and have tiny, wrinkled seeds.

Flowering Season: March to May

Habitat/Range: Yellow Evening Primrose is found in dry, sandy areas below 5,000 feet in Creosote Bush scrub, Joshua Tree woodland, and Pinyon-Juniper woodland in both the Mojave and Sonoran deserts to Texas and Sonora, Mexico.

Comments: Plants with grayish green leaves and 1–1½" petals are recognized as ssp. *bufonis;* these cannot self-pollinate. Those with green leaves and ¼–1" long petals are the self-pollinated ssp. *primaveris.*

Desert Gold-Poppy

STEPHEN INGRAM

JOHN REID

Brittle Spineflower

BRITTLE SPINEFLOWER
Chorizanthe brevicornu Torrey var. *brevicornu*
Buckwheat Family (Polygonaceae)

Description: This erect, 2–20" tall annual has a forked branching pattern. The lower stems are often reddish, while upper stems, branches, and flower stalks are yellowish green. When dried, the stems become very brittle. The linear, ¾–3" long basal rosette leaves wither and crumble early, leaving the plant leafless except for the leaflike, opposite bracts at the branching points on the stems. In each branch axil, whorls of 6 fused bracts form cylindrical but somewhat ribbed involucres, each with a very tiny flower with yellowish sepals barely protruding from the top.

Flowering Season: March to June

Habitat/Range: Brittle Spineflower is found on rocky slopes and gravelly flats below 5,000 feet in Creosote Bush scrub and Joshua Tree woodland. It occurs in deserts from Mono County to Baja California, Mexico.

Comments: *Chorizanthe brevicornu* var. *spathulata* grows from 5,000 to 7,000 feet in the desert mountains. Its calyx is not as ribbed, its stems are more reddish, and its leaves are broader than those of var. *brevicornu*.

Spiny-Herb

SPINY-HERB
Chorizanthe rigida (Torrey) Torrey & A. Gray
Buckwheat Family (Polygonaceae)

Description: This erect annual grows 1–6" tall. The stalked, broadly elliptic, ¼–1¼" long leaves occur in a basal rosette as well as on the stems, and they have woolly hairs on the undersurface. As the plant matures, narrow secondary leaves develop into a dense clump of hard thorns. Scattered between thorns are 3-angled tubes (the involucres), with 3 spine-tipped teeth, housing the tiny, yellowish, 6-parted flowers. The thorny, dark brown, dried plant bodies often remain intact through the following growth season.

Flowering Season: March to May

Habitat/Range: Spiny-Herb is common on rocky and gravelly soils below 6,000 feet in Creosote Bush scrub in deserts from Baja California, Mexico, north to the Owens Valley. It seems to occupy the most barren habitats and is especially prevalent on desert pavement.

Comments: Fossilized pack rat midden data record this species in the Marble Mountains between 4,000 and 9,000 years ago and in the Eureka Valley between 1,500 and 4,000 years ago.

STEPHEN INGRAM

July Gold

JULY GOLD
Dedeckera eurekensis Rev. & J. Howell
Buckwheat Family (Polygonaceae)

Description: This wide, rounded shrub grows
to 3' tall and 6' across. The alternate, elliptic,
yellowish green leaves are around ¼–½" long
on short petioles. The branched, 1–3" flower
clusters have 2–5 separate bracts at each node.
Each ⅛" long, yellow to reddish flower has 6
sepals and 9 stamens.

Flowering Season: June to August

Habitat/Range: July Gold is found on limestone talus between 4,000 to 7,200 feet along
the west-facing slopes of the White and Inyo
Mountains to the Last Chance Mountains
and Panamint Range. It is known from only
20 occurrences.

Comments: *Dedeckera* is a monotypic genus,
described in 1976 and discovered in the western White Mountains by botanist Mary
DeDecker. She was the author of *A Flora of the
Northern Mojave Desert* and a voice for plant
conservation in the eastern Sierras and northern Mojave Desert until her death in 2000.
July Gold is listed as state rare, and it appears
to have limited reproductive capabilities.
There is no evidence of vegetative reproduction, and seedlings have not been found; only
3% of its ovules develop into seeds.

TIM THOMAS

Desert Trumpet

DESERT TRUMPET

Eriogonum inflatum Torrey & Fremont var.
inflatum
Buckwheat Family (Polygonaceae)

Description: This unique, 4–60" tall perennial has stout, bluish green stems that are
inflated at the nodes. The upper stems have a
forked branching pattern, forming a leafless
and hairless canopied flower cluster. Each
small clump of flowers has a cup-shaped
whorl of fused bracts below, called the involucre, and each involucre has 5 teeth and its own
thin stalk connecting it to the stem. Each tiny
flower has 6 yellow sepals with white hairs.

Flowering Season: March to July, and also
September to October following summer rain

Habitat/Range: Desert Trumpet is very common on gravelly flats and in sandy washes
below 6,000 feet in Creosote Bush scrub,
Joshua Tree woodland, Blackbush scrub,
Sagebrush scrub, and Pinyon-Juniper wood-

land. It is found in the Mojave and Colorado
Deserts and throughout much of the southwestern United States.

Comments: The hollow, inflated stems were
used as pipes by some groups of Native Americans. Why are the stems inflated? One
hypothesis is that a gall-forming insect trig-
gers swelling by laying eggs in the stem. However, there are inflated stems where no insect
larvae are found, so it is more likely that the
inflation occurs during normal plant development. Some botanists recognize *Eriogonum
inflatum* var. *contiguum*, an annual with non-
inflated stems from Death Valley. Other
plants elsewhere without inflation are considered to be var. *deflatum*.

Palmer Buckwheat

PALMER BUCKWHEAT
Eriogonum palmerianum Rev.
Buckwheat Family (Polygonaceae)

Description: This 2–12" tall annual has a basal rosette of stalked leaves with round, ¼–1¼" blades and hairy undersurfaces. The slender stems arise from the base and branch to form a spreading crown. Pressed against the flowering stems are tiny, sessile, bell-shaped involucres with 5 teeth at the tips. The hairless, 6-parted flowers vary in color from light yellow to white to light pink. The outer 3 petal-like segments have spreading, fan-shaped tips, while the inner 3 are narrow and erect.

Flowering Season: April to October

Habitat/Range: Palmer Buckwheat is found in sandy or gravelly soils from 2,000 to 8,000 feet in both the Mojave and Colorado Deserts to California's Mono County, Colorado, and New Mexico.

Comments: The Whisk Broom *(Eriogonum nidularium)* is very similar to Palmer Buckwheat, but the flowers are apt to be a brighter yellow, and the flowering stem tips tend to curve inward instead of spreading, forming a birdcage effect.

Golden Carpet

GOLDEN CARPET
Gilmania luteola (Cov.) Cov.
Buckwheat Family (Polygonaceae)

Description: This low, branched annual forms loose, horizontal mats up to 8" in diameter. The round, hairless, ¼" leaf blades are on stalks up to ¾" long, in a rosette at the base of the plant. There are also clusters of narrow, leaflike, bristle-tipped bracts at branching points along the stem where the flower stalks arise. Several tiny, yellow, 6-lobed flowers are produced in each 5-parted involucre.

Flowering Season: March to April

Habitat/Range: Golden Carpet is known from only 5 occurrences on barren alkali slopes in Death Valley National Park, especially at Artist's Pallet and the surrounding hills.

Comments: This species is in the California Native Plant Society's *Inventory of Rare and Endangered Vascular Plants of California*. Its entire range is within Death Valley National Park. It is not threatened at this time.

Desert Portulaca

DESERT PORTULACA
Portulaca halimoides L.
Purslane Family (Portulacaceae)

Description: This ½–2½" tall annual has succulent, linear, ⅛–½" leaves, with ¼" long hairs in the leaf axils. The tiny flowers are produced in clusters of 2–10 at the ends of stems. Each flower has 2 sepals, 4–15 stamens, and 4–6 yellow petals that age to a pink or reddish color. The capsule opens by a lid to release numerous minute, black seeds.

Flowering Season: September, following summer rain

Habitat/Range: This plant grows in sandy soil and washes from 3,000 to 4,200 feet in Joshua Tree woodland in the Little San Bernardino Mountains and the mountains of the eastern Mojave Desert to Texas and northern Mexico.

Comments: Desert Portulaca is on the California Native Plant Society's watch list. It is rare and fairly endangered in California but is more common elsewhere.

Blackbush

BLACKBUSH
Coleogyne ramosissima Torrey
Rose Family (Rosaceae)

Description: Blackbush is a highly branched, somewhat spiny shrub that grows from 1–6' tall. Its gray bark turns black as it ages or when it gets wet, giving the plant its common name. The linear, entire, ¼–½" long leaves are in opposite clusters along the stems. The yellow flowers, which occur singly on the tips of branches, are unusual for the Rose Family in that they have 4 sepals instead of 5, and there are no petals. The small crescent-shaped, brown, hairless fruits are often found clinging to the shrub throughout the year.

Flowering Season: April to June

Habitat/Range: Blackbush occurs on dry slopes below 5,000 feet in Creosote Bush scrub, Joshua Tree woodland and Pinyon-Juniper woodland. It is the dominant shrub of Blackbush scrub vegetation, forming dense stands on north-facing slopes of the mountains of the eastern Mojave and on some of the desert slopes of the San Bernardino Mountains. Although it is found in the Sonoran Desert, it is much more common in the Mojave Desert to Colorado.

Comments: This is an important winter browse species for Mule deer and Bighorn sheep. Blackbush often grows on soil with a caliche layer, and it has a shallow root system; few of its roots can penetrate the caliche. Most of its leaves are shed during the hot summer months, but some leaves are usually retained on branch ends. A recent study showed that Blackbush is primarily wind pollinated, a strategy that should work well for a species that occurs in large dense stands. However, there are very few seedlings; they are usually killed during the summer heat and drought. Most germination appears to be from rodent seed caches. The dense stands of these highly resinous, tinderlike shrubs carry fire easily, but since they do not resprout or seed readily, they are often replaced by Turpentine Broom *(Thamnosma montana),* Bitterbrush *(Purshia glandulosa),* Desert Almond *(Prunus fasciculata),* or other species. One study showed that revegetation of Blackbush was aided by the addition of a fungus inoculant (arbuscular mycorrhizae).

Twining Snapdragon

TWINING SNAPDRAGON
Antirrhinum filipes A. Gray
Figwort Family (Scrophulariaceae)

Description: This hairless annual has very slender, twining stems with opposite, narrow, 1–2" long leaves. The bright yellow, 2-lipped, ½" long flowers with dark red spots on the lower lip are produced on 1–4" long, twisted stalks. The thin walls of the 2-chambered fruits rupture to release numerous seeds with 4–6 thick, parallel ridges.

Flowering Season: March to May

Habitat/Range: Twining Snapdragon grows through and over small shrubs in sandy soil below 5,000 feet in Creosote Bush scrub and Joshua Tree woodland in desert areas of southern California to Inyo County, Nevada, and Utah.

Comments: The plant in this photo is twining around the spines of a Barrel Cactus.

Snapdragon Penstemon, Yellow Keckiella

SNAPDRAGON PENSTEMON, YELLOW KECKIELLA

Keckiella antirrhinoides (Benth.) Straw var.
microphylla (A. Gray) N. Holmgren
Figwort Family (Scrophulariaceae)

Description: This erect, 2–8' tall shrub has spreading branches. The grayish green, inversely lanceolate, ¼–¾" long leaves are opposite and often in bundles, due to the development of the axillary buds. The yellow flowers are produced in loose, branched clusters. Each 2-lipped, ½–1" long flower has an inflated throat and a densely hairy, protruding staminode. The dry, ovate, 2-chambered fruits cling to the plant for a long time after splitting to release the seeds.

Flowering Season: April to June

Habitat/Range: Snapdragon Penstemon occurs in rocky soils below 5,000 feet in Joshua Tree woodland and Pinyon-Juniper woodland in the southern and eastern Mojave Desert and the western Sonoran Desert to San Francisco and Baja California, Mexico.

Comments: Snapdragon Penstemon is the food plant for the Desert Mountain Checkerspot butterfly *(Euphydryas chalcedona kingstonensis)*. These can be seen patrolling canyons in the eastern Mojave Desert in April and sometimes after summer rain. Rothrock's Keckiella *(Keckiella rothrockii)* is a shorter shrub (to 2' tall) with ¼–½" flowers that occurs in the mountains of the northern and eastern Mojave Desert.

Rock Lady

STEPHEN INGRAM

ROCK LADY

Maurandya petrophila Cov. & C. Morton
Figwort Family (Scrophulariaceae)

Description: The low, tufted perennial has slender, branched, hanging stems from a woody base. The leaves are rounded and palmately veined, with long, bristly teeth along the lobed margins. The 2-lipped, yellow, 1" long flowers are produced singly in leaf axils. The 4 stamens have 2 rows of tack-shaped glands on the filaments. The corolla tube is inflated at the base, and the corolla floor has 2 longitudinal folds. The seeds empty from holes at the tips of the ovate, 1-chambered fruit.

Flowering Season: April to June

Habitat/Range: Rock Lady is known from only 5 occurrences in limestone crevices between 3,500 and 5,800 feet in Creosote Bush scrub in Titus and Fall Canyons in Death Valley National Park.

Comments: Rock Lady is listed as state rare. The similar Violet Twining Snapdragon *(Maurandya antirrhiniflora)* has purple flowers and triangular leaves with basal lobes that turn outward. It is found on limestone at Kelso and the Providence Mountains to Texas and Oaxaca, Mexico.

LESSER MOHAVEA
Mohavea breviflora Cov.
Figwort Family (Scrophulariaceae)

Description: This erect, glandular, 2–8" tall annual has alternate, ovate leaves on short stalks. The deep yellow flowers have upper and lower flaring, fan-shaped lips and maroon spots on the swollen bases of the lower lip. The corolla encloses 2 fertile stamens, each with 1 anther sac, and 2 sterile staminodes. The dry, ovate fruits are ¼–½" long.

Flowering Season: March to April

Habitat/Range: Lesser Mohavea occurs on sandy and gravelly hillsides and washes below 2,500 feet in Creosote Bush scrub. It is found in the Mojave Desert east of Daggett and the Ord Mountains to the Colorado Desert and Baja California, Mexico.

Lesser Mohavea

Comments: These flowers look much like snapdragons (genus *Antirrhinum*), to which they are closely related. However, snapdragons have 4 stamens, each with 2 anther sacs.

Thick-Leaved Ground-Cherry

THICK-LEAVED GROUND-CHERRY
Physalis crassifolia Benth.
Nightshade Family (Solanaceae)

Description: Thick-Leaved Ground-Cherry is a sticky 8–20" tall perennial with ridged stems that are often branched in a zigzag pattern. The alternate, ovate, ½–1¼" long leaf blades have entire or wavy margins, and they are on petioles equally as long. The yellow, 5-parted, ½–¾" widely bell-shaped flowers are produced singly in leaf axils. The calyx dries and expands to nearly 1" long, enclosing the green, fleshy berry as it develops.

Flowering Season: March to May

Habitat/Range: This species is found in sandy, gravelly, and rocky areas below 4,000 feet in Creosote Bush scrub in both the Mojave and Sonoran Deserts to Nevada, Arizona, and New Mexico.

Comments: Other species of this genus are cultivated as ornamentals, such as the Chinese Lantern *(Physalis alkekengi),* and some are edible, such as Tomatillo *(Physalis philadelphica).*

Creosote Bush

CREOSOTE BUSH
Larrea tridentata DC. (Cov.)
Caltrop Family (Zygophyllaceae)

Description: This erect, 2–7' tall evergreen shrub has spreading, brittle, gray branches, which often have gummy, black, horizontal bands. The opposite, dark green, sticky leaves have 2 fused triangular leaflets, giving the appearance of a simple leaf with a butterfly shape. The 5-parted, ½–¾" flowers with yellow clawed petals are produced singly in leaf axils, followed by spherical, nearly ¼" fruits that are covered with white or rust-colored hairs.

Flowering Season: November to May

Habitat/Range: Creosote Bush is the dominant canopy shrub species across the Mojave, Sonoran, and Chihuahuan Deserts. It takes on slightly different shapes in the different deserts. In the Chihuahuan Desert the spreading branches form an inverted V-shape, while in the Mojave the Creosote Bush is very rounded, and the Sonoran Desert plants are intermediate. The chromosome number also increases from south to north; the Mojave Desert creosotes have 6 sets of chromosomes, while the Chihuahuan plants have 2 sets, and Sonoran plants have 4 sets.

Comments: Why are Creosote Bushes spaced so evenly apart? Recent research shows that the roots secrete a substance into the soil that keeps the roots of other adjacent Creosote Bushes and White Bur-Sage *(Ambrosia dumosa)* from elongating. This effect is removed when the substance is absorbed from the soil with an activated charcoal filter. You may find the tapered cases of Creosote Bagworm moth *(Thyridopteryx meadi)* stuck to branches. Bits of green leaves are attached while the larva feeds, but these turn yellow to brown after the adult moths leave the cases by June. You may also see the leafy balls of tissue the plant produces when the Creosote Leafy Gall midge deposits its eggs in the branchlets. The Lac Scale insect *(Tachardiella larrea)* is responsible for the common gummy, black bands on Creosote Bush stems. This substance was investigated as a possible source of shellac for the manufacture of varnish when the Japanese invasion of Burma in World War II cut off the supply, but it was found to be economically unfeasible.

Puncture Vine, Goathead

PUNCTURE VINE, GOATHEAD
Tribulus terrestris L.
Caltrop Family (Zygophyllaceae)

Description: The weak, prostrate, branched stems of this annual spread and trail to form mats up to 5' or more across. The opposite, hairy leaves are pinnately divided, with 6–12 ovate, ¼–½" long leaflets and a pair of leaflike stipules at the base. The yellow, 5-parted, ¼–½" wide flowers are produced singly in leaf axils. The fruit has 5 sections, which split apart into hard, 2–4-seeded, angular structures with sharp spines; these facilitate its dispersal by animals and vehicles.

Flowering Season: April to October

Habitat/Range: Puncture Vine is common in vacant lots, roadsides, and almost any disturbed area below 5,000 feet in most of the United States and Mexico, including the deserts. It is a native of the Mediterranean region.

Comments: Since its introduction around 1900, this pestiferous weed has spread extremely rapidly. The United States Department of Agriculture attempted to control it with herbicides for over 50 years, especially since it caused a serious disorder in livestock when they consumed it. Finally, in the early 1960s, two species of weevils were introduced from India, which have substantially reduced its populations.

Green and Brown Flowers

Silver Cholla

Many green and brown flowers do not attract animal pollinators but instead rely on wind or water to transfer pollen. Since the pollen grains are scattered by chance, the plants often produce massive amounts to increase the chances of pollen landing on a receptive stigma. The stigma surfaces are often feathery or very sticky, to increase the chances of catching the pollen; this is especially seen in the grasses.

Honey-Sweet

HONEY-SWEET
Tidestromia oblongifolia (S. Watson) Standley
Pigweed Family (Amaranthaceae)

Description: This rounded, 6–36" tall perennial has grayish white, ovate, ½–1¼" long leaves with wedge-shaped bases and a distinctive vein pattern. The tiny, inconspicuous flowers are in small clusters in leaf axils and are enclosed by bractlike leaves.

Flowering Season: April to December

Habitat/Range: Honey-Sweet is common in washes and on rocky hillsides in the eastern Mojave Desert to the Sonoran Desert, Texas, and northern Baja California, Mexico.

Comments: Honey-Sweet, a C_4 plant, has one of the highest rates of photosynthesis ever recorded. A related species, *Tidestromia lanuginosa,* is found in the mountains of the eastern Mojave to South Dakota and Mexico. It is an annual with leaves that are green on the upper surface. This genus was named for Ivar Tidestrom, a Swedish emigrant who earned a Ph.D. in botany and then worked for the United States Forest Service, the Smithsonian Institute, and the Bureau of Plant Industry. He authored *Flora of Utah and Nevada* in 1925.

Western Sand-Bur, Annual Bur-Sage

WESTERN SAND-BUR, ANNUAL BUR-SAGE

Ambrosia acanthicarpa Hook.
Sunflower Family (Asteraceae)

Description: This 1–3' tall, bristly annual has erect, slender stems and pinnately divided, 3" long leaves with winged petioles. The numerous, ¼" male flower heads, which are borne in clusters at the stem tips, have black lines along the midveins of the phyllary lobes. The single-flowered female flower heads are positioned below the male flowers. The fruits develop into spiny burs that readily cling to clothing.

Flowering Season: August to November

Habitat/Range: This plant is very common in loose or sandy soil on disturbed sites and may frequently be seen along roadsides throughout the desert at elevations below 7,000 feet. It has a wide range through many Western states.

Comments: Although it is a native, Western Sand-Bur has a weedy habit. This is one of the wind-pollinated ragweeds, all of which produce pollen in profuse quantities, triggering hay fever and allergy problems in humans. The species name literally means "spiny fruit," referring to the bothersome burs that hitchhike in shoes and socks.

White Bur-Sage, Burrobush

WHITE BUR-SAGE, BURROBUSH
Ambrosia dumosa (A. Gray) Payne
Sunflower Family (Asteraceae)

Description: This 8–36" tall shrub is drought-deciduous, losing its leaves when water is unavailable. The crowded, ¼–1½" long, pinnately divided leaves have white, woolly hairs. Separate male and female flowers occur on the same plant. The ¼" male flower heads are oriented downward so that pollen will dust the 2-flowered female heads below. Since the plants are wind-pollinated, massive quantities of pollen are produced. The fruit is a ¼" spherical bur with 30–40 flattened spines.

Flowering Season: March to June, and September to November following summer rain

Habitat/Range: White Bur-Sage is found in Creosote Bush scrub below 5,000 feet throughout the Mojave and Sonoran Deserts to northwestern Mexico.

Comments: The roots secrete a compound that inhibits the root growth of neighboring White Bur-Sage and Creosote Bushes, as shown by experiments using activated carbon to remove root secretions from soil. There is also evidence that White Bur-Sage roots can inhibit those of neighboring White Bur-Sage by root-to-root contact. These mechanisms contribute to the regular spacing pattern of shrubs often seen in Creosote Bush scrub. White Bur-Sage is often a codominant with Creosote Bush but is occasionally found without Creosote in areas where desert pavement or an impermeable, subsurface soil layer is found. Its shallow root system allows it to survive in these areas where the roots of Creosote Bush cannot penetrate deep enough to get adequate water. Repeat photography methods have documented that individual White Bur-Sage plants often live over 75 years. Fossilized pack rat midden data show that this species spread across the Mojave Desert between 9,000 and 5,000 years ago.

Big Sagebrush, Great Basin Sagebrush

BIG SAGEBRUSH, GREAT BASIN SAGEBRUSH
Artemisia tridentata Nutt.
Sunflower Family (Asteraceae)

Description: This aromatic, 3–9' tall, evergreen shrub has a short, thick trunk with hairy, gray bark. The narrow, wedge-shaped, ½–1½" long leaves have 3 lobes at the tip. Numerous, ¹⁄₁₀" flower heads with hairy phyllaries are produced in spreading, branched, 12" long clusters, followed by tiny, glandular or hairy fruits.

Flowering Season: August to October

Habitat/Range: Big Sagebrush occurs in dry sandy soils and desert washes from 1,000 to 10,000 feet in mountains in the western, northern, and eastern Mojave Desert and on north-facing slopes of the Transverse Ranges. Its range extends throughout the Western states.

Comments: Woolly bladder galls made by the Sagebrush Gall midge *(Asplondylia artemisiae)* are often quite obvious on the stems and leaves. Big Sagebrush had many uses in Native American culture. Leaves were chewed or made into a tea for colds, headaches, stomachaches, and to get rid of worms. The smoke from burning branches was used to disinfect the air at funerals, ceremonials, and sickbeds, and the wood was used for fuel and textiles. Seeds were eaten only in time of great need, since they are distasteful. This genus is named for the Greek goddess, Artemis, who was supposedly cured by a related species.

Bugseed

STEPHEN INGRAM

BUGSEED
Dicoria canescens A. Gray
Sunflower Family (Asteraceae)

Description: The stiff, white hairs of this 1–3' tall, widely branching annual give it a rough texture. The 1–2" triangular, toothed, 3-veined lower leaves are opposite, and the smaller, round, entire upper leaves are alternate. The nodding flower heads have several tiny male flowers with greenish corollas and 1–2 female flowers without corollas. The phyllaries are less than ¼" long, and they bend backward as they age. Two flattened, ¼" long akenes with toothed wings develop in each head.

Flowering Season: September to January

Habitat/Range: Bugseed is found in open areas on very sandy soils below 4,000 feet in Creosote Bush scrub and Joshua Tree woodlands in the Mojave Desert. It also occurs from the Colorado Desert to Sonora, Mexico.

Comments: The akenes resemble bugs, hence the common name Bugseed. The genus name literally means "two bugs" in Greek.

HERBA IMPIA, COTTONROSE
Filago californica Nutt.
Sunflower Family (Asteraceae)

Description: This hairy, erect, 2–12" tall annual has alternate, sessile, ¼–¾" long leaves. The upper leaves barely exceed the flower heads. Each ⅛" flower head has several tiny, inconspicuous, reddish purple disk flowers, and the 8–10 outer female flowers are partially enclosed by boat-shaped, woolly bracts. Each tiny, flattened akene has a ring of pappus bristles that falls off as a unit.

Flowering Season: March to June

Habitat/Range: Herba Impia is found in open Creosote Bush scrub and Joshua Tree woodland in the Mojave Desert. It also occurs throughout southern California to Texas and northern Mexico.

Comments: The genus name means "filament," referring to the hairs. Other species of

Herba Impia, Cottonrose

Filago can be found in the Mojave Desert, including *F. arizonica*, which differs from *F. californica* in that the upper leaves are much longer than the heads. *F. depressa* differs from *F. californica* in that the plants are spreading and not erect.

Hecastocleis

HECASTOCLEIS
Hecastocleis shockleyi Gray
Sunflower Family (Asteraceae)

Description: This unusual, rounded, 16–24" tall shrub is mostly hairless, except for tufts of hairs in the leaf axils. The alternate, ½–1¼" long linear leaves have spines at the tips and along the margins. The flowers are produced singly within each narrow head, but several heads together are also surrounded by leathery, spiny, ovate bracts that are nearly 1" long. The flower buds are reddish, but they turn greenish white after they open.

Flowering Season: May to June

Habitat/Range: This species is found in dry, rocky washes and on slopes from 4,000 to 7,000 feet in Creosote Bush scrub and Shadscale scrub in mountains of the northern Mojave Desert, especially in Death Valley National Park.

Comments: Hecastocleis was considered but rejected for listing by the California Native Plant Society, because it has since been found to be more common than previously known.

Cheesebush, Winged Ragweed

CHEESEBUSH, WINGED RAGWEED
Hymenoclea salsola A. Gray
Sunflower Family (Asteraceae)

Description: This yellowish green, resinous, scraggly shrub is usually 2–3½' tall. The linear, ¾–2" long leaves are mostly entire, but the lowest leaves may have a few, narrow, pinnate lobes. Crushed leaves and stem tips yield a foul, cheesy odor. Numerous, small, cuplike male flower heads are in spikelike clusters above the female heads, which are in leaf axils. The female heads have single flowers and winged, papery bracts that spread open as the ¼" long, spindle-shaped fruits develop.

Flowering Season: March to June

Habitat/Range: Cheesebush is very common on sandy flats, washes, and disturbed sites in Creosote Bush scrub, Shadscale scrub, Joshua Tree woodland, and Pinyon-Juniper woodland from Inyo County to northwestern Mexico.

Comments: The highest rates of photosynthesis take place in April, when Cheesebush plants in the Mojave Desert are fully leafed out. The stems also contribute significantly to photosynthesis, but by the end of summer the net photosynthesis rate drops to nearly zero, when they lose about half of their leaves and some of their twigs. Although native, this species has many weedy characteristics, including a high rate of seed production, a short life span, and the ability to rapidly establish in disturbed areas and resprout after burning. It may prove to be useful in revegetation efforts. Hybrids between Cheesebush and White Bur-Sage *(Ambrosia dumosa)* have been documented.

Silver Cholla

SILVER CHOLLA
Opuntia echinocarpa Engelm. & J. Bigelow
Cactus Family (Cactaceae)

Description: This 2–4' tall cactus has a short trunk below, branching above into a dense crown. The detachable, cylindrical joints have conspicuous bumps with 3–10, ¾–1¼" long spines. Each spine is enclosed in a silvery gray, papery sheath, which gives the plant a silver cast and its common name. The greenish yellow flowers with red-tinged outer segments are produced on branch tips, followed by ¾" long, dry, angular, spiny and malodorous fruits with white seeds. Very few of the fruits reach maturity, and immature fruits are often found in profusion, littering the ground beneath the plant.

Flowering Season: April to May

Habitat/Range: Silver Cholla is common in dry washes and flats below 6,000 feet in Creosote Bush scrub, Joshua Tree woodland, and Pinyon-Juniper woodland in deserts from Mono County to Baja California, Mexico.

Comments: Individuals of this same species may have spines with straw-colored sheaths, giving these plants a golden cast and the common name of Golden Cholla.

STEPHEN INGRAM

Iodine Bush

IODINE BUSH
Allenrolfea occidentalis (S. Watson) Kuntze
Goosefoot Family (Chenopodiaceae)

Description: This unusual, dark green shrub with succulent, jointed stems and alternate branches is usually less than 2' tall. The triangular, minute, scalelike leaves extend down the stem below their attachment points. The tiny flowers are arranged in a spiral pattern in the axils of bracts on the upper the fleshy stem tips, forming ¼–1" spikes.

Flowering Season: June to August

Habitat/Range: Iodine Bush is found at alkali seeps and edges of alkali dry lakes in very salty soils in the Great Basin, Mojave, and Sonoran Deserts to Oregon and northern Mexico.

Comments: Iodine Bush tolerates very salty conditions by storing salt in its stem tissues and absorbing water to dilute the salt. It can live in soil with over 6% salt, which is very high compared to the 2% limit of most salt-tolerant species. By the end of the summer, the terminal joints of stems have such a high salt concentration that they turn pink and fall off. This genus was named for Robert Allen Rolfe (1855–1921), who wrote the first book on orchid taxonomy.

Four-Wing Saltbush

FOUR-WING SALTBUSH
Atriplex canescens (Pursh) Nutt. ssp. *canescens*
Goosefoot Family (Chenopodiaceae)

Description: This densely branched, grayish green, 3–5' tall shrub has sessile, narrow, linear, ½–2" long leaves with inrolled margins. Like most saltbushes, the leaves have a scaly or mealy texture, and the male and female flowers are produced on separate plants. Two flattened, ½" long bracts enclose the female flowers, and there is a pair of longitudinal wings that emerge from the center of each bract. As the fruit develops, the bract margins and wings create a dry, 4-winged, stalked fruit.

Flowering Season: June through August

Habitat/Range: Four-Wing Saltbush inhabits washes and flats below 7,000 feet in alkali sinks, Creosote Bush scrub, and Pinyon-Juniper woodland. It is widely distributed throughout the Mojave Desert to Washington, South Dakota, Kansas, and Mexico.

Comments: The Shoshone and Paiute made arrows out of the wood of this species, and leaves were rubbed on sores to aid in healing. Near the Mojave River and at a few other scattered locations in California, Four-Wing Saltbush is a food plant for the rare San Emigdio Blue butterfly *(Plebejus emigdionis)*. The green or tan pupae attach to the foliage, and the adult butterflies may be found around the plant in the spring.

Shadscale

SHADSCALE
Atriplex confertifolia (Torrey & Fremont) S. Watson
Goosefoot Family (Chenopodiaceae)

Description: This spiny, rounded, 1–3' tall shrub has thick, scaly branchlets. The crowded, alternate, ½–¾" long, rounded leaves have entire margins and a grayish, scaly appearance. Male and female flowers are produced on separate plants. Female flowers usually occur singly in leaf axils, surrounded by 2 sessile, rounded, ¼–½" long convex bracts with entire margins. The tiny male flowers are produced in short spikes on the upper leaf axils.

Flowering Season: April to July

Habitat/Range: Shadscale is found in alkaline flats, sinks, and slopes below 7,000 feet in Shadscale scrub, Creosote Bush scrub, and Joshua Tree woodland in the Mojave Desert to eastern Oregon, North Dakota, and northern Mexico.

Comments: The Southern Paiute sometimes ate Shadscale seeds, and young leaves were crushed and applied to sores. This photo shows a male plant.

Desert Holly

STEPHEN INGRAM

DESERT HOLLY

Atriplex hymenelytra (Torrey) S. Watson
Goosefoot Family (Chenopodiaceae)

Description: The branchlets of this compact, rounded, 8–48" tall shrub have a white, scaly texture. The alternate, toothed, ½–1½" wide leaves have a silvery appearance from salts that collect and crystallize in surface hairs. Male and female flowers occur on separate plants. Female flowers are in short spikes, and each flower is surrounded by 2 round, compressed, ¼–½" bracts. The inconspicuous male flowers are produced in short, leafy clusters.

Flowering Season: January to April

Habitat/Range: Desert Holly is found in alkaline places, especially washes, in Creosote Bush scrub in the Mojave and Sonoran Deserts to Baja California, Mexico.

Comments: Desert Holly is the most drought-tolerant saltbush in North America.

It can tolerate hot temperatures and drought better than Creosote Bush, and it remains active throughout most of the year in the hottest, driest sites in Death Valley. The steep leaf angle and the highly reflective, silvery leaf color reduce the amount of solar radiation that can add to heat load. However, studies have shown that elevated ozone levels negatively affect Desert Holly, decreasing photosynthesis rates and possibly reducing its efficiency of water use. When cuttings of Desert Holly were transplanted to coastal southern California, the male and female flowers occurred on the same plant instead of separate plants, and they flowered in the summer months rather than in winter. The photograph illustrates a male plant.

Bractscale

BRACTSCALE

Atriplex serenana Nelson var. *serenana*
Goosefoot Family (Chenopodiaceae)

Description: This annual, semi-erect saltbush forms 1–3' high mats. The oblong, sessile, ½–1½" long leaves have green upper and lower surfaces, and they lack the scaly texture of most other saltbush species. Male and female flowers are in separate clusters on the same plant. The 2 bracts below each female flower are wedge shaped, fused to above the middle, and have prominent teeth at the top.

Flowering Season: May to October

Habitat/Range: Bractscale is occasionally found in alkali flats, seeps, and sinks in the Mojave and Sonoran Deserts. It is more common in low coastal and inland areas of California to Baja California, Mexico.

Comments: The conspicuous and somewhat unpleasant fishy odor may aid in identification of this species.

HOP-SAGE

Grayia spinosa (Hook.) Moq.
Goosefoot Family (Chenopodiaceae)

Description: This deciduous, 1–3' tall shrub has gray striped bark with twigs that harden into spines. The alternate, oblong, mealy-textured leaves are ½–1½" long, somewhat fleshy, and often gray at the tip. Male and female flowers are produced in dense clusters on separate plants, the female on branch tips and the male in leaf axils and on branch tips. Each female flower is surrounded by 2 round, green ¼–½" bracts, which turn red and very showy with age.

Flowering Season: March to June

Habitat/Range: Hop-Sage is common in Creosote Bush scrub, Joshua Tree woodland, Shadscale scrub, and Pinyon-Juniper woodland in the Mojave Desert to eastern Washington and Wyoming.

Hop-Sage

Comments: This genus was named in honor of Asa Gray (1810–1888), the leading American botanist of his day, who established the Gray Herbarium at Harvard.

Winter Fat

WINTER FAT
Krascheninnikovia lanata (Pursh) A. D. J.
Meeuse & Smit
Goosefoot Family (Chenopodiaceae)

Description: Winter Fat is a 1–2½' high shrub with slender, entire, ½–2" long leaves in alternating bundles along erect stems. The plant is covered with white or rust-colored, stellate hairs with occasional, interspersed, longer, simple hairs. Numerous tiny male flowers with protruding stamens occur in spikelike clusters at the tops of stems, and the ¼" long female flowers are in clusters in leaf axils below. Bracts under both female and male flowers have dense tufts of hair, giving the upper half of the plant a woolly appearance.

Flowering Season: April to August

Habitat/Range: Winter Fat is common on rocky and gravelly flats above 2,000 feet in Creosote Bush scrub, Joshua Tree woodland, Blackbush scrub, Shadscale scrub, and Pinyon-Juniper woodland in the Mojave Desert. It is widespread in the Western states to the Rocky Mountains.

Comments: Since Winter Fat is evergreen, wildlife and livestock are able to derive much nutrition from it during winter months, hence the common name. This genus was named for Stephan P. Krascheninnikov (1713–1755), a Russian botanist.

Arrow-Scale

ARROW-SCALE
Atriplex phyllostegia (Torry) S. Watson
Goosefoot family (Chenopodiaceae)

Description: This fleshy, branched, 4–16" tall annual has alternate, ½–1¾" long leaves that are triangular with outward-projecting lobes at the base, and they are green on both the upper and lower surfaces. Tiny, sessile, green flowers are produced in dense clusters at branch tips and in upper leaf axils.

Flowering Season: April to August

Habitat/Range: Arrow-Scale is found in alkaline soils and sinks below 5,000 feet in Creosote Bush scrub, Shadscale scrub, and Sagebrush scrub in the Mojave Desert to the eastern Sierra Nevada. Its range extends to the San Joaquin Valley, Oregon, and Utah.

Comments: The species may be confused with the very similar Poverty Weed *(Monolepis nuttalliana)*, which has flowers in axillary but not terminal clusters. The leaves tend to be narrower and not as triangular or fleshy as those of Arrow-Scale.

Amargosa Nitrophila

TIM THOMAS

AMARGOSA NITROPHILA
Nitrophila mohavensis Munz & Roos
Goosefoot Family (Chenopodiaceae)

Description: This 1–4" tall perennial has erect or spreading stems with paired branches. The crowded, opposite, ovate leaves are less than ¼" long. The tiny flowers are produced in leaf axils, surrounded by 2 unequal bracts.

Flowering Season: May to October

Habitat/Range: This species is known from only a few muddy sites with alkaline soil near Carson Slough in the northern Mojave Desert along the Nevada border.

Comments: Amargosa Nitrophila is listed as federally endangered, state endangered in California, and critically endangered in Nevada, due to habitat degradation and water diversion. Western Nitrophila *(Nitrophila occidentalis)*, a taller relative, is distinguished by having longer, linear leaves with long spaces between the nodes. It occupies moist soil below 7,000 feet in deserts and other areas in California to Nevada and Oregon.

Tumbleweed, Russian Thistle

TUMBLEWEED, RUSSIAN THISTLE

Salsola tragus L.
Goosefoot Family (Chenopodiaceae)

Description: This 1–3' tall annual becomes very round and bushlike with age. The young leaves are soft, slender, and 1–2" long. As the plant matures, the leaves become rigid, triangular, short, and scalelike, each with a sharp spine at the tip, and the branchlets acquire short, stiff hairs. The small, sessile, greenish flowers are produced in groups of 3 in the leaf axils. As the fruit develops, the membranous, pink-veined calyx expands to around ¼" wide. When the fruits are mature, the plant dries out and detaches from the roots near soil level. Its round shape facilitates rolling in the wind, which aids in seed dispersal.

Flowering Season: July to October

Habitat/Range: Russian Thistle is common and widely distributed in open and disturbed areas below 8,000 feet in the Mojave Desert and throughout western North America.

Comments: The genus name means "salty" in Latin, referring to the ability of this plant to tolerate salty soils. *Salsola tragus* is a native of Eurasia, as is another closely related species, *Salsola paulsenii*. *S. paulsenii* differs from *S. tragus* in that it has yellowish green young leaves up to 1" long and bumpy branchlets rather than stiff-hairy branchlets.

Greasewood

GREASEWOOD
Sarcobatus vermiculatus (Hook.) Torrey
Goosefoot Family (Chenopodiaceae)

Description: This rounded, spiny 3–6' tall shrub has linear, sessile, somewhat fleshy ¼–1" long leaves and yellowish to light gray stems. Male and female flowers are usually on separate plants. The male flowers consist of 2–3 stamens with rounded, shieldlike scales that are spirally arranged in 1" terminal spikes, while the tiny female flowers are in leaf axils. As the fruit develops, the calyx expands to form a ¼" wide wing.

Flowering Season: May to August

Habitat/Range: Greasewood is found in alkali soils from 3,000 to 7,000 feet in the far northern Mojave Desert as at Death Valley, the Nevada Test Site, Carson Slough, and Sarcobatus Flat in Nye County, Nevada. A small colony occurs at Rabbit Spring near Lucerne Valley, California, widely separated from the nearest neighboring population. Greasewood is much more common throughout the Great Basin Desert.

Comments: All of the plants at Rabbit Spring appear to be male. It is likely that this is a relict population from the last full glacial period, when the entire Mojave Desert was wetter and cooler.

Bush Seepweed, Ink-Blite

BUSH SEEPWEED, INK-BLITE

Suaeda moquinii (Torrey) E. Greene
Goosefoot Family (Chenopodiaceae)

Description: This muddy-looking, sparsely leafy, 1–4' tall subshrub has brown older stems and shiny, yellow-brown young stems. The dark green, linear, lower leaves are up to 1½" long, while upper leaves are shorter, lighter green, and succulent. Clusters of tiny, greenish, 5-parted flowers are produced on thin stems near the top of the plant. The flowers may have male or female parts or both. The stems of the flower cluster turn a dark reddish brown color when dried.

Flowering Season: May to September

Habitat/Range: Bush Seepweed occurs in alkaline soils below 5,000 feet in Creosote Bush scrub and alkali sink communities in the Mojave, Colorado, and Great Basin Deserts to Canada, Texas, and Mexico.

Comments: This species is salt tolerant and will grow closer to the edge of salty playas than Creosote Bush, but not as close as the halophytic Iodine Bush. Salts collect in the leaves during the growing season and are shed when the leaves fall off. This progressively increases the saltiness of the soil, eventually limiting the establishment of other seedlings and making the area uninhabitable by all but the most salt-tolerant species. Native Americans extracted a black dye from the stems that was used in basketry, giving the plant the common name of Ink-Blite.

California Croton

STEPHEN INGRAM

CALIFORNIA CROTON
Croton californicus Muell.
Spurge Family (Euphorbiaceae)

Description: This 1–3' tall, light olive green subshrub is covered with short, stellate hairs. The alternate, entire, elliptic leaves are 1–2" long on ½–1½" stalks. Male and female flowers usually occur on separate plants, but see comments below. The deciduous male flowers consist of around 10–15 stamens in a small, hairy, cuplike calyx. The female flowers have 5 sepals and no petals. The green, 3-lobed fruit is around ¼" long with 3 persistent styles that are split twice.

Flowering Season: March to October

Habitat/Range: California Croton is found in sandy soil at low elevations in the Mojave Desert, as at Kelso Dunes where it forms hummocks and stabilizes soil. It is widespread throughout southern California to Baja California, Mexico.

Comments: Most California Croton plants are usually either male or female, but some populations have up to 18% of the plants with both male and female flowers. A plant can also change gender within or between flowering seasons.

Annual Stillingia

ANNUAL STILLINGIA
Stillingia spinulosa S. Watson
Spurge Family (Euphorbiaceae)

Description: This 2–18" tall, densely clumped, milky-sapped plant has alternate, spiny-toothed, 1" long leaves with 3 veins emerging from the base. The tiny male flowers with 2 stamens each are produced in ¼–½" long spikes in leaf axils, with 1–2 female flowers below. The 3-lobed fruit has 3 styles and is less than ¼" long.

Flowering Season: March to May

Habitat/Range: Annual Stillingia grows in sandy soils and dunes below 3,000 feet in Creosote Bush scrub in the Mojave and Colorado Deserts.

Comments: This genus was named for the English naturalist B. Stillingfleet (1702–1771).

NOSEBURN
Tragia ramosa Torrey
Spurge Family (Euphorbiaceae)

Description: This 4–12" tall, clear-sapped perennial grows from a woody base. The branched and sometimes twining stems bear ½–¾" long, alternate, sharp-toothed leaves with tiny stipules. Each flower cluster contains 2–4 male flowers and 1 female flower. The male flowers have 4–5 recurved sepals and 3–6 stamens. The female flowers have 4–8 sepals and a 3-parted ovary with a style that is split into 3 parts from near the base.

Flowering Season: April to May

Habitat/Range: Noseburn is found on roadsides and in dry, rocky places from 3,000 to 5,500 feet in the mountains of the eastern Mojave Desert to Texas and Mexico.

Comments: The leaves of this innocent-looking plant can deliver a nasty sting that can raise welts and blisters.

Noseburn

TIM THOMAS

INDIAN RICEGRASS
Achnatherum hymenoides (Roemer & Shultes) Barkworth
Grass Family (Poaceae)

Description: This 1–2' tall, clumped, perennial bunchgrass has very narrow, rolled leaf blades and ¼" long ligules. It is beautiful in flower with its open, diffuse canopy of forked and spreading, threadlike branches with fat, fuzzy spikelets. Each plump seed has a prominent pair of bracts below it.

Flowering Season: April to July

Habitat/Range: Indian Ricegrass is common in sandy soils and flats below 11,000 feet in many vegetation types in the Mojave Desert. When found on rocky ridges, it usually occupies sandy patches between the rocks.

Comments: This was an important food source for native desert dwellers. In early summer, bunches of grass were piled up and beaten with sticks to release the small, dark seeds. Sometimes a stick was used to knock the seeds off the standing plants into baskets. The seeds were then roasted and ground into flour. Fire was often used to encourage growth of this plant.

Indian Ricegrass

STEPHEN INGRAM

Desert Needle Grass

TIM THOMAS

DESERT NEEDLE GRASS
Achnatherum speciosum (Trin. & Rupr.) Barkworth
Grass Family (Poaceae)

Description: The wiry-looking leaves of this 1–2' tall, tufted, perennial bunchgrass have hairy basal sheaths, narrow, inrolled blades, and membranous ligules. The branched, 4–6" long flower clusters occur in the fold of upper leaf sheaths. Each flower in the spikelet has a bent, 1½" long bristle, which has very soft, white, spreading hairs below the bend, giving the flower cluster a distinct, fuzzy appearance.

Flowering Season: April to June

Habitat/Range: Desert Needle Grass is widespread on slopes and rocky ridges below 6,500 feet in Joshua Tree woodland and Pinyon-Juniper woodland in the Mojave and Sonoran Deserts to Texas, Colorado, Mexico, and South America.

Comments: After the Owens Valley Paiute burned these plants, the stems and leaves were easily removed from the burned pile, but the seeds remained and were gathered. The boiled seeds absorbed water and were eaten like rice.

Needle Gramma

NEEDLE GRAMMA
Bouteloua aristidoides (Kunth.) Griseb. var. *aristidoides*
Grass Family (Poaceae)

Description: This 6–16" tall annual has hairless, solid, erect stems. The leaves have smooth blades and sheaths, with fringed or short-hairy ligules. They are flat or folded lengthwise, and they often have stiff hairs at the base. The flower cluster has 4–15 branches, each ½–1" long with 1–4 slender, appressed spikelets. The branches angle down from the main stem axis, and each falls off the plant as a unit.

Flowering Season: Late summer or fall, following summer rain

Habitat/Range: Needle Gramma is found in sandy soil below 5,500 feet in Joshua Tree woodland and Pinyon-Juniper woodland in the eastern and southern Mojave Desert to Texas and northern Mexico.

Comments: This plant is considered a nuisance in populated areas of some Western states, as its sharp, pointed branches become lodged in socks and clothing.

SIX-WEEKS GRAMMA
Bouteloua barbata Lagasca var. *barbata*
Grass Family (Poaceae)

Description: This tufted, 4–12" annual has spreading stems and narrow, flat, 1½" long leaves with hairless sheaths and narrow blades. The flower cluster has 4–7 alternate, ½" long spikes that resemble tiny, curved combs, with 25–40 spikelets coming off 1 side of the arched main axes.

Flowering Season: June to October, following summer rains

Habitat/Range: Six-Weeks Gramma is found on flats and in washes below 5,000 feet in the eastern Mojave Desert and Sonoran Desert to Colorado, Texas, and Mexico.

Comments: Like all of the "six weeks" grasses, this species is short-lived. They were given this name because they provided good grazing for cattle for about 6 weeks after rain.

Six-Weeks Gramma

Red Brome, Foxtail Chess

RED BROME, FOXTAIL CHESS

Bromus madritensis L. ssp. *rubens* (L.) Husnot
Grass Family (Poaceae)

Description: The erect or ascending stems of this 4–12" tall annual have closed leaf sheaths, ¼" ligules, and narrow leaf blades that are up to 4" long. The green, brushlike spikelets are cylindrical or slightly flattened and become reddish purple as they mature.

Flowering Season: March to June

Habitat/Range: Red Brome is widespread in many habitats below 6,000 feet throughout most of the United States and northern Mexico. It is native to Europe, Africa, and Asia.

Comments: This invasive species became established and widespread in California in the late 1800s and has become common in the Mojave Desert since the middle 1900s.

Although it is limited by lack of water and soil nutrients, especially nitrogen, it can be quite abundant beneath shrubs, along roadsides, and in crevices in rocky soil. Unlike many native wildflower species, which decompose fairly rapidly after their flowering season, dried Red Brome plants persist, in some areas promoting fire by creating a cover of highly flammable material. Since few desert shrubs survive or resprout following fire, the presence of Red Brome has caused type-conversion of some desert scrub communities into annual grass-lands. It is more abundant following succes-sive wet winters, as its seeds do not often survive more than 1 year of drought.

Saltgrass

STEPHEN INGRAM

SALTGRASS
Distichlis spicata (L.) E. Greene
Grass Family (Poaceae)

Description: The branched, trailing stems of Saltgrass spread over large areas by means of long, tough rhizomes. The stiff, 1–4" long leaf blades are alternate and regularly spaced at 60-degree angles from the stem. The leaf sheaths are split, not closed, and the ligule is fringed and membranelike. Saltgrass produces erect, branched clusters of compressed, firm, male and female spikelets at the tops of stems.

Flowering Season: April to July

Habitat/Range: Saltgrass is abundant around moist drainages, alkali seeps, springs, flats, rivers, and playas in the Mojave Desert. Its range includes most of the United States and Canada.

Comments: Saltgrass is extremely salt tolerant, getting rid of excess salt by secreting it onto its surfaces. The Kawaiisu scraped the salt off with sticks and formed a salt block, which was used sparingly for medicinal purposes. Some groups dried the plants on mats and beat the salt off with sticks. The Southern Paiute reportedly used this species as a fiber plant in woven items. The Great Basin Air Pollution Control District has ordered the Los Angeles Department of Water and Power to plant Saltgrass on the surface of the dry, salty Owens Lake bed to mitigate lake-surface wind erosion caused by long-term water diversion in the Owens Valley. Saltgrass is the only species that has yielded successful results.

DESERT FLUFF-GRASS
Erioneuron pulchellum (Kunth) Tateoka
Grass Family (Poaceae)

Description: This densely tufted perennial has inrolled, ½–2" long leaves at the base. It produces numerous naked, wiry, 2–5" tall stems with a terminal bundle of bractlike leaves that surround hairy, ¼–½" long spikelets. The terminal leaf bundles can eventually bend over and root in the ground, facilitating vegetative reproduction.

Flowering Season: February to May

Habitat/Range: Desert Fluff-Grass is found on gravelly soil on alluvial slopes and in washes in Creosote Bush scrub and Joshua Tree woodland in the Mojave Desert and in the Sonoran Desert to Colorado, Texas, and Mexico.

Comments: Following summer rains, the leaves produce some very unusual, soft, cobwebby hairs. These seem to be made of some material that dissolves in water, possibly a starch or sugar; they are not made of cells. These hairs are not usually present in the spring, and their function is unknown.

Desert Fluff-Grass

Porter's Muhly

PORTER'S MUHLY
Muhlenbergia porteri Beal
Grass Family (Poaceae)

Description: This 10–30" tall perennial is woody at the base. It has wiry, branched stems that often grow up through shrubs. The deciduous, 1–3" long leaf blades are flat and narrow. The flowers are produced in an open, branching cluster on very slender stalks. Each spikelet contains only 1 floret with a ¼–½" long terminal bristle.

Flowering Season: June to October

Habitat/Range: Porter's Muhly is found among shrubs and rocks on dry slopes from 2,000 to 5,000 feet in the Mojave Desert east of Twentynine Palms, and in the San Bernardino and San Jacinto Mountains to the Sonoran Desert, Colorado, western Texas, and Mexico.

Comments: Porter's Muhly may go unnoticed until late summer when the beautiful, delicate flower clusters turn red.

Common Reed

TIM THOMAS

COMMON REED
Phragmites australis (Cav.) Steudel
Grass Family (Poaceae)

Description: This thick, 6–12' tall, bamboo-like grass spreads from long rhizomes. The flat leaf blades are ½–2" wide and up to 20" long. Soft, beige, plumelike clusters of ½" long spikelets are produced on the upper 4–12" of the stems.

Flowering Season: July to November

Habitat/Range: Common Reed forms thickets along rivers and streams and in moist, alkaline places below 5,000 in the deserts. This plant is very widely distributed throughout the world, and it is weedy and invasive in many areas.

Comments: When Father Garcés visited the Vanyume in the 1700s, he reported that they had a type of grass they were using for sugar. This sugar was made from the sweet secretions of plant-sucking insects that lived on the reeds. The reeds were cut, dried, and then beaten to loosen the sticky substance. It was collected and rolled into large balls to be eaten as candy, insects and all! Other groups used variations of this technique. The plants were also used for arrows, pipes, and musical instruments.

Big Galleta

BIG GALLETA
Pleuraphis rigida Thurber
Grass Family (Poaceae)

Description: This coarse, long-lived, shrubby grass branches from a hard base of woody rhizomes to form clumps and hummocks that stabilize sand. The 1–3' tall, fuzzy stems are solid, even between the leaves (most grasses have hollow stems). The leaves have firm, 1–2½" long blades with curly hairs and edges rolled upward, hairless sheaths, and ligules that are membranous and fringed. The flowers are produced in 2–3" long, cylindrical, spike-like clusters. After the spikelets fall, the stalks to which they were attached remain on the plant and stick up as wavy, wiry extensions.

Flowering Season: May to June

Habitat/Range: Big Galleta is common on sandy soils, washes, and dunes below 4,000 feet in the Mojave and Sonoran Deserts to Sonora, Mexico.

Comments: *Pleuraphis jamesii* is a smaller herbaceous species with stems that are not fuzzy. It is common in the northern Mojave Desert.

Eureka Valley Dunes Grass

EUREKA VALLEY DUNES GRASS

Swallenia alexandrae Soderstrom & Decker
Grass Family (Poaceae)

Description: This stout, stiff perennial spreads to form extensive mats by means of thick, woody rhizomes with woolly nodes. The branched, 6–14" stems are hairless except near the tips. The leaves have flat, stiff, 2–6" long blades and hairy ligules, and the upper sheath margins are lined with long hairs. A narrow, flattened, 2–4" long cluster of ½" long spikelets is produced at the tops of stems.

Flowering Season: April to June

Habitat/Range: This species is found only in sand dunes from 3,000 to 3,500 feet in Eureka Valley, within Death Valley National Park.

Comments: Eureka Valley Dunes Grass is listed as state rare and federal endangered. In the past, dune recreation and off-highway vehicles degraded its habitat, but the area is now closed to vehicles and the population is recovering. It is difficult for the National Park Service to monitor activities in this remote area; any vehicular trespass or damage to plants should be reported. Eureka Valley Dunes Grass is the only species in the genus *Swallenia*, which was named for Jason R. Swallen (1903–1991), a student of American grasses. The specific name is in honor of Annie Alexander, a wealthy botanical explorer and benefactress who first collected this species with Louise Kellogg in May of 1949.

SIX-WEEKS FESCUE
Vulpia octoflora (Walter) Rydb. var. *hirtella*
(Piper) Henrard
Grass Family (Poaceae)

Description: Six-Weeks Fescue is a weak-stemmed, 2–16" tall, tufted annual. The alternate, flat, 1–3" long leaf blades roll upward, and the sheaths do not cover the entire internodes. The strongly flattened, ¼–½" long spikelets are produced in a densely crowded 1–4" long cluster at the stem tip.

Flowering Season: April to June

Habitat/Range: Six-Weeks Fescue is found in open, sunny places between shrubs and in burned areas below 4,500 feet in Creosote Bush scrub, Joshua Tree woodland, and Pinyon-Juniper woodland in the Mojave Desert to Colorado, Texas, and Baja California, Mexico.

Comments: This plant may be especially common following burns. This is another of the short-lived "six-weeks" grasses, which are so named because they supply about 6 weeks of cattle forage following a good rain.

Six-Weeks Fescue

FREMONT COTTONWOOD
Populus fremontii S. Watson ssp. *fremontii*
Willow Family (Salicaceae)

Description: Fremont Cottonwood is the tallest tree in the lower elevations of the desert, reaching heights of up to 90'. The trunk has whitish gray bark up to 5" thick, which becomes deeply furrowed with age. The 1½–3" long, bright green, hairless leaves are produced on flattened, 1–2" stalks. They are triangular in outline with pointed tips and irregular teeth or scallops on the margins. Male and female flowers are produced in 2" long catkins on separate trees. The plants are wind pollinated, and the downy seeds are also carried by wind.

Flowering Season: March to April, before or during the time the new leaves are forming

Habitat/Range: This species is common in riparian areas throughout the Mojave Desert and the Western states to the eastern Rocky Mountains.

Comments: Fremont Cottonwood is often infested with Big-Leaf Mistletoe *(Phoradendron macrophyllum)*. Also common is the Carpenter Worm moth larvae *(Prionoxystus robiniae)*, a 2–3" long, pink grub with a brown head. It lives in the crowns and trunks and exudes moist, sappy frass.

STEPHEN INGRAM

Fremont Cottonwood

Sand-Bar Willow, Narrow-Leaved Willow

SAND-BAR WILLOW, NARROW-LEAVED WILLOW
Salix exigua Nutt.
Willow Family (Salicaceae)

Description: This 6–12' tall shrub spreads by rhizomes, often forming large thickets. Younger twigs have soft hairs that wear off, leaving brown bark. The linear leaves are 2–5" long and ¼" wide with toothed margins. They are grayish on both surfaces due to the presence of silvery hairs. The hairy, 1–3" long, male and female flower catkins are produced on leafy twigs on separate plants.

Flowering Season: March to May, appearing with or after the leaves

Habitat/Range: Sand-Bar Willow is common along streams and in drainage channels below 8,000 feet in the Mojave Desert and throughout California to Texas and British Columbia.

Comments: The name *exigua* means "little," or "weak," referring to the small stature of the plants of this species, compared with many other willows. Aspirin (salicylic acid) is present in the bark and leaves of willows.

TIM THOMAS

Mojave Paintbrush

MOJAVE PAINTBRUSH
Castilleja plagiotoma A. Gray
Figwort Family (Scrophulariaceae)

Description: The 1–2' tall stems of this grayish green, erect perennial often grow up through low shrubs. The foliage has sparse, branched hairs. The linear, 1–2" long lower leaves grade into 3-lobed leaves and green, white-hairy bracts higher up the stem, and the bilateral flowers are enclosed in green, 3-lobed flower bracts. The ½" long, split calyx has straight lobes, and the hairy, tubular, greenish yellow corolla is nearly 1" long. The fruit is a 2-chambered capsule.

Flowering Season: April to June

Habitat/Range: Mojave Paintbrush is found from 1,000 to 7,500 feet in Joshua Tree woodland, Sagebrush scrub, and Pinyon-Juniper woodland on desert slopes of the San Bernardino and San Gabriel Mountains. It also occurs in scattered locations in Los Angeles, Kern, and San Luis Obispo Counties in California.

Comments: Mojave Paintbrush is uncommon enough to be on the California Native Plant Society's watch list, but the potential for extinction is very low at this time. Like other *Castilleja* species, Mojave Paintbrush is a root hemiparasite; that is, it is partially parasitic but makes some of its own food.

Crucifixion Thorn

CRUCIFIXION THORN
Castela emoryi (A. Gray) Moran & Felger
Quassia Family (Simaroubaceae)

Description: This thorny, densely branched shrub can be up to 3' tall and spreading, or 6–12' and erect. Juvenile plants have ½" long, scalelike leaves, but these drop early, leaving the older plants leafless. Male and female flowers are produced on separate plants. Each inconspicuous flower develops into a fruit with a spreading whorl of 5–6, ¼" long, 1-seeded parts, which often dry, split open to release seeds, and cling to the plant for 5–7 years.

Flowering Season: June to July

Habitat/Range: Crucifixion Thorn is found in gravelly soils in Creosote Bush scrub and dry playas below 2,000 feet. It is uncommon in the southern Mojave Desert in California, occurring only at Goffs, Ludlow, Amboy, and a few other locations, but it is fairly abundant in northeastern Arizona. It occurs occasionally in the Colorado Desert as at Hayfields and Coyote Well and becomes more abundant east and south to Sonora, Mexico.

Comments: This species is protected at Crucifixion Thorn Natural Area, a Bureau of Land Management administered area in Imperial County, California. This genus was named for Rene R. L. Castel (1759–1832) of France, who was a botanist, editor, and poet.

Desert Mistletoe

DESERT MISTLETOE
Phoradendron californicum Nutt.
Mistletoe Family (Viscaceae)

Description: Desert Mistletoe has 1–4' long, rounded, reddish stems, which appear in dense, branched clumps in the canopies of its host plants. It appears to be leafless, although there are small scalelike leaves present. The tiny, inconspicuous, green flowers develop into a profusion of ⅛" round, bright reddish pink berries.

Flowering Season: January to March

Habitat/Range: This species is found in the Mojave, Sonoran, and Great Basin Deserts to Baja California, Mexico. Its distribution depends on the availability of host plants. It is parasitic on Pea Family shrubs, including Cat-

claw *(Acacia greggi)* and Honey Mesquite *(Prosopis glandulosa)* in the Mojave Desert. In the Colorado Desert, hosts also include Palo Verde (*Cercidium* sp.) and Ironwood *(Olneya tesota)*. In some places where Catclaw is abundant as a regular host, Desert Mistletoe has been observed on Creosote Bush *(Larrea tridentata)*.

Comments: The fruits seem to be a favored food item of the Phainopepla, a shiny, crested, black bird with red eyes and white underwing patches. This plant's genus name literally means "tree thief" in Greek, referring to its parasitic habit.

Non-Flowering Plants

Bird's Foot Fern

California Juniper

CALIFORNIA JUNIPER
Juniperus californicus Carriere
Cypress Family (Cupressaceae)

Description: California Juniper is a 3–18' tall shrub with several trunks and thick, twisted branches, which trap wind-blown dirt. The grayish brown, grit-filled bark shreds and peels in wide strips. Tiny, green, scalelike leaves with rounded tips are flattened against the stem, overlapping so the internodes are not visible. Breaking a leafy twig shows that the leaves are in whorls of 3 per node, and the resinous gland in the center of each leaf can be observed with a 10X hand lens. The juvenile leaves are longer and not flattened to the stem. Male and female cones are produced on separate plants. The female cones, which have 1–3 seeds, have a bluish coating but are rusty brown underneath.

Reproductive Season: Cones are produced in fall, and the pollen is shed from February to March.

Habitat/Range: California Juniper is a dominant species of Pinyon-Juniper woodland. It is found at elevations below 6,000 feet in many mountain ranges throughout the Mojave Desert to Baja California, Mexico. It is especially common on north-facing slopes and adjacent flats of the Transverse Ranges.

Comments: An unpublished, 7-year study monitored the gender of several hundred California Junipers in Piñon Hills. About 2–3% of the plants switched gender each year. There was a tendency for larger plants to be female, but the smallest plants did not produce any cones.

Utah Juniper

UTAH JUNIPER
Juniperus osteosperma (Torrey) Little
Cypress Family (Cupressaceae)

Description: Utah Juniper is usually an 8–12' tall shrub, but it can take on a treelike form, reaching heights up to 24'. It has 1 thick trunk in addition to numerous thinner branches from near the base, and the opposite, overlapping leaves lack obvious resin glands. The male and female cones are produced on the same plant. The ¼–½" female cones contain 2–3 angled, pitted seeds.

Reproductive Season: Pollen is shed in the spring.

Habitat/Range: Utah Juniper is found on dry hillsides and flats from 4,000 to 8,000 feet on north-facing slopes of the Transverse Ranges east of Piñon Hills, and in the mountains of the eastern Mojave Desert to Mono County, Montana, Wyoming, and New Mexico.

Comments: Many of these plants are infested with tufts of the Juniper Mistletoe *(Phoradendron juniperinum)*, a yellowish green species with scaly leaves and dull white to pinkish berries.

NEVADA JOINT FIR, MORMON TEA
Ephedra nevadensis S. Watson
Ephedra Family (Ephedraceae)

Description: This grayish green, 1–4' tall shrub has branches that are nearly at right angles to the clumped stems. There are 2 scalelike leaves at each node, but these often fall, leaving the thick, gray leaf bases attached to the plant. There are 2 seed cones produced on short stalks at each node on female plants, and 1–3 pollen cones per node on male plants.

Habitat/Range: Nevada Joint Fir is very common in Creosote Bush scrub and Joshua Tree woodlands throughout the Mojave and Sonoran Deserts to Oregon.

Comments: Death Valley Ephedra *(Ephedra funerea)* resembles Nevada Joint Fir in color, but it has 3 leaves per node, and it has a very symmetrical, rounded shape. It is found in the northeastern Mojave Desert to Nevada.

Nevada Joint Fir, Mormon Tea

Long-Leaved Joint Fir

LONG-LEAVED JOINT FIR
Ephedra trifurca Torrey
Ephedra Family (Ephedraceae)

Description: Long-Leaved Joint Fir is readily distinguished by its sharp branch tips. It is pale green and it has 3 fibrous, persistent leaves at each node. The ½" long seed cones are pointed and have a papery texture.

Habitat/Range: This species can occasionally be found in sandy soils in Creosote Bush scrub in the eastern Mojave Desert, but it is much more common in the Sonoran Desert to Texas and Mexico.

Comments: California Joint-Fir *(Ephedra californica)* also has 3 leaves per node, but it does not have spiny branch tips. It is one of the commercial sources of ephedrine, a stimulant and decongestant.

Green Ephedra, Mountain Joint-Fir

GREEN EPHEDRA, MOUNTAIN JOINT-FIR
Ephedra viridis Cov.
Ephedra Family (Ephedraceae)

Description: The broomlike Green Ephedra is easily distinguished from other *Ephedra* species by its very erect, bright green stems. There are 2 leaves produced per node, but they drop, leaving behind the brown leaf bases. The female plants produce 2–6 seed cones at each node, and male plants bear 2–5 pollen cones per node.

Habitat/Range: Green Ephedra occurs from 2,500 to 7,000 feet in Sagebrush scrub, Blackbush scrub, and Pinyon-Juniper woodland on north-facing slopes of the Transverse Ranges and in mountains throughout the Mojave Desert to Colorado and northern Mexico.

Comments: The Paiute and Shoshone made a medicinal tea from both Green Ephedra and Nevada Joint Fir, although the flavor of Green Ephedra was preferred. They used it as a remedy for colds, urinary tract infections, and venereal diseases. Powdered stems were applied to sores. Some groups made flour from ground-up seeds.

Singleleaf Pinyon Pine

SINGLELEAF PINYON PINE
Pinus monophylla Torrey & Fremont
Pine Family (Pinaceae)

Description: The Singleleaf Pinyon Pine is a 10–50' tall tree that forms a wide, spreading crown. It doesn't seem to have the strong self-pruning feature of many species of pine, so the lower branches tend to remain attached. There is 1 needle at each node, with a paper leaf sheath around the bottom. The 2" long female cones are rounded, with thickened ends on the scales, while male cones are only about ¼" long.

Habitat/Range: Singleleaf Pinyon Pine is a dominant species of Pinyon-Juniper woodland. It occurs below 7,000 feet on north-facing slopes of the Transverse Ranges and in mountains of the Mojave Desert to Idaho and Baja California, Mexico.

Comments: Pinyon-Juniper woodland tends to burn only about every 150–300 years, but when it burns, it is usually quite devastating. The pinyon pines usually take longer than 100 years to recover, as they need nurse plants for protection while young. They are also susceptible to damage by beetles, especially the Pinyon Pine Engraver *(Ips confusus)*. The Two-Needled Pinyon Pine *(Pinus edulis)* occurs in the New York Mountains.

Coville's Lip Fern

BIRD'S FOOT FERN
Pellaea mucronata (D. Eaton) D. Eaton
Brake Fern Family (Pteridaceae)

Description: The rhizome scales of Bird's Foot Fern have a hardened, central stripe and pale, membranous margins. The dark brown, slender petioles tend to be flattened on the upper side. The 6–12" long leaves are 2–3 times pinnate, with elliptic, sharp-pointed ultimate leaflets that are about ¼" long. The spores are produced in bands along the inrolled margins of the undersurface of the leaflets.

Habitat/Range: This fern is occasionally found on rocky slopes and in rock crevices from Creosote Bush scrub to Pinyon-Juniper woodland in the Mojave Desert. It is more common in other areas in southern California to northern Baja California, Mexico.

Comments: Unlike flowering plants, which have sperm transported in pollen grains, ferns have sperm that must swim to the egg. This is why ferns commonly grow in very moist environments. Desert ferns are confined to moist microhabitats such as rock crevices, but even these dry out. Their strategy is to remain dormant for much of the year, then quickly rehydrate when water becomes available.

COVILLE'S LIP FERN
Cheilanthes covillei Maxon
Brake Fern Family (Pteridaceae)

Description: The short, thick rhizome of Coville's Lip Fern has tough, dark scales with narrow, lighter margins. The 3–10" long leaves are on brownish to purple, 1–4" petioles. They are 3–4 times pinnate, with rounded, beady ultimate leaflets. The upper surface is green, but the lower surface, which produces spores, is hidden by flattened, tan to white scales that have long, tangled hairs on the margins.

Habitat/Range: Coville's Lip Fern grows in sheltered rock crevices from 2,000 to 6,000 feet in the mountains and foothills of the Mojave Desert and throughout California to Baja California, Mexico.

Comments: The light fern spores are dispersed by wind. If they land in a moist, suitable location, they germinate and grow into a tiny, inconspicuous plant body that produces egg and sperm. Once an egg is fertilized, it can then grow into a complete, recognizable fern plant.

Bird's Foot Fern

GLOSSARY

Alternate—placed singly along a stem, one after another, usually each successive item on a different side of the stem from previous. As one traces the orientation from one item to the next above, a spiral is drawn around the stem. Usually used in reference to arrangement of leaves on a stem *(see* Opposite *and* Whorled *for comparison).*

Annual—a plant that completes its life cycle, from seed germination to production of new seeds, within a year, then dies *(see* Perennial *and* Biennial *for comparison).*

Anther—a sac at the tip of the stamen where the pollen is formed.

Axil—the region in the angle formed by the upper side of the leaf, or leaf stalk, where it joins the stem.

Banner—the upper petal in many of the flowers of the Bean Family *(see* "Pea" Flower), often bent upward or even backward, usually broader than the other petals, and always covering them in the bud; also called the standard or flag petal.

Basal—at the base or bottom of; generally used in reference to leaves located at the base of the stem, at ground level.

Beak—a conic projection or abruptly tapering end of a fruit.

Biennial—a plant completing its life cycle in two years and normally not producing flowers during the first year *(see* Annual *and* Perennial *for comparison).*

Bilateral—in reference to the shape of a flower as viewed "face on," a shortened term for "bilaterally symmetrical," and substitution for the technical term "zygomorphic." A bilateral flower is one that can be divided into mirror images in only one plane through the center of the flower. Mammals, fish, birds, and insects, for example, are bilaterally symmetrical *(see* Radial *for comparison).*

Blade—the broad, flat part of a structure, usually in reference to leaves or petals, often contrasting with the stalk of the structure.

Bract—reduced or modified leaf, often associated with flowers. May or may not be green, sometimes scalelike.

Bristle—a stiff hair, usually erect or curving away from its attachment point.

Bulb—underground plant part that is a short, swollen stem covered by fleshy, modified, food-storing, scalelike leaves that are usually nongreen (example is the onion).

Calyx—a collective term for the outer set of flower parts, composed of sepals, which may be separate or joined to one another; usually green. If there is only one set of parts outside the stamens or pistil, it is by definition the calyx, even though it may resemble a corolla *(see* Corolla *and* Petal-like Parts *for comparison).*

Capsule—a dry fruit that releases seeds through splits or holes; as used in this guide, usually not elongate *(see* Pod *for comparison).*

Catkin—a spike of male or female flowers that falls off the plant as a single unit after flowering or fruiting. Willows, oaks, and other wind-pollinated plants often bear catkins.

Clasping—surrounding or partially wrapping around a stem or branch.

Cluster—any grouping or close arrangement of individual flowers; "flower cluster" is used as a substitute for the commonly used but more technical term "inflorescence."

Compound Leaf—a leaf that is divided to its midrib or stalk into two to many leaflets, each of which resembles a complete leaf. A leaf will have a bud in its axil, whereas leaflets do not *(see* Palmately Compound Leaf, Pinnately Compound Leaf, *and* Simple Leaf *for comparison)*.

Corm—a fleshy, enlarged, underground stem base with scales.

Corolla—collective term for the set of flower parts interior to the calyx and exterior to the stamens (if present), composed of petals, which may be free or united; often white or brightly colored, rarely green *(see* Calyx and Petal-like Parts *for comparison)*.

Cotyledon—a fleshy leaf in the embryo of a seed that stores food for the eventual seed germination process.

Deciduous—a term referring to the more or less synchronized shedding of structures, usually leaves. Shrubs and trees that drop all their leaves at the end of the growing season are "deciduous," or leaves may be said to be "deciduous." Many desert plants are evergreen but will shed their leaves during severe drought and then are "drought deciduous" *(see* Evergreen *for comparison)*.

Disk Flower—small, tubular, usually trumpet-shaped flowers in the central portion of the flower head of plants in the Sunflower Family (Asteraceae) *(see illustration p. 39; see* Ray Flower, Ligule, *and* Strap-shaped Flower *for comparison)*.

Elliptical—in reference to the shape of a plane cut obliquely through the axis of a cone, usually in reference to leaf shape *(see illustration p. 38)*.

Entire—usually in reference to a leaf margin that is plain, not lobed or toothed *(see illustration p. 37)*.

Erect—standing more or less perpendicularly to the surface.

Evergreen—plants that bear green leaves throughout the year. Leaves may be shed asynchronously or synchronously, but in either case, new leaves are in place before old ones are shed *(see* Deciduous *for comparison)*.

Family—a group of related genera, usually easily recognized by sharing similar features (such as floral features, fruit types, stem anatomy, etc.).

Fascicle—A cluster or bundle of leaves or flowers.

Filament—the usually slender stalk of a stamen, tipped by the anther.

Flower Head—as used in this guide, a dense and continuous group of flowers, without obvious branches or spaces between them; often mistaken for a single "flower" until structure is understood. The term is used especially in reference to the grouping of flowers in the Sunflower Family (Asteraceae).

Fruit—the mature ovary of a plant, containing ripe seeds; a fruit may be fleshy or hard, large or small, and may consist of other parts of the flower or plant.

Genera—*see* Genus.

Genus—a group of closely related species, sharing many characteristics in common; plural "genera."

Glandular—bearing glands, which are structures that secrete something. Glands in plants are often borne at tips of hairs, and the exuded substance is usually moist or sticky and some-times odoriferous. Alternatively, they may be part of the surface layer and appear as darkened spots. Glandular secretions on the surface of plants usually inhibit or repel potential insects or other animals that might eat the plant.

Glochids—Bundles of very short, dense spines that may occur on cactus plants.

Herbaceous—a term that means "not woody." Such a plant is usually soft and green.

Hood—a curved or folded structure, often somewhat scoop shaped, associated with the corolla. In this guide "hoods" are those scoop-like structures interior to the petals and exterior to the stamens in milkweeds (Asclepiadaceae); since most milkweeds have reflexed petals, the hoods are typically the most prominent feature of the flowers. Species with bilateral flowers also often have the upper lip "hoodlike"; that is, much like a deeply cupped visor.

Inflorescence—the structure on which flowers are borne, in this guide called the "flower cluster"; various specialized terms describe the form of the inflorescence.

Inrolled—margins of leaves are rolled under, or revolute.

Involucre—a distinct series of bracts or leaves that subtend a flower or a flower cluster. Often used in the description of the flower head of the Sunflower Family (Asteraceae), where in this guide "whorl of bracts" is substituted.

Keel—referring especially to the two joined petals forming the lower part of the flower in the Bean Family (Fabaceae), which resembles the prow of a boat *(see illustration p. 39)*; any structure that is a sharp, narrow ridge.

Lanceolate—narrow and pointed at both ends, usually broader just below the middle, much like the tip of a lance. When describing a structure that is basically lanceolate, but

broader above the middle, in this guide the term "inversely lanceolate" is used, substituting for the technical term "oblanceolate."

Leaf—the flattened, usually photosynthetic and therefore "food-producing" organ of the plant, attached to the stem.

Leaf Blade—the broadened, flattened part of the leaf, in contrast to the leaf stalk.

Leaf Stalk—the slender portion of a leaf, distinguished from the blade, continuous with the midrib, and attaching the leaf to the stem; technically the "petiole."

Leaflet—a distinct leaflike segment of a compound leaf.

Ligule—a strap-shaped flower of plants in the chicory tribe of the Sunflower Family. These differ from ray flowers, which are also strap-shaped but surround disk flowers. *(see illustration p. 39; see* Ray Flower *and* Disk Flower *for comparison).*

Limb—the flared or expanded part of the corolla above the throat or tube.

Linear—long and very narrow, with parallel or nearly parallel sides *(see illustration p. 38)*.

Lobe—a segment of an incompletely divided plant part, typically rounded at tip; often used in reference to the partial segmentation of the leaf blade.

Margin—the edge of a leaf or other plant part.

Midrib—the central or main vein of a leaf.

Nectar Guides—markings on the flower of a contrasting color or that reflect ultraviolet light, to direct the pollinating animal to the center of the flower.

Nectar Spur—a tubular extension of a petal or sepal that secretes nectar.

Node—the region of the stem where one or more leaves are attached. Buds are commonly borne at nodes, in axils of leaves.

Nutlet—a term for a small, hard, one-seeded fruit or segment of a fruit.

Oblong—a shape with more or less parallel sides, longer in one direction that the other, as used here, with rounded ends; commonly used with leaf shape *(see illustration p. 38)*.

Opposite—paired directly across from one another along a stem or axis *(see* Alternate *and* Whorled *for comparison)*.

Ovary—the portion of the flower where seeds develop, usually a swollen area below the style (if present) and stigma; develops into the fruit.

Ovate—more or less egg-shaped in outline, often bluntly pointed at tip.

Pads—used here in reference to flattened stem-joints of *Opuntia*. The pads are part of the stem, the spine clusters (technically areoles) derived from branch systems, the needles modified from leaves.

Palmate—referring to an arrangement where segments attach to a common point, much like fingers attach to the palm of a hand. Used commonly to described lobing of a leaf (palmately lobed) or compound leaves (palmately compound). A palmately compound leaf is one that has three or more leaflets attached at the tip of the leaf stalk; an example is the leaves of lupines in the Bean Family (Fabaceae) *(see illustration p. 37)*.

Parallel—side by side, about the same distance apart for the entire length; often used in reference to veins or edges of leaves.

Parasitic Plant—a plant that lives on another plant, robbing it of nourishment.

Pappus—in the Sunflower Family (Asteraceae) the modified calyx, consisting of a crown of scales, bristles, or soft hairs at the top of the seedlike fruit.

"Pea" Flower—as used in this guide, a reference to the flower shape seen in many of the species in the Bean Family (Fabaceae); a flower that has a banner, two wings, and a keel *(see illustration p. 39)*

Perennial—a plant that normally lives for more than one year *(see* Annual *and* Biennial *for comparison)*.

Petal—a unit of the corolla, usually flattened and brightly colored.

Petal-like Parts—referring to parts of a flower that resemble petals but technically are not petals, or where the distinction between petals and sepals is not immediately evident; in technical works the term "tepals" may be used. In this guide "petal-like parts" is used in the Cactus Family (Cactaceae), where sepals are thoroughly intergradient with petals; in the Lily Family (Liliaceae), where sepals may be brightly colored like the petals; and in the Four O'Clock Family (Nyctaginaceae), where there are no petals, and the calyx is brightly colored and fragile, resembling a corolla.

Photosynthesis—the process by which plants use energy in light to rearrange and join molecules of carbon dioxide from the air, all to store the sun's energy in molecules of sugar built from the carbon dioxide and water; the plant's "food." Except for rare instances (such as around deep-sea vents), all life on Earth depends on this process.

Phyllaries—a series of bracts below the flower heads of Sunflower Family plants.

Pinna—the primary division of a compound leaf (plural pinnae), often equivalent to a leaflet (as in Astragalus and Lupinus). In the case of a twice compound leaf, this guide uses "segment" in place of pinna, the leaflets being the small leaflike structures resulting from division of the pinna.

Pinnate—referring to an arrangement where parts are aligned along opposite sides of an axis, much like the barbs of a feather are aligned along each side of the common central axis. Used commonly to describe lobing of a leaf (pinnately lobed) or compound leaves (pinnately compound). A pinnately compound leaf is one that has two or more leaflets arranged along opposite sides of a common axis; the leaves of many members of the Bean Family (Fabaceae) are an example of this *(see illustration p. 37).*

Pistil—the female part of the flower, consisting of ovary, style, and stigma; a flower may have one pistil or several pistils.

Pod—as used in this guide, a dry, elongate fruit that splits open upon maturity to release seeds *(see* Capsule *for comparison).*

Pollen—tiny, often powdery male reproductive cells formed in the anther, ultimately producing the sperm prior to fertilization of the egg within the ovary of the plant.

Pollination—the transfer of pollen from the anther of one flower to the stigma of another.

Prostrate—growing flat on the ground.

Pulvinus—a swelling at the base of a leaf stalk (petiole) or at the base of a leaflet, which often aids in the movement of leaves or leaflets.

Rachis—the main stem or axis of a pinnately compound leaf.

Radial—in reference to the shape of a flower as viewed "face on," a shortened term for "radially symmetrical," and substitution for the technical term "actinomorphic." A radial flower is one that can be divided into mirror images by several planes through the center of the flower. A starfish is radially symmetrical *(see* Bilateral *for comparison).*

Ray Flower—a flower at the periphery of the head of the Sunflower Family (Asteraceae), the corolla extended far to one side, flattened and shaped like a single petal; a flower head may have one, several, or many ray flowers, or it may have none; when several or many are present they usually extend outward like the rays of a star *(see illustration p. 39; see* Disk

Flower, Ligule, *and* Strap-shaped Flower *for comparison).*

Receptacle—the expanded portion of a stalk where flower parts are attached.

Recurved—Bent backward.

Reflexed—Abruptly bent backward.

Rhizome—a horizontal, underground stem.

Rosette—a dense cluster of leaves very closely spaced around the stem, often at ground level, but in members of the Agave Family (Agavaceae) sometimes at the top of a stout trunk.

Scale—any thin, membranous, usually translucent structure that somewhat resembles scales of fish or reptiles.

Scarification—the breaking of the seed coat prior to germination.

Seedlike—resembling a seed; in this guide used to refer to the fruits of various plants, especially members of the Sunflower Family (Asteraceae), where the "seed" (as in the sunflower "seed") is technically a one-seeded fruit, the outer covering consisting of ovary wall joined to the bases of other flower parts, the true seed contained inside.

Sepal—a unit of the calyx, typically flattened and green, but occasionally brightly colored *(see* Petal-like Parts" *for comparison).*

Serrate—saw-toothed, with teeth pointing toward the tip or front.

Shrub—a multi-stemmed woody plant of moderate to low height with stems arising at ground or near level.

Simple Leaf—a leaf that is not compound. A simple leaf may have a plain (entire) margin, or the margin may be toothed or deeply lobed. As long as clefts between the lobes do not extend to the midrib, the leaf is simple. A deeply lobed oak leaf, for example, is "simple."

Spatulate—referring to a shape broader in upper half, round at the tip *(see illustration p. 38)*.

Species—a group of very similar individuals that use their environment in a similar manner and that are capable of mating with one another to produce viable offspring. Because many plants reproduce asexually (e.g., dandelion, *Taraxacum*) or tend to self-pollinate and self-fertilize (e.g., some suncups, *Camissonia*), the definition is more difficult to apply in plants than in many animal groups. Species are internationally referred to by a scientific name, a binomial, such as *Taraxacum officinale*, where the first name is the genus name, and the second is the specific epithet, which modifies the genus name.

Specific Epithet—*see* Species.

Spike—an elongate, unbranched, often dense cluster of stalkless or nearly stalkless flowers.

Spikelet—the basic flower cluster unit of Grass Family plants. Each spikelet has two bracts called glumes at the base, with sessile flowers called florets above.

Stalk—as used in this guide, a stemlike structure supporting a leaf, flower, or flower cluster (technically "petiole," "pedicel," and "peduncle," respectively).

Stalkless—lacking a stalk; when stalkless, a leaf blade or a flower is directly attached to the stem.

Stamen—the male part of the flower, consisting of the slender stalklike filament and the saclike anther, in which pollen forms.

Staminode—a stamen which lacks an anther and is therefore sterile. Staminodes in the Figwort Family are often hairy.

Standard—*see* Banner.

Stellate Hairs—a starlike pattern of hair growth, with several slender hairs radiating from a common point of attachment at their bases.

Stigma—portion of the pistil receptive to pollen; usually at the top of the style, and often appearing fuzzy or sticky.

Stipules—a pair of attachments at the base of a leaf, often connected to each other. Leaves may or may not have stipules.

Stolon—an above-ground horizontal stem or runner.

Style—the portion of the pistil between the ovary and the stigma, often slender; each pollen grain will produce a tube that traverses the style, delivering sperm to the eggs within the ovary.

Strap-shaped Flower—in reference to the type of flowers found in the heads of dandelions *(Taraxacum)* and their relatives in the Sunflower Family (Asteraceae). The flowers throughout the head are strap-shaped, the corolla extended conspicuously toward the periphery of the head, the flowers in the center smaller than those near the edge of the head. Usually each corolla has five tiny teeth at the tip. These are contrasted with ray flowers, which are similar, but which are found only at the periphery of the flower head surrounding the disk flowers.

Subshrub—Plants with a shrubby appearance but with woody tissue only near the base and soft, green stems above.

Subspecies—a group of individuals within a species that have a distinct range, habitat, and structure; in plants usually not conceptually different from variety, but both terms remain in use due to historical reasons.

Subtend—situated below or beneath, often encasing or enclosing something.

Succulent—thickened, fleshy, and juicy.

Tendril—a slender, coiling structure that may be part of a stem or leaf. The tendrils of vines and climbing plants wind around other plants or objects for support.

Toothed—bearing teeth or sharply angled projections along an edge.

Tubercle—A small, rounded or conical projection.

Umbel—A flower cluster where each of the individual flower stalks attach at a common point at the tip of the main stalk of the flower cluster, much like the ribs of an umbrella attach at the top of the umbrella.

Variety—a group of individuals within a species that have a distinct range, habitat, and structure; in plants usually not conceptually different from subspecies, but both terms remain in use due to historical reasons.

Veins—bundles of small tubes, some of which carry water and minerals, others of which carry a sugar solution. Water and sugar solutions may move in opposite directions through different series of cells in the same vein.

Whorled—three or more parts attached at the same point around a stem or axis *(see* Alternate *and* Opposite *for comparison).*

Wings—a flat, thin, extended portion; in the Bean Family (Fabaceae), specifically referring to the two side petals of the flower, flanking the keel.

OR FURTHER READING

Mojave Desert vegetation and plant identification:

Abrams, Leroy. *Illustrated Flora of the Pacific States,* vols. 1–4. Stanford: Stanford University Press, 1940.

Arizona Rare Plant Field Guide. Edited by Lynn Richards. Arizona Rare Plant Committee, 2002.

Beatley, Janice C. *Vascular Plants of the Nevada Test Site and Central-Southern Nevada: Ecologic and Geographic Distributions.* Springfield, Va.: Technical Information Center, Energy Research and Development Administration, 1976.

Benson, Lyman. *The Native Cacti of California.* Stanford: Stanford University Press, 1969.

Benson, Lyman, and Robert A. Darrow. *The Trees and Shrubs of the Southwestern Deserts.* Tucson: The University of Arizona Press, 1954.

Bowers, J. E. *Flowers and Shrubs of the Mojave Desert.* Tucson: Southwest Parks and Monuments Association, 1999.

Britton, N. L. and J. N. Rose. *The Cactaceae,* vols. 1–4. Reprint, New York: Dover Publications, Inc., 1963. .

Cronquist, A., A. H. Holmgren, N. H. Holmgren, and J. L. Reveal. *Intermountain Flora,* vols. 1–4. Hafner Publishing Co., Inc., 1972; Reprint, New York: New York Botanical Garden, 1986.

DeDecker, Mary. *Flora of the Northern Mojave Desert.* Berkeley: California Native Plant Society, Special Publication Number 7, 1984.

Dodge, Natt N. *Flowers of the Southwest Deserts.* Globe, Ariz.: Southwestern Monuments Association, 1965.

Dole, Jim W., and Betty B. Rose. *An Amateur Botanist's Identification Manual for the Shrubs and Trees of the Southern California Deserts.* Big Bear Lake, California: Jim W. Dole and Betty B. Rose, 1994.

Epple, Anne Orth. *A Field Guide to the Plants of Arizona.* Mesa, Ariz.: LewAnn Publishing Company, 1995.

Frenkel, Robert E. "Ruderal Vegetation along some California Roadsides." *University of California Publications in Geography,* no. 20 (1989).

Henry, Mary Ann. "A Rare Grass on the Eureka Dunes." *Fremontia* 7 (2): 3-6 (1979).

Holland, V. L. and David J. Keil. *California Vegetation.* Dubuque, Iowa.: Kendall Hunt Publishing, 1995.

Jaeger, Edmund C. *Desert Wild Flowers.* Stanford: Stanford University Press, 1941.

The Jepson Desert Manual. Edited by Bruce G. Baldwin, Steve Boyd, Barbara J. Ertter, Robert W. Patterson, Thomas J. Rosatti, and Dieter H. Wilken. Berkeley: University of California Press, 2002.

Kearney, Thomas H. and Robert H. Peebles. *Arizona Flora.* Berkeley: University of California Press, 1964.

Knute, Adrienne. *Plants of the East Mojave.* Cima, Calif.: Wide Horizons Press, 1991.

Lamb, Samuel H. *Woody Plants of the Southwest.* Santa Fe, New Mexico: The Sunstone Press, 1977.

McMinn, Howard E. *An Illustrated Manual of California Shrubs.* Berkeley: University of California Press, 1939.

Mozingo, Hugh N. *Shrubs of the Great Basin: A Natural History.* Reno: University of Nevada Press, 1987.

Munz, Philip A. *California Desert Wildflowers.* Berkeley: University of California Press, 1969.

Munz, Philip A. *A Flora of Southern California.* Berkeley: University of California Press, 1974.

Phillips, B., A. M. Phillips, III, and M. A. Schmidt Bernzott. *Annotated Checklist of Vascular Plants of Grand Canyon National Park.* Grand Canyon Natural History Association, Monograph Number 7, 1987.

Raven, Peter H., and Daniel I. Axelrod. "Origins and Relationships of the California Flora," *University of California Publications in Botany,* no. 72 (1978).

Simpson, B. B. *Mesquite: Its Biology in Two Desert Ecosystems.* Stroudsburg, Pa.: Dowden, Hutchinson, and Ross, Inc., 1977.

Spellenberg, Richard, and S. R. Rodriguez Tijerina. "Geographic Variation and Taxonomy of North American Species of *Mirabilis,* Section Oxybaphoides (Nyctaginaceae)." *Sida* 19 (3): 539-570 (2001).

Stewart, Jon M. *Mojave Desert Wildflowers.* Albuquerque, New Mexico. 1998.

Taylor, Ronald J. *Desert Wildflowers of North America.* Missoula, Mont.: Mountain Press Publishing Company, 1998.

Turner, Raymond M. "Mohave Desert Scrub," vol. 4 of *Desert Plants,* ed. David E. Brown, no. 1–4, 1982.

Turner, Raymond M., Janice E. Bowers, and Tony L. Burgess. 1995. *Sonoran Desert Plants: An Ecological Atlas.* Tucson: The University of Arizona Press, 1995.

Twisselmann, Ernest C. *A Flora of Kern County.* San Francisco: University of San Francisco, 1967.

United States Department of Agriculture, Forest Service. *Range Plant Handbook.* (1937; Reprint, New York: Dover Publications, Inc., 1988.)

A Utah Flora. Edited by S. L. Welsh, N. D. Atwood, S. Goodrich, and L. C. Higgins. Provo: Brigham Young University, 1993.

Plant names and herbarium collection:

Bailey, L. H. *How Plants Get Their Names.* New York: Dover Publications, 1963.

Coombes, Allen J. *Dictionary of Plant Names.* Portland: Timber Press, 1997.

Nilsson, Karen B. *A Wildflower by Any Other Name.* Yosemite Association, Yosemite National Park, California, 1994.

Ross, Timothy S. "Herbarium Specimens as Documents: Purposes and General Collecting Techniques." *Crossosoma* 22 (1): 3-39 (1996).

Desert ecosystems, ecology, natural history, and conservation:

California Native Plant Society's Inventory of Rare and Endangered Plants of California, 6th ed. Edited by David P. Tibor. Sacramento: California Native Plant Society, 2001.

Clevenger, Sarah. *Flower Pigments.* Scientific American reprint, W. H. Freeman and Company, San Francisco, California. 1964.

Cooper, D. S., and D. L. Perlman. "Habitat Conservation on Military Installations." *Fremontia* 25 (1): 3-8 (1997).

Invasive Plants of California's Wildlands. Edited by Carla C. Bossard, J. M. Randall, and Marc C. Hoshovsky. Berkeley: University of California Press, 2000.

Jaeger, Edmund C. *The California Deserts,* 4th ed. Stanford: Stanford University Press, 1965.

Jaeger, Edmund C. *The North American Deserts.* Stanford: Stanford University Press, 1957.

Johnson, Hyrum B. "Plant Pubescence: An Ecological Perspective." *Botanical Review* 41 (3): 233-258 (1975).

Lovich, J. E. and D. Bainbridge. "Anthropogenic Degradation of the Southern California Desert Ecosystem and Prospects for Natural Recovery and Restoration." *Environmental Management* 24 (3): 309-326 (1999).

A Natural History of the Sonoran Desert. Edited by Steven J. Phillips and Patricia W. Comus. Tucson, Arizona: Arizona-Sonora Desert Museum, 2000.

Plant Biology of Eastern California. Edited by Clarence A. Hall Jr. and Victoria Doyle-Jones. University of California, White Mountain Research Station, 1988.

Schoenherr, Allan A. *A Natural History of California.* Berkeley: University of California Press, 1992.

United States Geological Survey. Western Ecological Research Center. *Presentation Abstracts: Mojave Desert Science Symposium.* February 25-27, 1999.

Historical information, ethnobotany, and medicinal uses of plants:

Bean, Lowell J., and Katherine S. Saubel. *Temalpakh: Cahuilla Indian Knowledge and Usage of Plants.* Banning, California: Malki Museum Press, 1972.

Earle, David D. "Indians of the Upper Mojave River and Victor Valley: The Historic Period." Victor Valley College, 1991.

Handbook of the American Indians North of Mexico, part 2. Edited by F. W. Hodge. Smithsonian Institution, Bureau of American Ethnology, Bulletin 30 (1912).

Handbook of North American Indians, Volume 10: Southwest. Edited by W. C. Sturtevant. Washington: Smithsonian Institution, 1983.

Handbook of North American Indians, Volume 11: Great Basin. Edited by W. C. Sturtevant. Washington: Smithsonian Institution,1986.

Johnston, Frank. *The Serrano Indians of Southern California.* Banning, Calif.: Malki Museum Press, 1965.

Kroeber, A. L. *Handbook of the Indians of California.* (1925; Reprint, New York: Dover Publications, Inc., 1976.)

Laird, Carobeth. *The Chemehuevis.* Banning, California: Malki Museum Press, 1976.

Lyman, L. "Historic Indians, Hispanic Incursions, and Other Travelers." 2002. Unpublished manuscript.

Moore, Michael. *Medicinal Plants of the Pacific West.* Santa Fe, New Mexico: Red Crane Books, 1993.

Rhode, David. *Native Plants of Southern Nevada: An Ethnobotany.* Salt Lake City: University of Utah Press, 2002.

"The Serrano Indians, Early Inhabitants of Victor Valley." *San Bernardino Museum Quarterly,* Winter 1962.

The Shoshoni Indians of Inyo County, Callifornia: The Kerr Manuscript. Edited by C. N. Irwin. Independence, California: Eastern California Museum, 1980.

Smith, Gerald A. and Ruth D. Simpson. 1964. *Basket Makers of San Bernardino County.* Redlands, California: San Bernardino County Museum, 1964.

Stickel, E. G., and L. J. Weinman-Roberts. *An Overview of the Cultural Resources of the Western Mojave Desert.* A special report prepared at the request of the United States Department of Interior, Bureau of Land Management. 1980.

Walker, Clifford J. *Back Door to California: The Story of the Mojave River Trail.* Barstow, Calif.: Mojave River Valley Museum Association, 1986.

Insects:

Colton, Harold S. "The Anatomy of the Lac Insect, *Tachardiella larrea." Museum of Northern Arizona,* Bulletin 21 (1944).

Emmel, Thomas C., and John F. Emmel. "The Butterflies of Southern California." *Natural History Museum of Los Angeles County,* Science Series 26 (1973).

Holland, W. J. *The Moth Book: A Guide to the Moths of North America.* New York: Dover Publications, Inc., 1968.

Powell, Jerry A. and Charles L. Hogue. *California Insects.* Berkeley: University of California Press, 1979.

Scott, James A. *The Butterflies of North America: A Natural History and Field Guide.* Stanford: Stanford University Press, 1986.

Stewart, Bob. *Common Butterflies of California.* Point Reyes Station, California: West Coast Lady Press, 1997.

Geology and pack rat middens:

Hunt, Charles B. *Death Valley: Geology, Ecology, Archaeology.* Berkeley: University of California Press, 1975.

Packrat Middens. Edited by Julio L. Betancourt, Thomas R. Van Devender, and Paul S. Martin. Tucson: The University of Arizona Press, 1990.

Horticulture:

Mabberley, D. J. *The Plant-Book.* New York: Cambridge University Press, 1987.

Mielke, Judy. *Native Plants for Southwestern Landscapes.* Austin, Texas: University of Texas Press, 1993.

INDEX

A

Abronia, Small-Flowered, 166
Abronia
  pogonantha Heimeri, 100
  villosa S. Watson var. *villosa,* 100
Acacia greggii A. Gray, 241
Acamptopappus sphaerocephalus (A. Gray) A.
  Gray, 188
Achnatherum
  hymenoides (Roemer & Shultes)
    Barkworth, 287
  speciosum (Trin. & Rupr.) Barkworth, 287
Achyronichia cooperi Torrey & A. Gray, 147
Acton Encelia, 197
Adenophyllum cooperi (A. Gray) Strother, 189
Adonis Lupine, 49
Ajamete, 128
Alkali Crucifer, 145
Alkali Goldenbush, 211
Alkali Mariposa Lily, 97
Allenrolfea occidentalis (S. Watson)
  Kuntze, 274
Allionia incarnata L., 101
Almond, Desert, 180
Alyssum, Desert, 144
Amaranthaceae
  Amaranthus fimbriatus (Torrey) Benth., 78
  Tidestromia oblongifolia (S. Watson)
    Standley, 266
Amaranth, Fringed, 78
Amaranthus fimbriatus (Torrey) Benth., 78
Amargosa Nitrophila, 281
Ambrosia
  acanthicarpa Hook., 267
  dumosa (A. Gray) Payne, 268
Amsinckia tessellata A. Gray, 226
Amsonia, 125
Amsonia tomentosa Torrey & Fremont, 125
Anacardiaceae
  Rhus trilobata Torrey & A. Gray, 124

Anemopsis californica (Nutt.) Hook., 182
Anisocoma acaulis Torrey & A. Gray, 189
Annual Bur-Sage, 267
Annual Stillingia, 286
Annual Turtleback, 217
Antelope Bush, 181
Antirrhinum filipes A. Gray, 258
Apache Plume, 119
Apiaceae
  Cymopteris deserticola Brandegee, 42
  Lomatium mohavense (J. Coulter & Rose)
    J. Coulter & Rose, 43
Apocynaceae
  Amsonia tomentosa Torrey & Fremont, 125
Apricot Mallow, 117
Argemone corymbosa E. Greene, 170
Arizona Lupine, 48
Arrow-Scale, 280
Artemisia tridentata Nutt., 269
Asclepiadaceae
  Asclepias erosa Torrey, 126
  Asclepias fascicularis Decne., 127
  Asclepias subulata Decne., 128
  Sarcostemma cyanchoides Decne ssp.
    hartwegii (Vail) R. Holm, 79
Asclepias
  erosa Torrey, 126
  fascicularis Decne., 127
  subulata Decne., 128
Aster
  Hoary, 44
  White, 132
Asteraceae
  Acamptopappus sphaerocephalus (A. Gray)
    A. Gray, 188
  Adenophyllum cooperi (A. Gray)
    Strother, 189
  Ambrosia acanthicarpa Hook., 267
  Ambrosia dumosa (A. Gray) Payne, 268
  Anisocoma acaulis Torrey & A. Gray, 189

Artemisia tridentata Nutt., 269

Atrichoseris platyphylla A. Gray, 128

Baccharis emoryi A. Gray, 129

Baccharis salicifolia (Ruiz Lopez & Pavon) Pers., 129

Baileya multiradiata A. Gray var. *multiradiata*, 190

Baileya pauciradiata A. Gray, 191

Bebbia juncea (Benth.) E. Greene var. *aspera* E. Greene, 192

Brickellia incana A. Gray, 130

Brickellia longifolia Wats., 130

Calycoseris parryi A. Gray, 193

Chaenactis fremontii A. Gray, 131

Chaetopappa ericoides (Torrey) G. Nesom, 132

Chrysothamnus nauseosus (Pallas) Britton ssp. *mohavensis* (E. Greene) H. M. Hall & Clements, 194

Chrysothamnus paniculatus (A. Gray) H. M. Hall, 195

Cirsium mohavense (E. Greene) Petrak, 80

Coreopsis bigelovii (A. Gray) H. M. Hall, 196

Dicoria canescens A. Gray, 270

Encelia actoni Elmer, 197

Encelia farinosa Torrey & A. Gray, 198

Encelia frutescens (A. Gray) A. Gray, 199

Enceliopsis covillei (Nelson) S. F. Blake, 200

Enceliopsis nudicaulis (A. Gray) Nelson var. *nudicaulis*, 201

Ericameria cooperi (A. Gray) H. M. Hall var. *cooperi*, 202

Ericameria cuneata (A. Gray) McClatchie var. *spathulata* (A. Gray) H. M. Hall, 203

Ericameria linearifolia (DC.) Urb & J. Wussow, 204

Eriophyllum mohavense (I. M. Johnston) Jepson, 205

Eriophyllum pringlei A. Gray, 206

Eriophyllum wallacei (A. Gray) A. Gray, 207

Filago californica Nutt., 270

Geraea canescens A. Gray, 208

Gutierrezia microcephala (DC.) A. Gray, 209

Hecastocleis shockleyi Gray, 271

Hemizonia arida Keck, 210

Hymenoclea salsola A. Gray, 272

Isocoma acradenia (E. Greene) E. Greene var. *acradenia*, 211

Lasthenia californica Lindley, 212

Layia glandulosa (Hook.) Hook. & Arn., 133

Lepidospartum latisquamum Wats., 212

Lepidospartum squamatum (A. Gray) A. Gray, 213

Machaeranthera arida Turner & Horne, 134

Machaeranthera canescens (Pursh) A. Gray var. *leucanthemifolia* (E. Greene) Welsh, 44

Malacothrix glabrata A. Gray, 214

Monoptilon bellidiforme A. Gray, 135

Monoptilon bellioides (A. Gray) H. M. Hall, 136

Nicolletia occidentalis A. Gray, 81

Palafoxia arida B. Turner & M. Morris var. *arida*, 82

Pectis papposa Harvey & A. Gray var. *papposa*, 215

Perityle emoryi Torrey, 136

Peucephyllum schottii A. Gray, 216

Psathyrotes annua (Nutt.) A. Gray, 217

Psathyrotes ramosissima (Torrey) A. Gray, 218

Psilotrophe cooperi (A. Gray) E. Greene, 219

Rafinesquia neomexicana A. Gray, 137

Senecio flaccidus Less. var. *monoensis* (E. Greene) B. Turner & T. Barkley, 220

Senecio mohavensis A. Gray, 221

Stephanomeria parryi A. Gray, 83

Stephanomeria pauciflora (Torrey) Nelson, 84

Syntrichopappus fremontii A. Gray, 222

Tetradymia axillaris Nelson var. *longispina* (M. E. Jones) Strother, 223

Thymophylla pentachaeta (DC.) Small var. *belenidium* (DC.) Strother, 224

Trichoptilium incisum A. Gray, 225

Trixis californica Kellogg var. *californica*, 225

Xylorhiza tortifolia (Torrey & A. Gray) E. Greene var. *tortifolia*, 45

Astragalus
  coccineus Brandegee, 116
  jaegerianus Per., 151
  lentiginosus Hook., 47

newberryi A. Gray var. *newberryi,* 91
Atrichoseris platyphylla A. Gray, 128
Atriplex
    canescens (Pursh) Nutt. ssp. *canescens,* 275
    confertifolia (Torrey & Fremont) S.
        Watson, 276
    hymenelytra (Torrey) S. Watson, 277
    serenana Nelson var. *serenana,* 278

B

Baccharis, Emory, 129
Baccharis
    emoryi A. Gray, 129
    salicifolia (Ruiz Lopez & Pavon)
        Pers., 129
Baileya
    multiradiata A. Gray var. *multiradiata,* 190
    pauciradiata A. Gray, 191
Bajada Lupine, 48
Ball Sage, Gray, 61
Banana Yucca, 158
Barrel Cactus, California, 233
Barstow Woolly Sunflower, 205
Basin Sagebrush, Great, 269
Bayonet, Spanish, 158
Beadpod, 228
Bean, Screw, 154
Beardtongue
    Limestone, 110
    White-Margined, 110
Beargrass, Parry's, 157
Beavertail Cactus, 89
Bebbia juncea (Benth.) E. Greene var. *aspera*
    E. Greene, 192
Bell, Desert Canterbury, 52
Bigelow's Coreopsis, 196
Bigelow's Monkeyflower, 108
Bigelow's Tickseed, 196
Big Galleta, 293
Bignoniaceae
    Chilopsis linearis (Cav.) Sweet ssp. *arcuata*
        (Fosb.) Henrickson, 85
Bignonia Family. *See* Bignoniaceae
Big Sagebrush, 269
Bill, Desert Heron's, 94
Bird's-Beak, Desert, 107
Bird's Foot Fern, 307
Bitterbrush, 181
Blackbush, 257
Black-Stem Rabbitchush, 195

Bladderpod, 228, 239
Bladder Sage, 58
Blazing Star, 245
Blazing Star, Sand, 245
Boerhavia triqueta S. Watson, 101
Booth's Primrose, 167
Borage Family. *See* Boraginaceae
Boraginaceae
    Amsinckia tessellata A. Gray, 226
    Cryptantha species, 138–39
    Heliotropium curassavicum L., 140
    Pectocarya penicillata, 141
    Pectocarya setosa, 142
    Plagiobothrys parishii Jtn., 143
    Tequilia plicata (Torrey) A. Richardson, 86
Bouteloua
    aristidoides (Kunth.) Griseb. var.
        aristidoides, 288
    barbata Lagasca var. *barbata,* 288
Box Thorn
    Cooper's, 184
    Pallid, 111
Bract, Punctured, 178
Bractscale, 278
Brake Fern Family. *See* Pteridaceae
Brandegea, 148
Brandegea bigelovii (S. Wats.) Cogn., 148
Brassicaceae
    Caulanthus inflatus S. Watson, 46
    Dithyrea californica Harvey, 144
    Lepidium flavum Torrey var. *flavum,* 227
    Lepidium fremontii S. Watson, 144
    Lesquerella tenella Nelson, 228
    Stanleya elata Jones., 229
    Stanleya pinnata (Pursh) Britton, 230
    Thelypodium integrifolium (Nutt.)
        Endl., 145
Brickellia
    Long-Leaved, 130
    Woolly, 130
Brickellia
    incana A. Gray, 130
    longifolia Wats., 130
Bristle-Lobed Sandmat, 151
Brittlebush, 198
Brittlebush, Green, 199
Brittle Spineflower, 250
Broad-Flowered Gilia, 68
Broad-Leaved Gilia, 103
Brome, Red, 289

Bromus madritensis L. ssp. *rubens* (L.)
  Husnot, 289
Broom-Rape, Cooper's, 66
Broom-Rape Family. *See* Orobanchaceae
Broom, Turpentine, 72
Brown-Eyed Primrose, 168
Buckhorn Cholla, 234
Buckwheat
  California, 177
  Flat-Topped, 176
  Palmer, 254
  Thomas, 255
Buckwheat Family. *See* Polygonaceae
Buddlejaceae
  Buddleja utahensis Cov., 231
Buddleja Family. *See* Buddlejaceae
  Buddleja utahensis Cov., 231
Bugseed, 270
Bur-Sage
  Annual, 267
  White, 268
Burrobush, 268
Bush, Antelope, 181
Bush, Creosote, 262
Bush, Indigo, 51
Bush, Iodine, 274
Bush, Panamint Butterfly, 231
Bush, Paper-Bag, 58
Bush Peppergrass, 144
Bush Seepweed, 284
Bush, Wait-a-Minute, 241
Bush, Wishbone, 102
Buttercup Family. *See* Ranunculaceae
Butterfly Bush, Panamint, 231
Butterweed
  California, 220
  Mojave, 221

C

Cactaceae
  Echinocactus polycephalus Engelm. & J.
    Bigelow var. *polycephalus,* 232
  Echinocereus engelmannii, 87
  Echinocereus triglochidiatus
    Engelm., 114
  Escobaria vivipara (Nutt.) F. Buxb. var.
    deserti (Engelm.) D. Hunt, 146
  Ferocactus cylindraceus (Engelm.) Orc. var.
    cylindraceus, 233
  Mammillaria tetrancistra Engelm., 88

Opuntia acanthocarpa Englem. & J.
  Bigelow var. *coloradensis* L. Benson, 234
Opuntia basilaris Engelm. & Bigel., 89
Opuntia chlorotica Engelm. & J.
  Bigelow, 235
Opuntia echinocarpa Engelm. & J.
  Bigelow, 273
Opuntia erinacea Engelm. & J. Bigelow
  var. *erinacea,* 236
Opuntia parishii Orc., 237
Sclerocactus polyancistrus (Engelm. & J.
  Bigelow) Britton & Rose, 115
Cactus
  Beavertail, 89
  Calico, 87
  California Barrel, 233
  Dead, 237
  Fringe-Flowered, 146
  Hedge-Hog, 87
  Mojave Mound, 114
  Nipple, 88
  Old Man, 236
  Pineapple, 115
Cactus Family. *See* Cactaceae
Calico Cactus, 87
Calico, Desert, 104
California Barrel Cactus, 233
California Buckwheat, 177
California Butterweed, 220
California Croton, 285
California Juniper, 302
California Poppy, 118
Calochortus
  kennedyi Porter var. *kennedyi,* 117
  striatus Parish, 97
Caltrop Family. *See* Zygophyllaceae
Calycoseris parryi A. Gray, 193
Calyptridium monandrum Nutt., 106
Camas, Death, 162
Cambess, Linear-Leaved, 179
Camissonia
  boothii (Douglas) Raven ssp. *desertorum*
    (Munz) Raven, 167
  brevipes (A. Gray) Raven ssp. *brevipes,* 246
  campestris (E. Greene) Raven, 247
  claviformis (Torrey & Fremont) Raven ssp.
    claviformis, 168
  pallida (Abrams) Raven ssp. *hallii*
    (Davidson) Raven, 248
Canaigre, 105

Canbya candida C. Parry, 171
Candle, Desert, 46
Candle, Our Lord's, 161
Canterbury Bell, Desert, 52
Canyon Petalonyx, 164
Caper Family. *See* Capparaceae
Capparaceae
    Cleomella obtusifolia Torrey &
      Fremont, 238
    Isomeris arborea Nutt., 239
Carpet, Golden, 255
Carpet-Weed, 165
Carpet-Weed Family. *See* Molluginaceae
Carrot Family. *See* Apiaceae
Caryophyllaceae
    Achyronichia cooperi Torrey & A.
      Gray, 147
Castela emoryi (A. Gray) Moran &
    Felger, 298
Castilleja
    angustifolia (Nutt.) G. Don, 120
    exserta (A. A. Heller) Chuang & Heckard
      ssp. *venusta* (A. A. Heller) Chuang &
      Heckard, 107
    plagiotoma A. Gray, 297
Catclaw, 241
Caulanthus inflatus S. Watson, 46
Cedar, Salt, 112
Chaenactis fremontii A. Gray, 131
Chaetopappa ericoides (Torrey) G. Nesom, 132
Chamaesyce
    albomarginata (Torrey & A. Gray)
      Small, 150
    setiloba (Torrey & A. Gray) Small, 151
Checker Fiddleneck, 226
Cheesebush, 272
Cheilanthes covillei Maxon, 307
Chenopodiaceae
    Allenrolfea occidentalis (S. Watson)
      Kuntze, 274
    Atriplex canescens (Pursh) Nutt. ssp.
      canescens, 275
    Atriplex confertifolia (Torrey & Fremont)
      S. Watson, 276
    Atriplex hymenelytra (Torrey) S.
      Watson, 277
    Atriplex serenana Nelson var. *serenana*, 278
    Grayia spinosa (Hook.) Moq., 278
    Krascheninnikovia lanata (Pursh) A. D. J.
      Meeuse & Smit, 279

    Monolepis nuttalliana (Schultes) E.
      Greene, 280
    Nitrophila mohavensis Munz & Roos, 281
    Salsola tragus L., 282
    Sarcobatus vermiculatus (Hook.)
      Torrey, 283
    Suaeda moquinii (Torrey) E. Greene, 284
Chess, Foxtail, 289
Chia, 60
Chicory, Desert, 137
Chilopsis linearis (Cav.) Sweet ssp. *arcuata*
    (Fosb.) Henrickson, 85
Chinch-Weed, 215
Chinese Houses, 73
Cholla
    Buckhorn, 234
    Club, 237
    Mat, 237
    Silver, 273
    Staghorn, 234
Chorizanthe
    brevicornu Torrey var. *brevicornu*, 250
    rigida (Torrey) Torrey & A. Gray, 251
Chrysothamnus
    nauseosus (Pallas) Britton ssp.
      mohavensis (E. Greene) H. M. Hall
      & Clements, 194
    paniculatus (A. Gray) H. M. Hall, 195
Cirsium mohavense (E. Greene) Petrak, 80
Claw, Devil, 115
Cleomella obtusifolia Torrey & Fremont, 238
Cliff Goldenbush, 203
Climbing Milkweed, 79
Clover, Purple Owl's, 107
Club Cholla, 237
Coleogyne ramosissima Torrey, 257
Collinsia bartsiifolia Benth. var. *davidsonii*
    (Parish) V. Newsom, 73
Colorado Desert Marigold, 191
Comb-Bur
    Hairy-Leaved, 141
    Stiff-Stemmed, 142
Common Reed, 292
Cooper's Box Thorn, 184
Cooper's Broom-Rape, 66
Cooper's Dyssodia, 189
Cooper's Glandweed, 189
Cooper's Goldenbush, 202
Cordylanthus eremicus Munz ssp.
    eremicus, 107

Coreopsis bigelovii (A. Gray) H. M. Hall, 196
Coreopsis, Bigelow's, 196
Cottonrose, 270
Cotton-Thorn, 223
Cotton-Top, 232
Cottonwood, Fremont, 295
Coville's Lip Fern, 307
Coyote Tobacco, 185
Cranesbill, 93
Crassulaceae
    Dudleya saxosa (M. E. Jones) Britton &
        Rose ssp. *aloides* (Rose) Moran, 90
Creosote Bush, 262
Crippler, Horse, 237
Croton, California, 285
Croton californicus Muell., 285
Crucifer, Alkali, 145
Crucifixion Thorn, 298
Cryptantha species, 138–39
Cucurbitaceae
    Brandegea bigelovii (S. Wats.) Cogn., 148
Cup, Mojave Sun, 247
Cupressaceae
    Juniperus californicus Carriere, 302
    Juniperus osteosperma (Torrey) Little, 303
Cuscutaceae
    Cuscuta denticulata Engelm., 149
Cuscuta denticulata Engelm., 149
Cymopteris, Desert, 42
Cymopteris deserticola Brandegee, 42
Cypress Family. *See* Cupressaceae

D
Daisy
    False Woolly, 222
    Naked-Stemmed, 201
    Panamint, 200
    Paper, 219
    Pringle's Woolly, 206
    Silver Lakes, 134
    Wallace's Woolly, 207
Dalea
    Parry, 50
    Silk, 92
Dalea mollisma (Rydb.) Munz, 92
Dandelion, Desert, 214
Datura, Sacred, 183
Datura wrightii Regel, 183
Dead Cactus, 237
Death Camas, 162

Death Valley Monkeyflower, 109
Death Valley Sage, 61
Death Valley Sandpaper Plant, 165
Dedeckera eurekensis Rev. & J. Howell, 252
Delphinium parishii A. Gray ssp. *parishii,* 71
Desert Almond, 180
Desert Alyssum, 144
Desert Bird's-Beak, 107
Desert Calico, 104
Desert Candle, 46
Desert Canterbury Bell, 52
Desert Chicory, 137
Desert Cymopteris, 42
Desert Dandelion, 214
Desert Five-Spot, 99
Desert Fluff-Grass, 291
Desert Gold-Poppy, 249
Desert Heron's Bill, 94
Desert Holly, 277
Desert Hyacinth, 64
Desert Larkspur, 71
Desert-Lavender, 57
Desert Lily, 156
Desert Live-Forever, 90
Desert Lupine, 50
Desert Mallow, 117
Desert Marigold, 190
Desert Marigold, Colorado, 191
Desert Milkweed, 126
Desert Mistletoe, 299
Desert Needle Grass, 287
Desert Needles, 82
Desert Paintbrush, 120
Desert Parsley, 43
Desert Plantain, 172
Desert Portulaca, 256
Desert Rock-Pea, 242
Desert Rue, 72
Desert Sage, 61
Desert Sand-Verbena, 100
Desert Senna, 243
Desert Star, 136
Desert Star, Small, 135
Desert Straw, 84
Desert Sunflower, 208
Desert Trumpet, 253
Desert Willow, 85
Desert Zygadene, 162
Devil Claw, 115
Devil's Lettuce, 226

Dichelostemma capitatum (Benth) A. W.
Wood ssp. *pauciflorum* (Torrey) Keator, 64
Dicoria canescens A. Gray, 270
Distichlis spicata (L.) E. Greene, 290
Dithyrea californica Harvey, 144
Dodder, 149
Dodder Family. *See* Cuscutaceae
Dogbane Family. *See* Apocynaceae
Dudleya saxosa (M. E. Jones) Britton & Rose
ssp. *aloides* (Rose) Moran, 90
Dunes Evening Primrose, Eureka, 169
Dunes Grass, Eureka Valley, 294
Dyssodia, Cooper's, 189

E

Echinocactus polycephalus Engelm. & J.
Bigelow var. *polycephalus,* 232
Echinocereus
engelmannii, 87
triglochidiatus Engelm., 114
Elegant Lupine, 48
Emory Baccharis, 129
Emory Rock-Daisy, 136
Encelia
Acton, 197
Rayless, 199
Encelia
actoni Elmer, 197
farinosa Torrey & A. Gray, 198
frutescens (A. Gray) A. Gray, 199
Enceliopsis
covillei (Nelson) S. F. Blake, 200
nudicaulis (A. Gray) Nelson var.
nudicaulis, 201
Ephedra
nevadensis S. Watson, 303
trifurca Torrey, 304
viridis Cov., 305
Ephedra, Green, 305
Ephedraceae
Ephedra nevadensis S. Watson, 303
Ephedra trifurca Torrey, 304
Ephedra viridis Cov., 305
Ephedra Family. *See* Ephedraceae
Eremalche, Small-Flowered, 98
Eremalche
exilis (A. Gray) E. Greene, 98
rotundifolia (A. Gray) E. Greene, 99
Eriastrum densifolium (Benth.) H. Mason
ssp. *mohavense* (Craig) H. Mason, 67

Eriastrum, Perennial, 67
Ericameria
cooperi (A. Gray) H. M. Hall var.
cooperi, 202
cuneata (A. Gray) McClatchie var.
spathulata (A. Gray) H. M. Hall, 203
linearifolia (DC.) Urb & J. Wussow, 204
Eriodictyon trichocalyx A. A. Heller var.
trichocalyx, 155
Eriogonum
deflexum Torrey var. *deflexum,* 176
fasciculatum Benth. var. *polifolium* (A.
DC.) Torrey & A. Gray, 177
inflatum Torrey & Fremont var.
inflatum, 253
palmerianum Rev., 254
Erioneuron pulchellum (Kunth) Tateoka, 291
Eriophyllum
mohavense (I. M. Johnston) Jepson, 205
pringlei A. Gray, 206
wallacei (A. Gray) A. Gray, 207
Erodium
cicutarium (L.) L'Her., 93
texanum A. Gray, 94
Eschscholzia
californica Cham., 118
glyptosperma E. Greene, 249
Escobaria vivipara (Nutt.) F. Buxb. var.
deserti (Engelm.) D. Hunt, 146
Eucnide urens (A. Gray) C. Parry, 163
Euphorbiaceae
Chamaesyce albomarginata (Torrey & A.
Gray) Small, 150
Chamaesyce setiloba (Torrey & A. Gray)
Small, 151
Croton californicus Muell., 285
Euphorbia incisa Engelm., 240
Stillingia linearifolia S. Watson, 116
Stillingia spinulosa S. Watson, 286
Tragia ramosa Torrey, 286
Euphorbia incisa Engelm., 240
Eureka Dunes Evening Primrose, 169
Eureka Valley Dunes Grass, 294
Evening Primrose
Eureka Dunes, 169
Golden, 246
Spring, 248
Yellow, 248
Evening Primrose Family. *See* Onagraceae
Evening Snow, 173

F

Fabaceae
  Acacia greggii A. Gray, 241
  Astragalus coccineus Brandegee, 116
  Astragalus jaegerianus Per., 151
  Astragalus lentiginosus Hook., 47
  Astragalus newberryi A. Gray var.
    newberryi, 91
  Dalea mollisma (Rydb.) Munz, 92
  Glycyrrhiza lepidota Pursh, 152
  Lotus rigidus (Benth.) E. Greene, 242
  Lotus strigosus (Nutt.) E. Greene, 242
  Lupinus arizonicus (S. Watson) S.
    Watson, 48
  Lupinus concinnus J. Agardh, 48
  Lupinus excubitus M. E. Jones var.
    excubitus, 49
  Lupinus shockleyi S. Watson, 50
  Marina parryi (Torrey & A. Gray)
    Barneby, 50
  Prosopis glandulosa Torrey var. *torreyana*
    (L. Benson) M. Johnston, 153
  Prosopis pubescens Benth., 154
  Psorothamnus arborescens (A. Gray)
    Barneby var. *minutifolius* (Parish)
    Barneby, 51
  Senna armata (S. Watson) H. Irwin &
    Barneby, 243
Fallugia paradoxa (D. Don) Endl., 119
False Woolly Daisy, 222
Fat-Leaf Phacelia, 55
Fat, Mule, 129
Fat, Winter, 279
Fern
  Bird's Foot, 307
  Coville's Lip, 307
Ferocactus cylindraceus (Engelm.) Orc. var.
  cylindraceus, 233
Fescue, Six-Weeks, 295
Fiddleneck, Checker, 226
Field Primrose, 247
Figwort Family. *See* Scrophulariaceae
Filago californica Nutt., 270
Filaree, Red-Stemmed, 93
Fir
  Long-Leaved Joint, 304
  Mountain Joint, 305
  Nevada Joint, 303
Firecracker, Utah, 121

Five-Spot, Desert, 99
Flat-Topped Buckwheat, 176
Flax, 65
Flax Family. *See* Linaceae
Fleshy-Fruited Yucca, 158
Flower, Onyx, 147
Flower, Parish's Popcorn, 143
Fluff-Grass, Desert, 291
Foot Fern, Bird's, 307
Forget-Me-Not, 138–39
Four O'Clock Family. *See* Nyctaginaceae
Four O'Clock, Giant, 103
Four-Wing Saltbush, 275
Foxtail Chess, 289
Freckled Milkvetch, 47
Fremont Cottonwood, 295
Fremont Phacelia, 55
Fremont Pincushion, 131
Fringed Amaranth, 78
Fringe-Flowered Cactus, 146
Frost Mat, 147

G

Galleta, Big, 293
Geraea canescens A. Gray, 208
Geraniaceae
  Erodium cicutarium (L.) L'Her., 93
  Erodium texanum A. Gray, 94
Geranium Family. *See* Geraniaceae
Ghost-Flower, 182
Ghost, Gravel, 128
Giant Four O'Clock, 103
Gilia
  Broad-Flowered, 68
  Broad-Leaved, 103
  Schott, 175
Gilia
  latiflora (A. Gray) A. Gray, 68
  latifolia S. Watson, 103
Gilmania luteola (Cov.) Cov., 255
Glandweed, Cooper's, 189
Glycyrrhiza lepidota Pursh, 152
Goathead, 263
Gold, July, 252
Goldenbush
  Alkali, 210
  Cliff, 203
  Cooper's, 202
  Interior, 204
  Linear-Leaved, 204

Golden Carpet, 255
Golden Evening Primrose, 246
Goldenhead, 188
Goldfields, 212
Gold-Poppy, Desert, 249
Goodding's Verbena, 76
Goosefoot Family. *See* Chenopodiaceae
Gourd Family. *See* Cucurbitaceae
Gramma
    Needle, 288
    Six-Weeks, 288
Grape Soda Lupine, 49
Grass, Desert Needle, 287
Grass, Eureka Valley Dunes, 294
Grass Family. *See* Poaceae
Gravel Ghost, 128
Greasewood, 283
Great Basin Sagebrush, 269
Green Brittlebush, 199
Greenbroom, 212
Green Ephedra, 305
Gray Ball Sage, 61
Grayia spinosa (Hook.) Moq., 278
Ground-Cherry, Thick-Leaved, 261
Gutierrezia microcephala (DC.) A. Gray, 209

H

Hairy-Leaved Comb-Bur, 141
Hecastocleis, 271
Hecastocleis shockleyi Gray, 271
Hedge-Hog Cactus, 87
Heliotrope, 140
Heliotropium curassavicum L., 140
Hemizonia arida Keck, 210
Herba Impia, 270
Heron's Bill, Desert, 94
Hesperocallis undulata A. Gray, 156
Hoary Aster, 44
Hole-in-the-Sand Plant, 81
Holly, Desert, 277
Honey Mesquite, 153
Honey-Sweet, 266
Hop-Sage, 278
Horse Crippler, 237
Houses, Chinese, 73
Hyacinth, Desert, 64
Hydrophyllaceae
    Eriodictyon trichocalyx A. A. Heller var.
        trichocalyx, 155
    Nama demissum A. Gray var. *demissum,* 94

Phacelia campanularia A. Gray ssp.
    vasiformis Gillett., 52
Phacelia crenulata Torrey, 53
Phacelia curvipes S. Watson, 54
Phacelia distans Benth., 55
Phacelia fremontii Torrey, 55
Phacelia ivesiana Torrey, 155
Phacelia parishii A. Gray, 56
Phacelia pedicillata A. Gray, 57
Phacelia rotundifolia A. Gray, 156
Hymenoclea salsola A. Gray, 272
Hyptis emoryi Torrey, 57

I

Impia, Herba, 270
Incienso, 198
Indian Ricegrass, 287
Indian Tobacco, 186
Indigo Bush, 51
Ink-Blite, 284
Interior Goldenbush, 204
Iodine Bush, 274
Isocoma acradenia (E. Greene) E. Greene
    var. *acradenia,* 211
Isomeris arborea Nutt., 239
Ives Phacelia, 155

J

Jimson Weed, 183
Joint Fir
    Long-Leaved, 304
    Mountain, 305
    Nevada, 303
Joshua Tree, 159
July Gold, 252
Juniper
    California, 302
    Utah, 303
Juniperus
    californicus Carriere, 302
    osteosperma (Torrey) Little, 303

K

Keckiella antirrhinoides (Benth.) Straw var.
    microphylla (A. Gray) N. Holmgren, 259
Keckiella, Yellow, 259
Krameria
    erecta Shultes, 95
Krameriaceae
    Krameria erecta Shultes, 95

Krascheninnikovia lanata (Pursh) A. D. J. Meeuse & Smit, 279

L

Lace-Leaf Phacelia, 55
Lady, Rock, 260
Lakes Daisy, Silver, 134
Lane Mountain Milkvetch, 151
Langloisia setosissima (Torrey & A. Gray) E. Greene ssp. *punctata* (Cov.) S. Timbrook, 69
Lamiaceae
  Hyptis emoryi Torrey, 57
  Monardella exilis E. Greene, 96
  Salazaria mexicana Torrey, 58
  Salvia carduacea Benth., 59
  Salvia columbariae Benth., 60
  Salvia dorrii (Kellogg) Abrams var. *pilosa* (A. Gray) J. L. Strachan & Rev., 61
  Salvia funerea M. E. Jones, 61
  Salvia mohavensis E. Greene, 62
Larkspur, Desert, 71
Larrea tridentata DC. (Cov.), 262
Lasthenia californica Lindley, 212
Layia glandulosa (Hook.) Hook. & Arn., 133
Lax-Flower, 191
Lennoaceae
  Pholisma arenarium Hook., 63
Lennoa Family. *See* Lennoaceae
Lepidium
  flavum Torrey var. *flavum,* 227
  fremontii S. Watson, 144
Lepidospartum
  latisquamum Wats., 212
  squamatum (A. Gray) A. Gray, 213
Lesquerella tenella Nelson, 228
Lesser Mohavea, 261
Lettuce, Devil's, 226
Lettuce, Wire, 84
Licorice, Wild, 152
Lilac Sunbonnet, 69
Liliaceae
  Calochortus kennedyi Porter var. *kennedyi,* 117
  Calochortus striatus Parish, 97
  Dichelostemma capitatum (Benth) A. W. Wood ssp. *pauciflorum* (Torrey) Keator, 64
  Hesperocallis undulata A. Gray, 156

Nolina parryi S. Watson, 157
  Yucca baccata Torrey, 158
  Yucca brevifolia Engelm., 159
  Yucca shidigera K. E. Ortgies, 160
  Yucca whipplei Torrey ssp. *caespitosa* (Jones) Haines, 161
  Zigadenus brevibracteatus (M. E. Jones) H. M. Hall, 162
Lily
  Alkali Mariposa, 97
  Desert, 156
  Mariposa, 117
Lily Family. *See* Liliaceae
Limestone Beardtongue, 110
Linaceae
  Linum lewisii Pursh, 65
Linanthus
  Mojave, 70
  Parry's, 70, 174
Linanthus
  breviculus (A. Gray) E. Greene, 70
  dichotomus Benth., 173
  parryae (A. Gray) E. Greene, 70, 174
Linear-Leaved Cambess, 179
Linear-Leaved Goldenbush, 204
Linear-Leaved Stillingia, 116
Linum lewisii Pursh, 65
Lip Fern, Coville's, 307
Little Sunbonnets, 175
Live-Forever, Desert, 90
Lizard's-Tail Family. *See* Saururaceae
Loasaceae
  Eucnide urens (A. Gray) C. Parry, 163
  Mentzelia albicaulis Hook., 244
  Mentzelia involucrata S. Watson, 245
  Mentzelia laevicaulis (Hook.) Torrey & A. Gray, 245
  Petalonyx nitidus Wats., 164
  Petalonyx thurberi ssp. *gilmanii* (Munz) Davis & Thompson, 165
Loasa Family. *See* Loasaceae
Locoweed, Scarlet, 116
Loeseliastrum
  matthewsii (A. Gray) S. Timbrook, 104
  schottii (Torrey) S. Timbrook, 175
Lomatium mohavense (J. Coulter & Rose) J. Coulter & Rose, 43
Long-Leaved Brickellia, 130
Long-Leaved Joint Fir, 304
Lord's Candle, Our, 161

Lotus
  rigidus (Benth.) E. Greene, 242
  strigosus (Nutt.) E. Greene, 242
Lotus, Stiff-Haired, 242
Lupine
  Adonis, 49
  Arizona, 48
  Bajada, 48
  Desert, 50
  Elegant, 48
  Grape Soda, 49
  Shockley, 50
Lupinus
  arizonicus (S. Watson) S. Watson, 48
  concinnus J. Agardh, 48
  excubitus M. E. Jones var. *excubitus,* 49
  shockleyi S. Watson, 50
Lycium
  cooperi A. Gray, 184
  pallidum Miers var. *oligospermum* C.
    Hitchc., 111

M

Machaeranthera
  arida Turner & Horne, 134
  canescens (Pursh) A. Gray var.
    leucanthemifolia (E. Greene) Welsh, 44
Machaeranthera, Slender, 214
Malacothrix glabrata A. Gray, 214
Mallow
  Apricot, 117
  Desert, 117
Mallow Family. *See* Malvaceae
Malvaceae
  Eremalche exilis (A. Gray) E. Greene, 98
  Eremalche rotundifolia (A. Gray) E.
    Greene, 99
  Sphaeralcea ambigua A. Gray var.
    ambigua, 117
Mammillaria tetrancistra Engelm., 88
Man Cactus, Old, 236
Mansa, Yerba, 182
Marigold
  Colorado Desert, 191
  Desert, 190
Marina parryi (Torrey & A. Gray)
  Barneby, 50
Mariposa Lily, 117
Mariposa Lily, Alkali, 97
Mat Cholla, 237

Matchweed, 209
Mat, Frost, 147
Mat, Purple, 94
Maurandya petrophila Cov. & C.
  Morton, 260
Mealy Rosette, 217
Menodora spinescens A. Gray, 166
Menodora, Spiny, 166
Mentzelia
  albicaulis Hook., 244
  involucrata S. Watson, 245
  laevicaulis (Hook.) Torrey & A. Gray, 245
Mesquite, Honey, 153
Mexican Whorled Milkweed, 127
Midget, Rock, 109
Mignonette Family. *See* Resedaceae
Milkvetch
  Freckled, 47
  Lane Mountain, 151
  Newberry, 91
  Scarlet, 116
Milkweed
  Climbing, 79
  Desert, 126
  Narrow-Leaf, 127
  Mexican Whorled, 127
  Rush, 128
Milkweed Family. *See* Asclepiadaceae
Mimulus
  bigelovei (A. Gray) A. Gray, 108
  mohavensis Lemmon, 121
  rupicola Cov. & A. L. Grant, 109
Mint Family. *See* Lamiaceae
Mirabilis
  californica A. Gray, 102
  multiflora (Torrey) A. Gray var. *glandulosa*
    (Standley) J. F. Macrb., 103
Mistletoe, Desert, 299
Mistletoe Family. *See* Viscaceae
Mohavea
  breviflora Cov., 261
  confertiflora (Benth.) A. A. Heller, 182
Mohavea, Lesser, 261
Mojave-Aster, 45
Mojave Butterweed, 221
Mojave Linanthus, 70
Mojave Monkeyflower, 121
Mojave Mound Cactus, 114
Mojave Paintbrush, 297
Mojave Pennyroyal, 96

Mojave Prickly-Pear, 236
Mojave Sage, 62
Mojave Sand-Verbena, 100
Mojave Spurge, 240
Mojave Stinkweed, 238
Mojave Sun Cup, 247
Mojave Thistle, 80
Mojave Yucca, 160
Molluginaceae
  Mollugo cerviana (L.) Ser., 165
Mollugo cerviana (L.) Ser., 165
Monardella exilis E. Greene, 96
Monkeyflower
  Bigelow's, 108
  Death Valley, 109
  Mojave, 121
Monolepis nuttalliana (Schultes) E.
  Greene, 280
Monoptilon
  bellidiforme A. Gray, 135
  bellioides (A. Gray) H. M. Hall, 136
Mormon Tea, 303
Mound Cactus, Mojave, 114
Mountain Joint-Fir, 305
Mountain Milkvetch, Lane, 151
Muhlenbergia porteri Beal, 291
Muhly, Porter's, 291
Mule Fat, 129
Mustard Family. *See* Brassicaceae

N

Naked-Stemmed Daisy, 201
Nama demissum A. Gray var. *demissum*, 94
Narrow-Leaf Milkweed, 127
Narrow-Leaved Willow, 296
Needle Gramma, 288
Needle Grass, Desert, 287
Needles, Desert, 82
Nettle, Rock, 163
Nevada Joint Fir, 303
Newberry Milkvetch, 91
Nicolletia occidentalis A. Gray, 81
Nicotiana
  obtusifolia Martens & Galeotti, 185
  quadrivalvis Pursh, 186
Nightshade Family. *See* Solanaceae
Nipple Cactus, 88
Nitrophila, Amargosa, 281
Nitrophila mohavensis Munz & Roos, 281
Nolina parryi S. Watson, 157

Nolina, Parry's, 157
Noseburn, 286
Notch-Leaved Phacelia, 53
Nyctaginaceae
  Abronia pogonantha Heimeri, 100
  Abronia villosa S. Watson var.
    villosa, 100
  Allionia incarnata L., 101
  Boerhavia triqueta S. Watson, 101
  Mirabilis californica A. Gray, 102
  Mirabilis multiflora (Torrey) A. Gray var.
    glandulosa (Standley) J. F. Macbr., 103
  Tripterocalyx micranthus (Torrey)
    Hook., 166

O

O'Clock, Giant Four, 103
Oenothera
  californica (S. Watson) S. Watson ssp.
    eurekensis (Munz & Roos) Klein, 169
  primaveris A. Gray, 249
Old Man Cactus, 236
Oleaceae
  Menodora spinescens A. Gray, 166
  Oligomeris linifolia (M. Vahl) J. F.
    Macbr., 179
Olive Family. *See* Oleaceae
Onagraceae
  Camissonia boothii (Douglas) Raven ssp.
    desertorum (Munz) Raven, 167
  Camissonia brevipes (A. Gray) Raven ssp.
    brevipes, 246
  Camissonia campestris (E. Greene)
    Raven, 247
  Camissonia claviformis (Torrey & Fremont)
    Raven ssp. *claviformis*, 168
  Camissonia pallida (Abrams) Raven ssp.
    hallii (Davidson) Raven, 248
  Oenothera californica (S. Watson) S.
    Watson ssp. *eurekensis* (Munz & Roos)
    Klein, 169
  Oenothera primaveris A. Gray, 249
Onyx Flower, 147
Opuntia
  acanthocarpa Englem. & J. Bigelow var.
    coloradensis L. Benson, 234
  basilaris Engelm. & Bigel., 89
  chlorotica Engelm. & J. Bigelow, 235
  echinocarpa Engelm. & J. Bigelow, 273

erinacea Engelm. & J. Bigelow var.
   erinacea, 236
   parishii Orc., 237
Orobanchaceae
   Orobanche cooperi (A. Gray) A. A.
      Heller, 66
Orobanche cooperi (A. Gray) A. A. Heller, 66
Our Lord's Candle, 161
Owl's Clover, Purple, 107
Oxytheca perfoliata Torrey & A. Gray, 178

P

Paintbrush
   Desert, 120
   Mojave, 297
Palafoxia arida B. Turner & M. Morris var.
   arida, 82
Pale Primrose, 248
Pallid Box Thorn, 111
Palmer Buckwheat, 254
Palmer's Penstemon, 75
Panamint Butterfly Bush, 231
Panamint, Daisy, 200
Panamint, Penstemon, 74
Panamint Plume, 229
Pancake-Pear, 235
Papaveraceae
   Argemone corymbosa E. Greene, 170
   Canbya candida C. Parry, 171
   Eschscholzia californica Cham., 118
   Eschscholzia glyptosperma E. Greene, 249
Paper-Bag Bush, 58
Paper Daisy, 219
Parachute Plant, 128
Parish's Phacelia, 56
Parish's Popcorn Flower, 143
Parry Dalea, 50
Parry Rock-Pink, 83
Parry's Beargrass, 157
Parry's Linanthus, 70, 174
Parry's Nolina, 157
Parry's Stephanomeria, 83
Parsley, Desert, 43
Peach Thorn, 184
Pea Family. *See* Fabaceae
Pectis papposa Harvey & A. Gray var.
   papposa, 215
Pectocarya
   penicillata, 141

setosa, 142
Pellaea mucronata (D. Eaton) D. Eaton, 307
Pennyroyal, Mojave, 96
Penstemon
   Palmer's, 75
   Panamint, 74
   Snapdragon, 259
   Utah, 121
Penstemon
   albomarginata M. E. Jones, 110
   calcareous Brandegee, 110
   fruticiformis Cov. var. *fruticiformis,* 74
   palmeri A. Gray var. *palmeri,* 75
   utahensis Eastw., 121
Peppergrass, Bush, 144
Pepper-Grass, Yellow, 227
Perennial Eriastrum, 67
Perityle emoryi Torrey, 136
Petalonyx
   nitidus Wats., 164
   thurberi ssp. *gilmanii* (Munz) Davis &
      Thompson, 165
Petalonyx, Canyon, 164
Peucephyllum schottii A. Gray, 216
Phacelia
   Fat-Leaf, 55
   Fremont, 55
   Ives, 155
   Lace-Leaf, 55
   Notch-Leaved, 53
   Parish's, 56
   Round-Leaf, 156
   Specter, 57
   Washoe, 54
Phacelia
   campanularia A. Gray ssp. *vasiformis*
      Gillett., 52
   crenulata Torrey, 53
   curvipes S. Watson, 54
   distans Benth., 55
   fremontii Torrey, 55
   ivesiana Torrey, 155
   parishii A. Gray, 56
   pedicillata A. Gray, 57
   rotundifolia A. Gray, 156
Phlox Family. *See* Polemoniaceae
Pholisma arenarium Hook., 63
Phoradendron californicum Nutt., 299
Phragmites australis (Cav.) Steudel, 292
Physalis crassifolia Benth., 261

Pigweed Family. *See* Amaranthaceae

Pima Rhatany, 95

Pinaceae

  Pinus monophylla Torrey & Fremont, 306

Pincushion, Fremont, 131

Pine Family. *See* Pinaceae

Pine, Singleleaf Pinyon, 306

Pineapple Cactus, 115

Pink Family. *See* Caryophyllaceae

Pinus monophylla Torrey & Fremont, 306

Pinyon Pine, Singleleaf, 306

Plagiobothrys parishii Jtn., 143

Plant, Death Valley Sandpaper, 165

Plant, Hole-in-the-Sand, 81

Plant, Parachute, 128

Plant, Scaly-Stemmed Sand, 63

Plant, Smooth Sandpaper, 165

Plantaginaceae

  Plantago ovata Forsskal, 172

Plantago ovata Forsskal, 172

Plantain, Desert, 172

Plantain Family. *See* Plantaginaceae

Pleuraphis rigida Thurber, 293

Plume

  Panamint, 229

  Prince's, 230

  Tall Prince's, 229

Plume, Apache, 119

Poaceae

  Achnatherum hymenoides (Roemer &
    Shultes) Barkworth, 287

  Achnatherum speciosum (Trin. & Rupr.)
    Barkworth, 287

  Bouteloua aristidoides (Kunth.) Griseb. var.
    aristidoides, 288

  Bouteloua barbata Lagasca var. *barbata,* 288

  Bromus madritensis L. ssp. *rubens* (L.)
    Husnot, 289

  Distichlis spicata (L.) E. Greene, 290

  Erioneuron pulchellum (Kunth) Tateoka, 291

  Muhlenbergia porteri Beal, 291

  Phragmites australis (Cav.) Steudel, 292

  Pleuraphis rigida Thurber, 293

  Swallenia alexandrae Soderstrom &
    Decker, 294

  Vulpia octoflora (Walter) Rydb. var. *hirtella*
    (Piper) Henrard, 295

Polemoniaceae

  Eriastrum densifolium (Benth.) H. Mason
    ssp. *mohavense* (Craig) H. Mason, 67

Gilia latiflora (A. Gray) A. Gray, 68

Gilia latifolia S. Watson, 103

Langloisia setosissima (Torrey & A. Gray)
    E. Greene ssp. *punctata* (Cov.) S.
    Timbrook, 69

Linanthus breviculus (A. Gray) E. Greene,
    70

Linanthus dichotomus Benth., 173

Linanthus parryae (A. Gray) E. Greene,
    70, 174

Loeseliastrum matthewsii (A. Gray) S.
    Timbrook, 104

Loeseliastrum schottii (Torrey) S.
    Timbrook, 175

Polygonaceae

  Chorizanthe brevicornu Torrey var.
    brevicornu, 250

  Chorizanthe rigida (Torrey) Torrey & A.
    Gray, 251

  Dedeckera eurekensis Rev. & J. Howell, 252

  Eriogonum deflexum Torrey var.
    deflexum, 176

  Eriogonum fasciculatum Benth. var.
    polifolium (A. DC.) Torrey & A.
    Gray, 177

  Eriogonum inflatum Torrey & Fremont var.
    inflatum, 253

  Eriogonum palmerianum Rev., 254

  Gilmania luteola (Cov.) Cov., 255

  Oxytheca perfoliata Torrey & A. Gray, 178

  Rumex hymenosepalus Torrey, 105

Popcorn Flower, Parish's, 143

Poppy

  California, 118

  Prickly, 170

  Pygmy, 171

Poppy Family. *See* Papaveraceae

Populus fremontii S. Watson ssp.
    fremontii, 295

Porter's Muhly, 291

Portulacaceae

  Calyptridium monandrum Nutt., 106

  Portulaca halimoides L., 256

Portulaca, Desert, 256

Portulaca halimoides L., 256

Prickly-Pear, Mojave, 236

Prickly Poppy, 170

Primrose

  Booth's, 167

  Brown-Eyed, 168

Eureka Dunes Evening, 169
Field, 247
Golden Evening, 246
Pale, 248
Spring Evening, 248
Yellow Evening, 248
Prince's Plume, 230
Prince's Plume, Tall, 229
Pringle's Woolly Daisy, 206
Prosopis
glandulosa Torrey var. *torreyana* (L.
Benson) M. Johnston, 153
pubescens Benth., 154
Prunus fasciculata (Torrey) A. Gray var.
fasciculata, 180
Psathyrotes
annua (Nutt.) A. Gray, 217
ramosissima (Torrey) A. Gray, 218
Psilotrophe cooperi (A. Gray) E. Greene, 219
Psorothamnus arborescens (A. Gray) Barneby
var. *minutifolius* (Parish) Barneby, 51
Pteridaceae
Cheilanthes covillei Maxon, 307
Pellaea mucronata (D. Eaton) D.
Eaton, 307
Punctured Bract, 178
Puncture Vine, 263
Purple Mat, 94
Purple Owl's Clover, 107
Purshia tridentata (Pursh) DC. var.
glandulosa (Curran) M. E. Jones, 181
Purslane Family. *See* Portulacaceae
Pygmy-Cedar, 216
Pygmy Poppy, 171

Q

Quassia Family. *See* Simaroubaceae

R

Rabbitbrush
Black-Stem, 195
Rubber, 194
Rafinesquia neomexicana A. Gray, 137
Ragweed, Winged, 272
Ranunculaceae
Delphinium parishii A. Gray ssp.
parishii, 71
Rattlesnake Weed, 150
Rayless Encelia, 199
Red Brome, 289

Red Rock Tarplant, 210
Red-Stemmed Filaree, 93
Reed, Common, 292
Resedaceae
Oligomeris linifolia (M. Vahl) J. F.
Macbr., 179
Rhatany Family. *See* Krameriaceae
Rhatany, Pima, 95
Rhubarb, Wild, 105
Rhus trilobata Torrey & A. Gray, 124
Ricegrass, Indian, 287
Rock-Daisy, Emory, 136
Rock Lady, 260
Rock Midget, 109
Rock Nettle, 163
Rock-Pea, Desert, 242
Rock-Pink, Parry, 83
Rock Tarplant, Red, 196
Rosaceae
Coleogyne ramosissima Torrey, 257
Fallugia paradoxa (D. Don) Endl., 119
Prunus fasciculata (Torrey) A. Gray var.
fasciculata, 180
Purshia tridentata (Pursh) DC. var.
glandulosa (Curran) M. E. Jones, 181
Rose Family. *See* Rosaceae
Rose-Heath, 132
Rosette
Mealy, 217
Velvet, 218
Round-Leaf Phacelia, 156
Rubber Rabbitbrush, 194
Rue, Desert, 72
Rue Family. *See* Rutaceae
Rumex hymenosepalus Torrey, 105
Rush Milkweed, 128
Russian Thistle, 282
Rutaceae
Thamnosma montana Torrey &
Fremont, 72

S

Sacred Datura, 183
Sage
Bladder, 58
Death Valley, 61
Desert, 61
Gray Ball, 61
Mojave, 62
Thistle, 59

Sagebrush
  Big, 269
  Great Basin, 269
Salazaria mexicana Torrey, 58
Salicaceae
  Populus fremontii S. Watson ssp.
    fremontii, 295
  Salix exigua Nutt., 296
Salix exigua Nutt., 296
Salsola tragus L., 282
Saltbush, Four-Wing, 275
Salt Cedar, 112
Saltgrass, 290
Salvia
  carduacea Benth., 59
  columbariae Benth., 60
  dorrii (Kellogg) Abrams var. *pilosa* (A.
    Gray) J. L. Strachan & Rev., 61
  funerea M. E. Jones, 61
  mohavensis E. Greene, 62
Sand-Bar Willow, 296
Sand Blazing Star, 245
Sandblossoms, 174
Sand-Bur, Western, 267
Sand-Cress, 106
Sandmat
  Bristle-Lobed, 151
  White-Margin, 150
Sandpaper Plant
  Death Valley, 165
  Smooth, 164
Sand Plant, Scaly-Stemmed, 63
Sand-Verbena
  Desert, 100
  Mojave, 100
Santa, Yerba, 155
Sarcobatus vermiculatus (Hook.) Torrey, 283
Sarcostemma cyanchoides Decne ssp. *hartwegii*
  (Vail) R. Holm, 79
Saururaceae
  Anemopsis californica (Nutt.) Hook., 182
Scale-Broom, 213
Scale-Bud, 189
Scaly-Stemmed Sand Plant, 63
Scarlet Locoweed, 116
Scarlet Milkvetch, 116
Schott Gilia, 175
Sclerocactus polyancistrus (Engelm. & J.
  Bigelow) Britton & Rose, 115
Screw Bean, 154

Scrophulariaceae
  Antirrhinum filipes A. Gray, 258
  Castilleja angustifolia (Nutt.) G. Don, 120
  Castilleja exserta (A. A. Heller) Chuang &
    Heckard ssp. *venusta* (A. A. Heller)
    Chuang & Heckard, 107
  Castilleja plagiotoma A. Gray, 297
  Collinsia bartsiifolia Benth. var. *davidsonii*
    (Parish) V. Newsom, 73
  Cordylanthus eremicus Munz ssp. *eremicus*,
    107
  Keckiella antirrhinoides (Benth.) Straw
    var. *microphylla* (A. Gray) N.
    Holmgren, 259
  Maurandya petrophila Cov. & C.
    Morton, 260
  Mimulus bigelovei (A. Gray) A. Gray, 108
  Mimulus mohavensis Lemmon, 121
  Mimulus rupicola Cov. & A. L. Grant, 109
  Mohavea breviflora Cov., 261
  Mohavea confertiflora (Benth.) A. A.
    Heller, 182
  Penstemon albomarginata M. E. Jones, 110
  Penstemon calcareous Brandegee, 110
  Penstemon fruticiformis Cov. var.
    fruticiformis, 74
  Penstemon palmeri A. Gray var. *palmeri*, 75
  Penstemon utahensis Eastw., 121
Seepweed, Bush, 284
Senecio
  flaccidus Less. var. *monoensis* (E. Greene)
    B. Turner & T. Barkley, 220
  mohavensis A. Gray, 221
Senna
  Desert, 243
  Spiny, 243
Senna armata (S. Watson) H. Irwin &
  Barneby, 243
Shadscale, 276
Shockly Lupine, 50
Silk Dalea, 92
Silver Cholla, 273
Silver Lakes Daisy, 134
Simaroubaceae
  Castela emoryi (A. Gray) Moran &
    Felger, 298
Singleleaf Pinyon Pine, 306
Six-Weeks Fescue, 295
Six-Weeks Gramma, 288
Skeleton Weed, 176

Skunkbrush, 124
Small Desert Star, 135
Small-Flowered Abronia, 166
Small-Flowered Eremalche, 98
Smooth Sandpaper Plant, 165
Snakeweed, Sticky, 209
Snapdragon Penstemon, 259
Snapdragon, Twining, 258
Snow, Evening, 173
Soda Lupine, Grape, 49
Solanaceae
    Datura wrightii Regel, 183
    Lycium cooperi A. Gray, 184
    Lycium pallidum Miers var. *oligospermum*
        C. Hitchc., 111
    Nicotiana obtusifolia Martens &
        Galeotti, 185
    Nicotiana quadrivalvis Pursh, 186
    Physalis crassifolia Benth., 261
Southwestern Verbena, 76
Spanish Bayonet, 158
Spectacle-Pod, 144
Specter Phacelia, 57
Sphaeralcea ambigua A. Gray var.
    ambigua, 117
Spiderling, 101
Spineflower, Brittle, 250
Spiny-Herb, 251
Spiny Menodora, 166
Spiny Senna, 243
Spring Evening Primrose, 249
Spurge
    Mojave, 240
    Yuma, 151
Spurge Family. *See* Euphorbiaceae
Staghorn Cholla, 234
Stanleya
    elata Jones., 229
    pinnata (Pursh) Britton, 230
Star, Blazing, 245
Star, Desert, 136
Star, Sand Blazing, 245
Star, Small Desert, 135
Stenotopsis, 204
Stephanomeria
    parryi A. Gray, 83
    pauciflora (Torrey) Nelson, 84
Stephanomeria, Parry's, 83
Stick-Leaf, White-Stemmed, 244
Sticky Snakeweed, 209

Stiff-Haired Lotus, 242
Stiff-Stemmed Comb-Bur, 142
Stillingia
    Annual, 286
    Linear-Leaved, 116
Stillingia
    linearifolia S. Watson, 116
    spinulosa S. Watson, 286
Sting-Bush, 163
Stinkweed, Mojave, 238
Stonecrop Family. *See* Crassulaceae
Straw, Desert, 84
Suaeda moquinii (Torrey) E. Greene, 284
Sumac Family. *See* Anacardiaceae
Sunbonnet, Lilac, 69
Sunbonnets, Little, 175
Sun Cup, Mojave, 247
Sunflower
    Barstow Woolly, 205
    Desert, 208
Sunflower Family. *See* Asteraceae
Swallenia alexandrae Soderstrom &
    Decker, 294
Sweetbush, 192
Syntrichopappus fremontii A. Gray, 222

T

Tack-Stem, Yellow, 193
Tall Prince's Plume, 229
Tamaricaceae
    Tamarix ramosissima Ledeb., 112
Tamarisk, 112
Tamarisk Family. *See* Tamaricaceae
Tamarix ramosissima Ledeb., 112
Tarplant, Red Rock, 210
Tea, Mormon, 303
Tequilia, 86
Tequilia plicata (Torrey) A. Richardson, 86
Tetradymia axillaris Nelson var. *longispina*
    (M. E. Jones) Strother, 223
Thamnosma montana Torrey & Fremont, 72
Thelypodium integrifolium (Nutt.) Endl., 145
Thick-Leaved Ground-Cherry, 261
Thistle
    Mojave, 80
    Russian, 282
Thistle Sage, 59
Thorn
    Cooper's Box, 184
    Crucifixion, 298

Pallid Box, 111
Peach, 184
Thorn-Apple, 183
Thymophylla, 224
Thymophylla pentachaeta (DC.) Small var.
  belenidium (DC.) Strother, 224
Tickseed, Bigelow's, 196
Tidestromia oblongifolia (S. Watson)
  Standley, 266
Tidy-Tips, White, 133
Tobacco
  Coyote, 185
  Indian, 186
Tornillo, 154
Tragia ramosa Torrey, 286
Tree, Joshua, 159
Tribulus terrestris L., 263
Trichoptilium incisum A. Gray, 225
Tripterocalyx micranthus (Torrey) Hook., 166
Trixis, 225
Trixis californica Kellogg var. *californica*, 225
Trumpet, Desert, 253
Tumbleweed, 282
Turpentine Broom, 72
Turtleback, 218
Turtleback, Annual, 217
Twining Snapdragon, 258

U

Utah Firecracker, 121
Utah Juniper, 303
Utah Penstemon, 121

V

Valley Dunes Grass, Eureka, 294
Valley Monkeyflower, Death, 109
Valley Sage, Death, 61
Valley Sandpaper Plant, Death, 165
Velvet Rosette, 218
Verbena
  Goodding's, 76
  Southwestern, 76
Verbenaceae
  Verbena gooddingii Briq., 76
Verbena gooddingii Briq., 76
Vervain Family. *See* Verbenaceae
Vine, Puncture, 263
Viscaceae
  Phoradendron californicum Nutt., 299
Visnaga, 233

Vulpia octoflora (Walter) Rydb. var. *hirtella*
  (Piper) Henrard, 295

W

Wait-a-Minute Bush, 241
Wallace's Woolly Daisy, 207
Washoe Phacelia, 54
Waterleaf Family. *See* Hydrophyllaceae
Weed, Jimson, 183
Weed, Rattlesnake, 150
Weed, Skeleton, 176
Western Sand-Bur, 267
White Aster, 132
White Bur-Sage, 268
White-Margined Beardtongue, 110
White-Margin Sandmat, 150
White-Stemmed Stick-Leaf, 244
White Tidy-Tips, 133
Whorled Milkweed, Mexican, 127
Wild Licorice, 152
Wild Rhubarb, 105
Willow
  Narrow-Leaved, 296
  Sand-Bar, 296
Willow, Desert, 85
Willow Family. *See* Salicaceae
Windmills, 101
Winged Ragweed, 272
Winter Fat, 279
Wire Lettuce, 84
Wishbone Bush, 102
Woolly Brickellia, 130
Woolly Daisy
  False, 222
  Pringle's, 206
  Wallace's, 207
Woolly Sunflower, Barstow, 205

X

Xylorhiza tortifolia (Torrey & A. Gray) E.
  Greene var. *tortifolia*, 45

Y

Yellow Evening Primrose, 249
Yellow-Heads, 225
Yellow Keckiella, 259
Yellow Pepper-Grass, 227
Yellow Tack-Stem, 193
Yerba Mansa, 182
Yerba Santa, 155

Yucca
   Banana, 158
   Fleshy-Fruited, 158
   Mojave, 160
Yucca
   baccata Torrey, 158
   brevifolia Engelm., 159
   shidigera K. E. Ortgies, 160
   whipplei Torrey ssp. *caespitosa* (Jones)
      Haines, 161
Yuma Spurge, 151

Z
Zigadenus brevibracteatus (M. E. Jones) H.
   M. Hall, 162
Zygadene, Desert, 162
Zygophyllaceae
   Larrea tridentata DC. (Cov.), 262
   Tribulus terrestris L., 263

ABOUT THE AUTHOR

Pam MacKay is a professor of biology at Victor Valley Community College in Victorville, California, where she teaches population and environmental biology, botany, plant identification, microbiology, and tropical natural history courses. She is involved in Mojave Desert conservation efforts and has been instrumental in founding the new Mojave Desert Chapter of the California Native Plant Society, serving as field trip chair and past president. She is also a volunteer naturalist for the Golden Trout Natural History Association, leading hikes and natural history workshops in the backcountry of the southern High Sierra. Pam has Bachelor of Science degrees in biology and botany as well as a Master of Science degree in biology from California State Polytechnic University in Pomona. She has also completed coursework towards a doctorate degree at the University of California at Riverside.

ABOUT SOME OF THE PHOTOGRAPHERS

John S. Reid has been a professional commercial and advertisement photographer for over fifteen years. For the last five years he has been involved in a study of the insects of the tropical rain forest leaf litter in Belize, where he has taken the first photographs of several insects new to science. He has published photographs and nature articles in numerous magazines and has produced photographic calendars. He currently teaches commercial and outdoor nature photography at Victor Valley College in Victorville, California.

Stephen Ingram, a professional photographer, has traveled extensively, including trips to Kenya, Alaska, Australia, and to Costa Rica, where he completed his graduate studies on cloud forest epiphytes. Previously he was the herbarium curator for Selby Botanical Gardens in Florida. His photographs are published in numerous books, calendars, field guides, and magazines. He currently lives in the Eastern Sierra between Bishop and Mammoth Lakes.

Tim Thomas is a botanist with the United States Fish and Wildlife Service. He has written listing proposals and recovery plans for numerous rare plant species of California and has been an outspoken voice for plant conservation. His plant photographs have been published in numerous books, including *California's Wild Gardens* and *Plants of the Santa Monica Mountains*. He is currently the president of the Mojave Desert Chapter of the California Native Plant Society.

RT Hawke is a naturalist and outdoor education specialist for the Los Angeles County Office of Education. He has taught numerous field workshops and adult education classes for the Audubon Society and various community colleges. He is the primary photographic author of *Rare Plants of the San Gabriel Mountains*. He teaches Natural History of the Mojave Desert at Victor Valley College in Victorville, and he is very active with the California Native Plant Society. He resides in the San Bernardino Mountains.